THE BOOK OF JUDAS

THE
BOOK
OF
JUDAS

A POEM BY
Brendan Kennelly

BLOODAXE BOOKS

ISBN: 1 85224 170 5   hardback edition
1 85224 171 3   paperback edition
1 85224 172 1   limited signed edition of 30 copies

First published 1991 by
Bloodaxe Books Ltd,
P.O. Box 1SN,
Newcastle upon Tyne NE99 1SN.

Bloodaxe Books Ltd acknowledges
the financial assistance of Northern Arts.

Cover reproduction by V & H Reprographics, Newcastle upon Tyne.

Printed in Great Britain by
Bell & Bain Limited, Glasgow, Scotland.

For all good dreams
    twisted, exploited and betrayed.
For all those
    conveniently and mindlessly damned
        by you and me.
And for all those writing and unwriting
        poets of humanity
            who have a bash
                at comprehending the incomprehensible.

THE BOOK OF JUDAS

A Poem

PREFACE

The imagination provides the most effective means of confronting and express-
ing the prejudices and inherited hatreds buried in the self until they exist
before our eyes like so many lucid accusations confirming Ibsen's belief that
poetry is a court of judgment on the soul. But it's more, much more than
that. In a long poem, *Cromwell* (1983), I tried to open my mind, heart and
imagination to the full, fascinating complexity of a man I was from childhood
taught, quite simply, to hate. A learned hate is hard to unlearn. It would be
easy enough to go through life hoarding and nourishing such hate, feeding
it dutifully with endless "proofs", thus keeping alive the explosive frenzies
that fuel political situations such as that in Northern Ireland. But when one
tries to substitute the uncertainties of altruistic exploration for the certainties
of inherited hate, one is immediately disrupting and challenging one's "cult-
ural legacy", spitting in the faces of the authoritative fathers and their revered,
unimpeachable wisdom. The process of unlearning hate is a genuine insult
to some, particularly those whose prejudices are called convictions.

There is something in Irish life which demands that you over-simplify
practically everything. This is another way of saying that everybody must
be labelled, made readily accessible, explainable. Protestant, Catholic, Dub,
Northerner, Culchie, etc, are such labels. Stick any of these labels on a man
or a woman, a boy or a girl, and you needn't bother yourself with further
enquiry into their characters or minds. The problems of complex personality
are easily solved. The label tells you all you need to know. Kerryman, Jew-
boy, Proddie Dog, Southsider, Northsider. 'Ah, sure, the bowsie never read
a book in his life!' *Label.* Judas. Now, we know. We have him in his place.
The rest is as clear as daylight. We know him to the core.

But there is an electricity in the air that burns the labels and restores the
spirit of investigative uncertainty. Poetry tries to plug in to this electricity,
to let it thrill and animate one's ways of feeling and thinking and seeing.
This electricity is what the labels fear. This electricity makes room for all
the voices of the damned and outcast, the horrible archetypes for whom, in
the opinion of many "decent people", there is no ear, no hope of redemp-
tion; and because no hope is allowed, these "horrible souls" can be blamed
for practically anything. Recently, an English football manager was scream-
ingly headlined JUDAS in an English paper because he changed his mind
or 'went back on his word'. Judas was in no position to write a protesting
letter to that newspaper. If he had, would the editor have published it? And
in what spirit?

How must men and women who cannot write back, who must absorb the full thump of accusation without hope of reply, who have no voices because we know they're "beyond all hope", feel in their cold, condemned silence? In *The Book of Judas* I wished to create the voice of a condemned man writing back to me, trained and educated to condemn him. How shall I listen to someone who, I am told, has no right to a voice? If I could stretch myself to let the butcher Cromwell speak for himself, articulate his position across centuries of mechanical, hate-filled condemnation, and in the process discover that he had a lot of things to point out to me, to my shame and illumination, might I not also learn to let the outcast scapegoat Judas, suddenly electrified with protean virtuosity, yet remaining dubious, speak back and out from his icy black corner of history, or my pathetic little mind scraping at that black ice? The moment I surrendered to the voice from that icy black corner, the electricity began to flow, the questions erupted, the answers ran away to hide in some cosy little corner of their own. We all learn the nature of the possibilities of our own particular little corner.

The damned soul has a special perspective on us all, but how can we believe him, how can we believe one who is a liar and traitor by instinct? Above all, how can this be poetry? The questions kept coming as I wrote and rewrote the poem over eight years. Was Judas a fall guy in some sublime design he didn't even begin to understand? What was he trying to prove? Was he a not-so-bright or a too-bright politician? A man whose vision of things was being throttled by another, more popular vision? A loner in an organised bunch? One who knew the dynamising power of a timely moment of betrayal? Simply an envious bastard? One who knew how to shock others into a new awareness of their situation? A man wanting to test the limits of his own intelligent, speculative, vicious potential? A spirit not confined to the man who bore the name Judas but one more alive and consequential now at the famined, bloated, trivialised, analytical, bomb-menaced, progressive, moneymad, reasonable end of the twentieth century than ever before? Is Judas by definition the most contemporary of contemporaries? The Judas-voice is odd and ordinary, freakish and free, severed and pertinent, twisting what it glimpses of reality into parodies of what is taken for granted, convinced (if it's convinced of anything) that we live in an age almost helplessly devoted to ugliness, that the poisoned world we have created is simply *what we are*, and cannot be justified or explained away by science or industry or money or education or progress. To this extent, Judas knows nothing is external: where we are is who we are, what we create is merely the symmetry of our dreams. It is therefore insane to blame anybody but ourselves. But can we believe Judas? Or what he calls his poetry? How can the damned man be, even for a moment, admitted into our hearts and minds? Should he be? Why? Does he not deserve not to be heard?

The Gaelic novelist Máirtín Ó Cadhain once said to me that in Ireland we divert attention from serious issues by creating a hubbub about trivial matters. I never cease to be amazed and amused at the power of triviality over serious minds. (I include myself, insofar as I can claim to be serious-minded.) In this poem I wanted to capture the relentless, pitiless anecdotalism of Irish life, the air swarming with nutty little sexual parables, the platitudinous bonhomie sustained by venomous undercurrents, the casual ferocious gossip, the local industry of rumour-making and spreading, always remembering that life is being parodied, that this Christian culture itself is a parody of what may once have been a passion. There's an atrocious tendency in Irish life, especially in Dublin, to dismiss people by turning them into sad or clownish parodies of themselves. I believe that the culture of these islands, is, broadly speaking, Christian. I have no wish to offend non-Christians, I'm merely stating a belief. I also believe that this culture is now in an advanced state of self-parody. Or, if you wish, in an advanced state of self-betrayal, playing Judas to itself. In this poem I wanted this man to talk to himself, this culture to mutter to itself of what is lost or forgotten or betrayed or grotesquely twisted in memory. And appallingly obvious now. Yet there are no answers.

I wonder if many people feel as I do – that in the society we have created it is very difficult to give your full, sustained attention to anything or anybody for long, that we are compelled to half-do a lot of things, to half-live our lives, half-dream our dreams, half-love our loves? We have made ourselves into half-people. Half-heartedness is a slow, banal killer. It is also, paradoxically, a creepy pathway towards "success", especially if the half-heartedness is of the polished variety. I think it was D.H. Lawrence who said that the real tragedy of modern man is the loss of heart. I don't think so. I believe our tragedy is the viability of our half-heartedness, our insured, mortgaged, welfare voyage of non-discovery, the committed, corrosive involvement with forces, created by ourselves, that ensure our lives will be half-lived. There's a sad refusal here. A rejection of the unique, fragile gift.

Have we refused some love-offering we should have accepted? Have we organised and unionised ourselves into semi-paralytics? Is Judas a shrewd refuser of what might have made him loveable and vulnerable rather than – whatever he is? How much of our law of success is bound up with knowing what and how to refuse? Is this refusal-betrayal necessary if one is to be numbered among "decent people"? How "respectable" is Judas? To what extent have we elected Judas to be our real redeemer from the consequences of what we have ourselves created but like to blame somebody else for, when "things go wrong?"

In asking these questions, in following the Judasvoice as it appeared in words before my eyes, I tried to deal with, or let Judas deal with the idea of intention or purpose or ambition, children, a notion of love, history, apostles, you, money, sex, selfhood, Some Lads, politicians and politics, and the possibility that Judas may be the spirit of language, of poetry. This last section shocked me. Everybody knows that the literary world everywhere, be it Dublin, London, Paris, New York, or even Sidcup or Skibbereen, can be hate-riddled to an astonishing degree. I've heard people say, 'Poets are self-centred, malignant bastards, aren't they, really?' These same people frequently go on to say that it's a great wonder, and a paradoxical cause for gratitude, that such malignant, self-centred bastards are capable of producing 'such beautiful stuff'. The implication is that poetry is produced *in spite of* the nature of these 'self-centred, malignant' souls. *The Book of Judas* explores the possibility that "beauty" is produced *because* of it. Judas has a permanent residence on the human tongue. His potential vitality in every word known to us is incalculable, thrilling and fascinating. Who can fully trust the words out of any mouth, especially his own?

This scapegoat, critic of self and society, throws chronological time out the window. Before his ancestors arrived on the scene, he was. After the unborn will have ceased to exist, he'll be. As others arrive, exist and perish, he tholes. Time is merely a stage where his reticent yet theatrical spirit is repeated and refined as it continues to endure the stones of blame thrown by those who really know the score. If I'd stuck to chronology in this poem I'd have lost the voices of that spirit. By treating time in the ways a blamed person treats it, that is, with the ceaseless nervous agility of the accused-from-all-sides, the poem became open to the stimulating effects of that electricity which saves most thinking people from the pornography of labels. And the man could talk and mutter as he wished, or was compelled to. I have always associated unbridled, passionate muttering with freedom. There is something more attractively genuine in such mutterings than in most of the bland interchanges that go by the name of "communication". Wherever I see men and women furiously muttering to themselves in the streets of Dublin I am saddened by their loneliness, touched by their sincerity, awed by their freedom.

I would like to thank Terence Brown for his readings of this poem and suggestions concerning it. Thanks also to Gerald Dawe for his reading and comments. And finally my gratitude to Neil Astley for his many ideas on how to shape and re-shape this work. It was he, chiefly, who gave the poem whatever shape it can claim to have.

BRENDAN KENNELLY

ONE

Do it

Lips

What words emigrate through these:

Promises threats salutations curses lies
Protestations of love and hate
Memories wording to new shapes
Attempts at prayer
Cant and ranting
Money-counting
Enraged obscenities.

They work in my sleep.
I lie there, lost and vulnerable,
No longer in control.
The words escape into the darkness
Like hunger-strikers finding the gates open
Or cries from children swallowing hunger
On a mountain of excrement and death.

If I have a soul they tell it.
If I have a heart they let you know it.
Do they?

How often have they betrayed me
And told my little truth. Have they?

When I see trout flashing through water
They close in wonder.
When my blood is chill with anger
They are po-faced diplomats.
When I see pictures that make heaven a possibility
They ooze platitudes like spittle.
When I see precision bombers at work
They suck horror like mother's milk.

They think
Food and drink.
They breathe
Distinctions of stink.

They murder with chuckles and outbursts
Of laughter laughing at innocence.
They make hell what it is –
Ordinary, polished with commonsense.

They operate like a surgeon or a shark.
They electrify her body in the dark.

When they utter the beautiful words of others
They sneer at their own skill.

They listen. They lie in wait, daylight
Assassins.

They kill at will.
They kiss when pressed.

They subvert the moon's truest tunes,
They whistle music inside out
Making doubt certain, certainty doubt.

They permit pain to find a voice.
They stiffen when no one listens.
They freeze in the presence of what sees through them.

More than anything else
They understand silence.

They taste it, licking themselves
Till they are wet enough for pain
To utter itself all over again.

They slave for me, ask nothing in return.
The harder they work the more I wonder
If I believe them.

Do It

Do it, I said, do it for sure,
What in hell are you waiting for?

You could sit around forever
Dreaming plotting scheming thinking
Sensitively festering, saying

      I want to change the situation
      I want others to see the change

I want unborn eyes to see the difference
I want you to see how destructive you are
When you love and pray
And lead the ignorant natives astray
And save the animals from death

I want to scrub dead gratitudes
Clarify the bitter feuds
Burn the murderous plans
To help the vulnerable children

I want to shred every mind
That ever dreamed of money

Money

I want to know that I am here

– Not a leaf in the wind
Not a dead neighbour nor yesterday's headlines
Not the slitting words of a busy cynic
Nor a political speech at some self-acclaiming conference

Not a girl's bloodgush in her growing
Not a shrunken hope
Nor a dogsvomit despair

        And I don't want to turn away
Into a home a job a bank a promise
A weekend retreat
A night
With the most fabulous little fucker in the land

And Jesus is she great

And I don't want to make a statement
Or write a poem
Or paint a picture
Or hack a shape from stone
Or win a prize for the skilled quality of my lies

I want to do it
And I will I will

It's only what the me-me world deserves

Just give me a second to steady my nerves

Service

The best way to serve the age is to betray it.
If it's a randy slut slooping for hump
Hide in a dark ditch, wait, waylay it
And land where no one can extradite you.

If it's a moneyman with a philosophy like
'There's only cash and as many fucks as you can get'
Inspire him to talk of Daddy's tenderness
Till his eyes are wet.

Be a knife, bullet, poison, flood, earthquake;
Cut, gut, shrivel, swallow, bury, burn, drown
Till someone senses things ain't as they should be.

If betrayal is a service, learn to betray
With the kind of style that impresses men
Until they dream of being me.

An Attack

I once had an attack of sincerity
And to tell you nothing but the truth
It made a confirmed eejit of me
For a night. The scene is a hotel in Beirut,
I have tipped (generously for me) the night-porter
Who knows the value of averted eyes
When I enter with the Russian Ambassador's daughter.
I'm feeling inventive, randy and wise
And five hours later in the steamy
Genius of that never-to-be-forgotten bed,
Sincere, for the only time in my life.

Poetry flows like lava, I am dreamy
And volcanic, my proposal is classically phrased,
She refuses, thank Vesuvius, I might have suffered a wife.

Insincerity as a Detector of Human Worth

Men have a passing interest in each other
Though only a few care about anyone else.
This does not prevent them seeing themselves
As lovers, and feeling love upon the pulse.

Such love is the perfect way not to know
Anyone, because of its fatal sincerity.
Marriages collapse because they're based on what's true
At the time. Fulfilment is another name for atrophy.

If on the other hand you experiment with lies
Salted with what is deftly insincere
You'll see their hearts as your words come and go.
Let them take the bait. Assume a wise
Look. Be hurt, if necessary. Say you're queer
Or a Jesusfreak. Their eyes will tell you all you
Need to know. What do you need to know?

Abraham's Bosom

I've died many times,
Not always because of well-conceived
And well-executed crimes
But because, being undeceived,
I glimpse a little, understand much
And hang myself
Out of a tingling mixture of boredom and shame.
The ninth time I died
I shot straight to Abraham's bosom,
A smelly place in West Heaven. I saw
Adam and Eve chatting about apples, Cain
And Abel editing a study of Brotherly Love,
Various Popes discussing greed lust envy pride
Hitler organising the resurrection of the Jews
Dante and Beatrice refusing to get out of bed.

'Welcome to my bosom, Judas' Abraham said,
'Despite your atrocious name I appreciate your worth.'

'I don't like your bosom, Abe' I replied
'It's too large, damp, unacceptably hairy.
I'm dropping back to earth.'

Back to this dear criminal dump I came
Glad of my good fortune, my bad name,
Sceptical of my next outing to Abraham's bosom.

If I Could

If I could I would betray the silence
That plants in me thoughts of betrayal.
My mind is a tiny fruitful garden
More professionally manicured than Eden

And grows voices rather than flowers.
Or perhaps flowers are voices
Of money holidays profit gossip sneering
Clever contempt, choice obscenities such as

Judas is the shrewdest whore
That ever stacked a man with galloping disease,
Judas makes evil gardening an immortal art,
Judas soulmocks the planets dividing rich and poor,
Judas troubles heaven with vile ideas,
Judas does brisk business with his heart.

Halcyon Days

I find the four gospels a darned good read
Though I don't come well out of the scene.
I saw what I saw, did what I did
And shed no tears over what might have been.

These were halcyon days, sane, insane,
Small farmers and fishermen leaving home
On impulse, just up and out, quick adventurous men.

I liked Peter, first Pope and Bishop of Rome.

Far from all that the same Peter was born and bred.
Leaving the wife and kids must have been hard

But Peter always did what Peter had to do.

In this, we were not unalike. I'm glad
These gospels show him in a kindly light.
I once wrote in my scrapbook that what I approve of I tend to regard as true.

Beards

I grew a beard once, labyrinthine thing
Wandering all over my mind like a Viking saga
Or an old Hebrew song without an ending.
I realised I'd something to hide so I
Put my trust in voracious facial hair.
My mouth vanished, most of my face was lost,
My eyes took in the world, my soul smirked at staring
Children, my beard galloped, I'd be undressed
Without it. Then certain of the apostles began
To imitate me, beards began to flourish,
Common as lepers rotting towards the grave.
After all, they had nothing to hide, these men
Chosen by heaven to fulfil its wish.
It was time to distinguish myself. I decided to shave
So I hopped into a supermarket in Nazareth
And bought a dozen disposable razors
With lemonsoap and aftershave lotion.
Foamed before a mirror, measuring my breath,
I shaved long years' growth from my treacherous mug.
The face began to appear, Jesus the chin,
The pitty cheeks, infamous lips,
The inventive pallor of the skin.
For a moment I was in touch with my old self,
Boy, young man, vigorous entrepreneur.
And yet my restored face seemed weird
To me. Then I remembered all the pictures
Of God the Father I'd seen as a child
In which the Creator had sported a beard.
I forgave myself everything, began to feel undefiled.
O beardy weirdy Father, your son is criss-cross wild.

The Devil's Lilies

Seeing a cat crucified to a telegraph pole
The latest fast cars gulping the highways
I realise God created the world
In a psychedelic haze

I see the spaced-out heroes hacking
Each other to pieces in the scenic glens
While sprawled poets invent the Bible
In opium dens

Little remains for me but to set out again
After coffee on a contemplative stroll
Through timeless weeds and daffydowndillies,
My mind much like the minds of other men
From Bethlehem and Bradford and Listowel.
These men are flowerless. I pick the devil's lilies.

Inescapable

Now in a grave moment I am considering
Inescapable decay. Despite
The joyous fact that Flanagan will drink
Poteen out of my skull at his light-
hearted flings, I feel the odd existential pang
Though I lack an approved philosophical background.
Dust, I whisper to myself, dust which in winter
Becomes muck on rain-lashed roads that seem
The black twisting arteries of a dream
Endured in fierce intensity
Buried in triviality,
Is what I am. Such thoughts ring
In my treacherous head as I see my
Favourite politician visit itinerant camps,
Look softly at the women, kiss the filthy children,
Denounce the PLO, the Red Brigade, the IRA,
Grow indignant on telly for the inner city poor
Console deserted wives and selected cripples.
And what do I do? Sweet fuckall, sing dumb,
Think of dust, selfish get, lazy lump, cute whore.
Is dust, old winter muck, worth living for?

I promise not to ask that question again.
It has bamboozled the best efforts of prize-winning men.

(they think)

To be the thing you are – there's the temptation.
With some deluded souls this is an aim.
I am deluded, I know that, knowing makes it worse,
I say my god my father Judas is my name.

I'm destined for a special fame
I am myself and that's a special burden
You made me, god, let not your godheart harden
Worms eat earth in first and last gardens
Men chew sins that is they play the game
The scene changes the game is still the same

Game-players need a hero
Someone who plays it more despicably than they
Standard exemplar model paradigm o hang it god
Not just adolf stalin napoleon nero
But someone flawless absolute and sly
(they think). Could I be that? M'mmm. I do believe I could.

An O.K. Guy

So much depends on a TV appearance.
It's true it's true it's absurd.
I practised for days but clean
Forgot how my beard
Stuck like a watery turd to my chin
And what a seedy sneaky voice I have
And darting ratty eyes
Infecting the light of surburban paradise.
No one believed me, I was dressed in lies.
And yet in spite of these disasters
I might have come across as an OK guy
Were it not that at a vital moment
I picked my nose. The whole fucking nation
Rang the station and said I should be crucified.
Today a blob of snot on my forefinger
Recalls an agony on which I shall not linger.

Good Book

Good Book was depressed. Where was its ancient happy self?
'I am neglected,' Good Book said, 'You read me but most
Of the rest of the world spits me on the shelf.
What do people read? Novels by beefy
Women, cynical men, pukey novels so fat
They make me feel despairing and griefy.
How did human intelligence slum to that?
What abysmal stupor has enveloped the minds of men
They no longer wish to hear a word of truth?
Abel Cain Abraham Isaac Job Moses – where are they?'

'Don't worry, Good Book,' I replied, 'You are more known
Than you know. I just met Cain in the murderous flush of his youth
And am acquainted with several others of your *dramatis personae*.'

Good Book seemed relieved, smiled, went away.

Only...

In the Kingdom of God, there are no men and women.
There are only...
                    The radio switched to Bach,
I was thinking of competition in business
Between Solomon Tuft and Felicity Flack.

                    Solomon bred sheep
For the European market. He was also into cows.
Felicity, being lyrical, loved to watch the dawn creep
Into her bed where she was wont to linger and browse
On the state of the cattle and sheep market
And on the special talents of Solomon Tuft
Who, when Felicity began to compete
With him, became, though seasoned, familiar with defeat.
In purely business terms, Felicity roughed
Solomon up. This morning, I thought it odd
When a voice with a soft monetary rhythm
Said there were no men and women in the Kingdom of God
Only...

In That Moment

There must have been a first time.
Something was broken, a grace lost,
A man sidestepped himself, a woman lied.

In that moment, persecution and martyrdom
Happened, two hearts learned not to trust,
A remarkable person was betrayed.

Beatification

When I was a Chat Show Host,
My nationwide programme
Approaching its nightly end,
I would suddenly up my interest
In the proceedings. Leaning
Towards the face of the most
Beautiful woman in the place,
I would say with an urgent air
'We have thirty seconds left!
Who, in your view, is the best
Chat Show Host in the colourful
History of television?'
The beautiful creature would hesitate
For one staggering moment
And explode,
'You, Judas, you alone, you are God!'
The nation swilled her words.
I, angelically bright,
Kissed ten million hearts good-night
From My undisputed place,
Smiling as a blush modesty
Beatified my face.

My Image Throws No Shadow

Give me the one image I dare not share with any other
Because the source ordained it was mine alone
And could not be repeated among men.

The weakling Cain had to murder his brother
But couldn't banish the shadow out of his bones.
My image throws no shadow, it is clear and clean.

Anew

Dose me with Last Rites, I live again, I
Sit up in bed though you plan to bury me
Complete with spectacles and marriage-ring.

Lubricate me with Final Oils, ram me with prayers
For the dying, I break out like the bad weather
And sprout anew in the young and daring.

This Radioactive Morning

I've met the Patron Saint of Animals
The Patron Saint of Workers
The Patron Saint of Hopeless Cases
The Patron Saint of Terrorists
The Patron Saint of Lapsed Believers
The Patron Saint of Drunken Drivers.

This radioactive morning in my bedsit
I nominate myself
The Patron Saint of Traitors.

I have in mind sleek battalions
Of itchy aspirants, the accomplished few,
The threatening promise of the unborn.

Offer novenas on the penitential stones
Let various tribunals hear Judas and his crew
The stars will get cancer if I don't get my turn.

Christmas 1986

At the entrance to the church, in black
Spare lettering: GUNS NOT PRAYER.

Which Matters?

This had all the ingredients of an epic story:
A God, immortal beauty and power,
Perfect above deficient human machinery
Cranking away, keeping an obstinate grip on wonder,
Imagining itself for battle, leaving the heart open
To consequential attacks of passion.
We dreamed ourselves, dreams were the lives of men,
When lives were dreamed how real were hell and heaven.
            But even as I defined the cosmos
I ceased to tell the story and became
Interested in myself, self-seeking, what my feelings were.
Friendships frayed, I liked each new neurosis,
Sticky confessions whimpered my way to fame,
The scene splattered apart in rags and tatters.
Epic story? Whimpering scene? Which matters?

TWO

Are the poems honest, doctor?

Appetite

Collecting urine-samples in outer Rathmines
In the name of Church, country and God
Became my duty when I was made
Head of the Vice-Squad
Sniffing out heroin and synthetic-opiate addicts
In the heart of the Supermarket jungle.
These ravenous children, victims from the womb, sick
And ecstatic, are mad
For money as farmers, darlings of Mummy Earth.
          Like a virtuous Revenue Officer
So contemptuous of fame
No slippery victim will ever know my name,
        I ferret them out,
      Drag them into the light
Where they skeletonstand, chewed by their own appetite.
      These are the true poets,
        Each one
Skilled in the art of self-crucifixion,
       Hung up on
Spoofy proofs of self-fabrication,
       Mangy angels of smelly damnation,
       Freak dreams of an ego
       Shivering in a doorway
       Lousy with lyricism,
       No end to their lust
Only the patient, wearing, heartless, absolute,
     Brotherly, smothering, vindictive
      Pity of dust.

She's There

My soul is her lower lip but only for
A moment, then it's the story she becomes
Before my eyes in the coughing street where
I am trying to remember her name.

'Ginnie, Ginnie Greene, sir. I takes this blanket, yes,
An' I makes through the streets, I'm a beggar,
I looks right into the tourists' eyes
An' I takes what I can for me sisters an' brothers.

An' why am I tellin' you this? Once, a bad day
You gave me bread, gave me white bread,
That's why I'm talkin' like this.'

My soul is an old crow perched in a tree.
Ginnie, Ginnie Greene, what do you mean to me?
White bread for living you begged, white bread I gave.
Who'll give the bread you'll beg for the grave?

Butter

The morning I thought I might live forever
Yvonne Casey was sentenced to a year in jail
For stealing a pound of butter
Spreadable as a melting whore.

Striding through Pontius Pilate Square
Nothing in front of me but eternity
I pondered the golden significance of butter
And how the poor will suffer jail for it, gladly.

Sunlight on Pontius Pilate Square
Flowed warmly as justice. I felt at home there
For a moment but then my mind said

Suppose eternity is butter, nothing but butter,
Are you still willing to live forever?

That's the kind of question I'm not prepared to answer.

The Distinct Impression

'I was delivering a child
In this kip of a bedroom in Keogh Square.
The woman jerked and groaned in the bed
Sweat wetting her hair.

Six children lumped and stared at me
As I worked on her.
In the bed with the woman was her man,
Face to the wall, an occasional snore.

"Is it out yet?" he asked of a sudden.
If I'd a bucket o' boilin' water then
I'd have emptied it over his skin.

I had the distinct impression
That the moment the child was out of the woman
That bastard would be back in.'

Eily Kilbride

On the North side of Cork city
Where I sported and played
On the banks of my own lovely Lee
Having seen the goat break loose in Grand Parade

I met a child, Eily Kilbride
Who'd never heard of marmalade,
Whose experience of breakfast
Was coldly limited,

Whose entire school day
Was a bag of crisps,
Whose parents had no work to do,

Who went, once, into the countryside,
Saw a horse with a feeding bag over its head
And thought it was sniffing glue.

I Knew Janet Once

In Colenta Hospital, Bucharest,
Hope is drugs
Orphans with AIDS are guinea pigs.

A hundred infants lie in their cots.
Some suck their bottles, some cry,
All wait to be injected
With FLV23/A.

According to Save the Children Fund in Sweden
The experiments are being conducted
Without proper protocol and expertise.

'We have no alternative' say the Hospital Authorities
'There is no vaccine, no treatment.
Maybe this will work. It's non-toxic.
We are following the highest standards
In our efforts to fight this ravaging disease.'

An AIDS baby, frail and thin, sits on Janet's knees.
I knew Janet once. She's deep in the baby's eyes.

A Pit of Dead Men

Dr Bridgeman said 'What are we to do
If ten-year-old poets insist
On writing of these midnight meetings
With their fathers' lust,
    Randy shaggers invading their daughters' beds
Trying to hush the whole thing up at the same time?
The daughters are writing about it, using their heads,
Telling the world of their fathers' crimes,
Keeping nothing back, all spilled out, can you imagine
What it'll do to these families?

When I was at school we did Shakespeare and Milton,
I learned *Paradise Lost* and all its epic beauties,
Adam and Eve and God, Heaven, Hell and Satan
But these children's poems stink like a pit of dead men.'

'Are the poems honest, Doctor? Should the young girls tell?'

'What good is honesty if home is hell?'

Seven Years

Because I'd walked by the side of the man
Who'd grown out of the heavenly boy
I snuffed out my interest in pop-song and can-can
And laboured for seven years at my *Ode to Joy*.

People I knew insisted there was joy in this world.
My *Ode* led me through a multitude of styles.
As the years melted I began to lose conviction
And was not inspired by regular plagues of piles.

Many are the forces moulding my notion of joy –
Pneumonia, moneylending, Asian flu, forms of pox,
Apostles, crucifixions, celibates, all things political:

After seven years I found I had nothing to say.
My *Ode* never even became an interesting fake.
All I could imagine was nothing at all.

A Deeper Tyrant

'Beware of mothers.
My father came in late at night
Saying he'd screwed three women.
She listened

Gave nothing away
Obeyed.
He screwed and screwed and screwed.
She bowed her head,

A deeper tyrant than he.
If I had to choose a man to teach me
How to screw it would be my father,

We'd be in a kiphouse together,
He'd give me his skill, his unwilling pity.
I'd pass these on to my son, or try to.'

Night Air

'My friend Rebecca returned from a party,
Glad of the peace of home, sat in
Her living-room listening to music.
After a while she decided to check the children,
Softly upstairs towards Jonathan's bedroom.
He was twelve, her favourite. She found him
Lying in bed, naked, asleep, his penis
Erect in the light thrown from the landing.
Before she knew it she was at the bedside,
Wanting the boy's penis inside her. Breathing
"Jonathan! Jonathan!" she leaned towards him, then realising
Herself, turned, closed the door, rushed downstairs, out
Into the garden, gulped the night air, her shocked mind shivering.'

Out of Sight

When language breaks children find it
Easy to kill. James Wade
Whose house began to burn one night
Phoned the fire-brigade,

It came and fought the fire
Or tried to. Out of the dark
Stones came hurtling from children's hands
And put an end to work.

The firemen ran, the house burned,
The flames dayed night
Burning like hate, like unappeasable desire

And who'll forget the curses curses curses
Of children out of sight
Stoning the men road engines James Wade his fire?

Cardboard Child

As I sniffed my way through the midnight smoggy
I saw children sleeping
In doorways of the rubbishy city –
Almost enough to set me weeping.
I approached a cardboard child and asked
'Why are you not at home in bed?'
'No home,' she said 'No home', again and again.
She lay like a litterbag
Near the river thickening to the sea.
No champion of justice I, yet I swear
Rare rage boiled up. I was wild.
'The wrong people,' I said, 'own all the silver,
All the silver.' She looked at me. She didn't care.
What do I care for the cardboard child?

An Ardent Lad

It's not often we get snow in Nazareth
But when it falls it makes me brood
On purity and the transitional character of death
Pointing to flawless God.

There I was, chickenstepping down the road,
Spellbound by the stainless evidence
Of what my blood longed for, my cold blood,
When a bad snowball assassinated me

And refrigerated even my seventh sense.
I turned, it was an ardent lad, he
Laughed, I walked over, kicked him in the balls,
He screamed, I kicked him in the arse
Twice, it's only fun he yelled, I know that I
Said, it's only fun, I must go now, duty calls.

Sludge

I am warning parents
Not to allow their children to bathe
In parts of Dublin Bay where
Sludgy build-ups of rotting algae accumulate.

The sludge, black with a white crust
When the top dries, and proffering a stench
Is reported by walkers on strands
At Sandymount, Booterstown, Dollymount.

The sludge appears each year in Dublin Bay.
High tides wash up green algae
That grows on mudflats and starts to decay.

Sewage, unnoticed, slouches home through the sludge
Putting all who touch it
In danger of various infections.

Birds eat the sludge. Walkers along the Bay
Should report to the Eastern Health Board
If they see birds staggering in the slime
'Behaving as if they were drunk'.

Birds can be cured if caught in time.

The Innocence of Slaughterers

You didn't set out with dagger and axe
After midnight stealing into towns and villages
To murder the sleeping children; nor did you hire
Hit-men to do the job while your averted eyes

Embraced the raped landscape of your childhood.
No, you stayed at home and, armchaired, read
The UNICEF Report. You were moved, moved,
And saving schemes bombarded your head.

Such schemes! Passionate as your youthful dreams!
Revolutionary, they came to nothing, how could
Such ardour fail to make one loaf of bread?

36

The children die, die, no screams
Split you or me, the innocent blood
Of slaughterers spits on the huge small dead.

The Sound

Sheltering from a shower of consciousness
I crouched in Limbo where the thought was born;
A perfect wound bespeaks a perfect thorn
And bleeding more begins with bleeding less.

Of all the haunting words I choose *forlorn*,
I feel I own it like a costly house
Where I can think or sleep or rot or burn
In solitude remote and dangerous.

The shower has stopped, I'm taking the new sun,
Traitorous words are banished underground.
Sick of disease the god goes healing men
Who might be better treated by a gun,
Their ills dying like the sound
Of gunfire. Give me that sound again, again,

words

what's words ozzie assed me
sounds dat kum outa peepul's mouths i said
where dey kum from first sez ozzie
dunno i replied

fukken fish have no words ozzie went on
but dey enjoy de fukken sea
and fukken tigers have no words
but dey enjoy eatin you and me

only peepul has words ozzie said
an luk at de shit dey talk
if i kud reed i'd say buks are shit as well

words are to kummynikate sez i

like shit sez ozzie won good bomm
blow de whole fukken world ta hell

sumtimes ozzie

sumtimes ozzie get very odd indeed
he get mad for money or girls or blood
he come over ta me here at my place
he say wudja pleez jeez for de luvvagod

have a bitta crack with me tonite
when i see dat luk in his eye
i wanna tell him relax take it easy
but i might as well be talkin to a fly

upside down on de seelin
funny way ta luk at de world
so i go with ozzie down ta york street

and he snatch a bag from an old wumman
take out de money trow de bag away
buy a lotta cider go to his place turn out de lite

madmanalive

sumtimes ozzie get dis fierce urge
ta go fast tru dublin really fast man
so he cum over ta my place in a surge
of anger or sumtin an he say kummon

so i go we try merryon square an
leeson street den we walk out
ta ballsbridge very rich peepul dayre
an sumtimes we find de car we're lukkin for

shiny an black ozzie luv cars black like
midnite he sez dis time, we drive
tru dublin in a merk in spite

o' de fakt we havvent a tosser
between us ozzie is madmanalive
god help anyone get in our way tonite

no trubbal

no trubbal ta ozzie ta lead a gang
a twenty yewts as if dey was wun
rob ole peepul de day a de penshun
an den have fun

well furst ozzie go down de keys ta dat pub
an buy duzzens a bottals a cider
find an empty house an swig like hell
till de hole gang is mad tagedder

den de gang hoot an howl tru de town
till sumwun fritened fone de pulleece

ozzie an de gang hav pokkets fulla stones

de pulleece drive up wid sirens blarin mad
ozzie wait a while den he giv de word
de twenty yewts scream
                              'stone dere fukken bones'.

prades

ozzie is stonemad about prades
so he say kummon ta belfast
for de 12th an we see de orangemen
beatin de shit outa de drums
beltin em as if dey was katliks' heads

so we set out from dublin
an landed in belfast for de fun
it was brill
dere was colour an music an everyone
was havin a go at sumtin i dunno

what but i'll never forget ozzie in
de middul of all de excitement
pickin pockets right left and centre

on de train back to dublin he was laffin his head
off, dere shud be more fukken prades he said

flushed

ozzie kum to me all flushed sez he
i want a fukken ride
i was lukken at de telly lass nite
sumwun played here kums de bride

sum fukken bride i can tell ya boy
i very nearly hopped inta de box
kummon now sez ozzie we'll go ta
our pub down de keys an get our rocks

off so down we toddle like a pair
o' young bulls up from de cuntry

fifteen pints o' cider a man i never lied
about drink in me life we pick up two
fine tings an screw em crosseyed up in de park
ozzie said tis hard ta whack de fukken ride

ozzie smiled

ozzie got six months in spike island for sundry offences
de judge sez ozzie was a wild animal
dat was most o' de time outa his senses
when ozzie was sentenced i thought he'd go wild

dayre he stud between two coppas
i lukked at him i felt sick but ozzie smiled
when ozzie smiles like dat dere's danger ahead
he smiled at de judge den he walked

politely outa de court my head
was spinnin after three months ozzie
turned up at my place he said two screws

got spiked in spike island he said he wanted
ta visit his fayvrit allied irish bankbranch
before leavin ireland for a long hollyday in england

bang

ozzie herd sumwun in a pub
sayin ireland shud be yewnighted
de man who did dat wud be faymuss
ozzie was delighted

so he joined de i.r.a.
dey trew him out
don't ask me why
ozzie didn't give a shite

dat hidriggin bomm sez he
explodin over england
wud make de hell of a bang
an yewnight ireland

freedom sez ozzie is knowin what ta do
if i can get wun bomm sez he i can always get two

skool

dis jesus fella sez ozzie who was he
how de fuck do i know sez i
you went ta skool forra bit sez ozzie
didn't learn much dayre sez i

but he died on de cross sez i
for you an for me de teetchur said
what de fuck you talkin about sez ozzie
de man is dead dat's all de man is dead

but everywun sez jesus dis an jesus dat
pay de jesus rent by us a jesus pint
till i get de jesus dole

but who de jesus hell was he sez ozzie
i dunno sez i yoor jesus iggerant sez he
shuv yoor iggerance up yoor bleedin hole

work

ozzie never worked in his life
he juss draws de jesus dole
in tree diffrent playces
he sez money is good for de soul

he sez work is de wickedest word in
de world it shud never be menshunned
he sez work is de only drug he don't like
its all right for peepul in de suburbs

i asked ozzie what would he do
if he got cot in his little trix
he said he'd apply for legal aid

an what are you doin at de moment
i assed him ozzie smiled an said
i'm workin on a home-made hand grinade

42

marridge

lil cassidy take de whip ozzie said
jim cassidy give it to her every night
i hear her scream an cry
she calm down after a while

deyre married y'know
marridge take place in churches
girls in nice dresses men in soots
preests prayers booze grub big speeches

lil cassidy dressed in white one day
now she cry when she get de whip
she try ta run from jim she juss fall

she scream fuck you she get hurt she curse she pray
he lift de fist he gave her a dunt in de lip
i dunno why peepul get married at all

Jobs

'Me first mistake was stealin' two bob
Off me daddy. If I'd a bit o' common
Jimmy Rafferty I'd a told him straight
But I hedged an' he hit me an' got me a job

As a messenger-boy in a shop in Duke Street,
I stuck it for two years, then I went workin'
For a cloth-maker shoulderin' rolls
O' cloth all over me city o' Dublin, sweatin'.

Left that, too. Lugs Brannigan gave me a cuff
On the ear one night when I crashed a queue
Outside the Odeon, then got me a job as an usher.
Lugs was a great man, helped the poor

Especially women beaten by animalmen.
I left that too. At nineteen I started to drink
Porter Phoenix Carlsberg Smithwicks Power Jameson

Anything then. Then I stopped it,
Got a job in the sewers. With
Helmet gloves rubber clothes flashlamp
I went down below Dublin

From Kingsbridge into O'Connell Street
Flashin' me lamp in the eyes o' rats
Diabolical as tomcats. Rats don't like light
In their eyes. I waded through shit,

Women's jamrags and men's rubbers stuck
To my rubbery clothes. Rubber clings to rubber.
The ends men will go to for a fuck!
The sewers o' Dublin are flush with the relics o' lovers.

Motherogod, what flowed between me legs!
I left that too, I wrote a song and a hymn
Called *My Lady in Blue*
I wanted Micky Mocke to sing it, that fell through,

I have four grandchildren now, I love 'em, I'm fifty-five,
I've a security job, I'm happy, I'm workin', I'm alive.'

By Any Other Name

The famous theologian, chatting with Herod and myself
Was silent a moment, then infallibled to us,
'It's clear, from whatever angle you consider the matter,
Judas by any other name would be as treacherous.'

Stimulated, I dived into my own mind,
That bottomless pit of fatuous impressions
Fascinating as money, countless as grains of sand
In Salthill or Calais or Brighton or Ballybunion
Where the rascal Atlantic threatens the Golf Links.

'By any other name...' François Jacques Marie Iscariot –
I rolled it on my lying tongue, my tongue said no.
I thought of Henry Cecil Cyril Sebastian Vidkun Idi Dick
Harry Tom Seamus Horace Ted Slim Pat
Barney Ernie Gulliver Knacker Snowball Brendan Holy Joe.

Not right, I thought, not right. Then up popped Irish Mick.
All other names were burnt-out stars. Mick did the trick.

Herod's Way

Herod's way of coping with children?
'Knife the little fuckers, one by one.'

Herod's Epitaph

Time's children gave him plenty rope:
While there's death there's hope.

The Little Trick

So much to say, so little said.
The children's souls are roses after rain.
I think tonight of the world's dead –
        Suppose they lived again

And saw the consequences of their attempts to be
Fathers and mothers to the likes of me.
Let me not dwell on that, the story
Is of men or monsters, have it your way.

Even if I said what I have to say
It'd be a lie in the end, long before the end,
One word after another, tale, song, poem, lie;

I must operate on myself, the question is how.
Do I apply the knife and find
The little trick that makes me live or die?

Or admit my words betray my pain,
Throw pennies at them, tinkers in the rain?

That's Where

Why then did I know I should let my blood
Flow down the main street of that small town
Where a bomb in a doorway killed a milkman
And seven children?

And why, out of that blinding red stream,
Was I compelled to lift with my right
Forefinger a single drop,
Hold it up to the light

　　Where it slowly formed itself into a star?
A star at the end of my finger!
Star of my blood! My pathetic blood!

That's where the milkman and the seven children were
Beginning to understand the mind of the bomber
That's where my mind went right and wrong for good

And ill, that's where I saw things
As I knew I should.

Murty's Burning Hands

I heard the questions gunning past
Like assassins in search of a target.
I thought of Murty Galvin in the slow class,
The sweat on his forehead unable to answer
And Murty shaking at

　　Why did God make hell?
　　What do you mean by angels?
　　What is Original Sin?
　　On what day did God become man?
　　Where was Christ's body while his soul was in Limbo?
　　What is the greatest of all misfortunes?
　　What is forbidden by the ninth commandment?
　　For what end did God make us?
　　What is the happiness of heaven?

46

When the questions got no answer
Murty was beaten by the teacher.
'Take me to the fountain,' Murty said.
I pumped the water over Murty's burning hands.
He dried his hands on his jumper.
Whinbushes blazed madyellow, God knows why.
There was money for hares that must escape or die.
'All the fuckin' questions,' Murty said.
'An' me without an answer in me head.'

Feed the Children

Let my story feed the children
Who need a monster to hate and fear.
Arrange them in a classroom
Pour me into each innocent ear.
Be sure they know exactly what I've done
How I inflicted my own punishment
On myself, in a ropey place, alone.
Describe my face, my hands, my hair. Say I was sent
By darkness to commit the ultimate crime
Against the light and am the only man
Other men have not forgiven.
Tell the children all this, and more, so that their time
On earth will prove to all how no one
Of my kind can get within an ass's roar of heaven.

Tricks

The problem with having a dog is kids
I'm hearing noises I never heard before
Sure you could be killed crossin' the street
Must get in touch with Mary's organisation
Install a Chubb Alarm over the front door

When people speak of a victim
They have in mind
A frail elderly lady
With bad arthritis and partly blind

They rarely think of a strong brute like me
Strolling along a street
When two knife-wielding muggers attack
Grab all my cherished pieces of silver
Give me a valedictory stab in the back.

My mind is playing tricks, my bedsit is an abyss.
I'll see someone hangs for this.

Staring

'He stood at my bedroom door
Put his left forefinger against
The thin mean line of his mouth.
I was staring at a cross that said
      Ssshh!'

When I Was Three

'He was my father in that land and he was odd
Although he said the rosary at evening
And confessed his sins to God
Or someone representing God listening
In the absolving twilight the first
Saturday of every month of every year.
When I was three he came into my room
At night, switched off the light on my cold fear

And stuck his finger up my bum.
He said stick out your tongue, he put his
Tongue to my tongue in a hideous kiss,
Shoved his finger between my thighs,
Same thing every night, and I was dumb
And when he went I bit and swallowed all the cries
But I kept gasping-living and I don't know why.

O daddy daddy, rain at the window is breaking out my eyes.'

Vigil

'The lady of the house is a notorious drug-pusher
The police know she's been at it for years
Our vigil at her door is to persuade her
To get out of here.
        I can't prove it but she killed my son.
It took him three years to die.
The lady has a husband two brothers a daughter and three sons:
A happy family
Planting misery in people, watching it grow
And deepen in the youngsters' eyes
While the lady of the house counts her money.
Why not call in the law, you ask. We tried that.
Whatever law is, it's in our hands now.
Law may be right and strong, law may be wise
But when a rat attacks me I kill the rat.'

Faces

'An easy birth, a daughter, my fourth child,
I hated her from the start
And resolved there and then
I'd hate her all my life with all my heart
Though something in my heart rebelled at that.
I beat her, I wanted to kill her, I beat her
Night and day, bloody black and blue,
I wanted to strangle her, knife her, poison her, I
Wanted to save her too

From me, my icy eyes, my killing mind,
I beat her where bruises can't be seen,
Why did I do it? I wanted to find
Out why I resolved myself to be obscene.

One bruising night, in my favourite beating-place,
My daughter's face became my mother's hate-filled face.'

Youngsters Today

'You can be sure o' nothin' now, sir.
You might get a knife in the chest or a hammer
On the head if you open the door to a stranger.
Young boys an' girls are stuck into crime, sir.

Mick Magee, an ould butty o' mine an' his sister
Julia, are livin' in a flat out in Cork Street.
Three girls, Legion o' Mary workers,
They said, knocked at their door. Mick and Julie

Greeted 'em heart-an'-a-half into the flat.
One o' the girls slipped upstairs, ransacked the place,
Stole every penny me friends'd managed to save.

Mick is arthritic, Julia's eyes are failin'.
D'you know what, sir? The youngsters today
Would steal a corpse outa the grave!'

A Specially Gifted Child

Mental gymnastics displayed in the cradle
Shrewd questions asked instead of acting giddy or wild
Convinced my mother I was unusually able
And deserved the status of A Specially Gifted Child.

At five I understood the currencies of the world
At seven I made a Marxist friend brain-weary
With a profitable revision of
His party's major economic theory.

Words craved my interest. I gave it.
That multi-volumed Oxford was a joy.
Monumental. Pathetic too. I was the first to see.

I saw through father mother home, I knew the time to leave it,
I sought pure gold, to hell with base alloy.
And then I met a man who puzzled me.

THREE

I hear the pages crying

Grey-Back

Bulleting down
From his private sky
He ripped the eyes
Out of the lamb
Half-way out of the sheep.

The old grey-backed crow!

O my father full of advice
   My brother tremulous with yearning
      My lovers in lost ballrooms
         My exams my job my pension
            My fear I might lose it all
               My friend-enemy insulting me
                  My body pumping with dream
                     My head in a pit of defeat
                       My hand ready to kill

Whatever came between me and the man
I believed I loved?

Between Bottles

What they say of his blood is true of the man:
It spattered all over the place
From lips nose head back shoulders buttocks hands face,
Nobody wiped it up, it lay in the sun,
Faded into the ground
Rained upwards towards the stars
Down on the bodies of soldiers killed in wars
And girls giving birth in productive lands.

In the minds of men the blood became clichés
And the clichés were the most powerful
Forces the world has known.

I spent a week with Hitler after the Fall of Paris
Helping him to polish his clichés in an old Château
Between bottles of Chablis, Beaujolais, Beaune.

No Image Fits

I have never seen him and I have never seen
Anyone but him. He is older than the world and he
Is always young. What he says is in every ear
And has never been heard before.
I have tried to kill him in me,
He is in me more than ever.
I saw his hands smashed by dum-dum bullets,
His hands holding the earth are whole and tender.
If I knew what love is I would call him a lover.
Break him like glass, every splinter is wonder.
I had not understood that annihilation
Makes him live with an intensity I cannot understand.
That I cannot understand is the bit of wisdom I have found.
He splits my mind like an axe a tree.
He makes my heart deeper and fuller than my heart will dare to be.
He would make me at home beyond the sky and the black ground,
He would craze me with the light on the brilliant sand,
He is the joy of the first word, the music of the undiscovered human.
Undiscovered! Yet I live as if my music were known.
He is what I cannot lose and cannot find
He is nothing, nothing but body and soul and heart and mind.

So gentle is he the gentlest air
Is rough by comparison
So kind is he I cannot dream
A kinder man
So distant is he the farthest star
Sleeps at my breast
So near is he the thought of him
Puts me outside myself

So one with love is he
I know love is
Time and eternity
And all their images.
No image fits, no rod, no crown.

I brought him down.

Compiling a Life

I'm compiling a life tonight
Of this and that: family letters, a rent-book,
Joan Connolly's articles on love and marriage
Culled from New Years in the outback,
A sermon given somewhere, two pages missing,
Random thoughts scribbled on envelopes,
Postcards from Laura, an invitation to dinner,
Pencil-drawings of Spanish Armada ships,
An Expressionist painting of The Unforgivable Sinner's lips,
The limp débris of what may have been passion
Once, enough to make my imagination tear
Into a relationship between man and God
And I'll write it down by Jesus I'll write it down
And some pedantic old wanker somewhere
Will think it a scholarly miracle
When he proves I'm a fraud.
A fraud? Of course I am. That's my part in the plot.
Most men are frauds, somehow, though they speak as if they're not.

A Second's Eternity

Even when he was acting the tough around Jerusalem
He had a good word for the bad women
Who liked him for how he saw them
And talked to them in their poxy dens.

Late at night when the screwing has to start
In the moaning towns, villages and cities
Where a longing prick is a pain in the heart
And no one is near to give you the kiss of life

And you, like him, might be out walking by
A river, staring at lights, thinking of simple misery
And the ubiquitous insult to simple dignity

Then he, like you, sees a dead dog in the street,
Bends down, touches, you believe he sighs
As he looks for a second's eternity through the dead eyes.

God of Insult

If I come to believe in a god again
I will believe in the god of insult.
That way, the obscene lords won't have an unruffled ride,
The uncouth boorish truth will spit in the listening bone
To see respectable faces melt
Into an understanding of why
Lovers have always lied. Dare I say
That once in the grinning cliques, I tried?

Beyond It All

Have you ever been in the company of one
Who seemed
Beyond it all
As though he'd dreamed
The vilest atrocity
We lot are capable of?
Not only that, but he has this notion of love
To make us free:

Free, despite the evidence, O the evidence,
Let me not think of that,
That lived-in, lived-with pit

Of men women children beasts
Here, gone in a blink.
Someone beyond it all? Or too much in it?
I met him, I think.

Stretcher Case

What they think is love is not what love is.
Every thought is an act of Judas and a plea to Christ
Or an act of Christ and a plea to Judas
Whose heart was never iced

Over like the seminary in our town
During the no-go winter of sixty-three.
The milk froze in the cows;
Dreams in folks' heads, waves on the living sea

And the Great Philosophical Tradition were cramped
As an aging footballer who can't handle extra time
So the young winger blots him out,
The St John's Ambulance men stretcher him off.
He knows it's the end and the end is no shame
Because he gave it all he had for as long as he could.
What more can a stretcher-case do? Cover his head.
Supporters will tell you he loved what he did.
'A broken back? Jesus, he was a game kid!'

Crucifix-Kisser

There are those who can't live without love
Or tell themselves so,
Must have Pagan amour or Christian caritas
Or it's no bloody go.
Some model themselves on Adonis
Some on Christ
But for Bartley McNally the swish
Of himself must suffice.

Down in the ratty tenements
Tubercular girls sigh
For one strong fucking push,
The old and the new testaments
Ring hollow, a gospelly lie
Worth only the bum's rush
Into the streets where multitudes shove
And the huge-bosomed, red-lipped crucifix-kisser
Is shrieking of love.

God As An Unmarried Mother

God fell in love with this Limerick fella
Who, although a good Confraternity Man,
Fell in love with God also
And wanted to have a baby with Her.

It happened one night in a field outside Glin.
God got pregnant and the Confraternity Man
Changed because he re-fell in love with the old sin-
stuff. God was left on Her own.

God gave birth to a darling child
And struggled to rear him all by Herself.
Some people were kind but quite a few condemned Her

Writing to the papers to say She was defiled
And deserved to be left on the shelf
By the Confraternity Man who was safe in England somewhere.

That Multiple Cold

Unlike God I am everywhere
And surprise myself with my ubiquity;
I hear myself in a lover's whisper
Thrusting into the old mystery.
I hear myself in a phone-call
From the other side of the Atlantic;
Words banal and magical
Will make Melissa Sweeney shake
With fear in the small house by the choked canal
Where I see myself in a teacher's eyes
Explaining me to Melissa's child.

How shall I convince you explanation is all lies?
How shall I tell what I know to be real
When I am I, and everywhere, and properly, y'know, reviled?
It is my voice stabs me most. That multiple cold...

A Moment of Love

Should I permit myself a moment of love
It would be for the way
He explodes in the face
Of dominant mediocrity
                   – a bomb of a man
Ticking in the timid corners of time.
     Is he the first terrorist
Warring against all that I am?

I am forcing my heart to open to the fact
That of all those I've known and half-known
He's the one who refuses to hide

Anything. Terrifying. He must be attacked
From all angles, get him, do him, he's the one
To be shot knifed hanged strangled drowned crucified.

     We'll praise him when he's dead
Honour the truth of every word he said
Make his name inseparable from the name of God.

The Heart of Nothingmatters

At the heart of nothingmatters, love is born.
He walks with the world's emptiness in his face
Not pausing to look at children
Huddled in the shade of the blackthorn

Bush, somewhere you'd never look twice.
If the curious animals followed him he wouldn't look.
Next year's snow is falling through his eyes
And as he walks he is the silence of a rock.

Creatures might recoil, sensing his indifference,
The last of our beautiful cities melt,
Our sweetest singers be all forlorn.

Instead, the seasons turn to entrance
Each other, a perfect form is shaped through fault,
At the heart of nothingmatters, love is born.

Holiday

It was years later, I was on holiday,
Late Autumn, one of my favourite towns
In the south-east corner of Africa,
Doing research in rare monkeys' skeletons.

I was strolling down a crowded street
Musing in that warm style, nostalgic and dim,
When (I swear to God my heart missed a beat)
I saw him

Passing about seven yards to my right side,
Looking straight ahead, clothed in white,
Calm, purposeful, tall.

I stared, then ran through the crowd,
Touched his shoulder, blurted my question straight.
'Sorry' he smiled, 'Sorry. That's not my name at all.'

I froze back to rare monkeys' skeletons, human fool.

The Beautiful Sentiments

The beautiful sentiments comfort me like Johnson's
Babypowder motherkissing my skin.
I could cry when I hear 'Love thy neighbour',
Secret of home, civilisation.

Yet my neighbour is less than loving
Saying and doing things not greatly to my taste
Such as expecting me to breakfast on
Choice cutlets of nuclear waste.

For behold my neighbour dumpeth his opulent waste on me
Oozing like fat tributes from his poison-palaces
Humming with good works in his unmean and pleasant land.
How shall I love this neighbour who murders the sea
And in murdering it propagates oily lies?
My love, I fear, turns sour. Will my neighbour understand?
My neighbour. Neighbour. Might I not spend

An average dicey winter
Brooding on that word? Nay! Burr!
No. Neighbour. Who is my neighbour?
After two thousand years on earth, I ask
Who is my neighbour? Lost God, let me choose
One, he was blind, his brother had the task
Of guiding him down the village street to Mass
Where he, blind and slight, gazed at the tabernacle.
That's where God is, the priest and teacher said.
House of Gold
        Ark of the covenant
            Morning Star
Remember o most tender…so blind and small,
My neighbour's words were eyes, eyes blind with blood,
He died, his brother died, my mind is where they are,
If I forget or banish them, they never were,
If the fierce dream weakens, I have no neighbour,
If I have no neighbour, I am no lover,
If the fierce dream weakens, I am loveless ever.

I Hear the Pages Crying

'My dear Ted, I followed him
For several years through the country
Trying to keep track of his parables and miracles,
His love mercy pity
For the most leprous types this place can produce.
I watched him closely, taking regular notes.
I looked at him looking
Into people's hearts, sifting their minds,
Giving them gifts of light, hearing and sight.
I listened to the voices of his friends and enemies.
I decided to write.

I've been busy with my own work, it's not easy
Being a country G.P.
But I think I caught something of him
Or did I half-catch the merest glimpses?
It's hard to say, the book seemed to write itself,
Had to be there, a cat cleaning itself in the sun,
A knowledge that flesh is mercy covering the bone,
Becoming its own history, its own mythology.

He was heartbreakingly human, I won't write again,
There is no language that is not in vain,
No beautiful line that is not profane,
Ignorance showers through my heart and brain
Like this endless sickness in men women children,
My book stinks of sickness, a sweaty sense of dying
Into the notion that truth becomes helpless lying,
He moved through that, I tried for the right words,
They twisted, gibbered, where are the words for him?
At every sickbed now I hear the pages crying.'

Superman

I may have mentioned I lay at my own side,
Friendly, trying to create in me a little rest.
On th'other hand, being for icy centuries unblessed,
I may have been lying. If I say my mind aloud

And admit that walking an average tatty street
Becomes a heady odyssey in non-existence
Punctuated by an interest in deplorable antiques,
Trite minds in print, old stamps, old shillings and pence,

I can hardly expect you to follow me
When I superman out of myself to a star behind stars.
The sound of kisskisskissing greets my brain

And multicoloured flowers of treachery
Scream to be plucked and sold to visitors
Willing me, on this remote spot, to repeat myself
                                        Again and again
Till I have purged my heart of whatever drove me
To lie at my own side, as if I were someone who loved me.

Versions

Before the known, within, beyond it, mocking, the unknown:
I wear that hat because it fits me.
He was a man
With an extra-terrestrial air of mystery.

Once in a worldtime you meet a man like that.
Such was the impression he made on me
And on my metaphysical hat
I resolved to commission a biography.

Through an agent I spoke to Matthew,
Mark, Luke, John.
Each said he'd write a book and make it true.

I read each book in turn. All four
Give mesmerising versions of the man
But not the man I knew.

My Mind of Questions

Did Jesus have brothers and sisters?
　　　　Did they give him a rough time?
What was it like on a Saturday night
　　　　In the Holy Family home?

Did they mock his God-like talents?
　　　　Laugh at wise things he said?
Did he fight with them for an extra spud
　　　　Or a cut o' brown bread?

Did he have a favourite sister
　　　　Who understood him better than most
And agreed that he was the Father
　　　　Son and Holy Ghost?

If challenged, would he fight back,
　　　　Square up to a bully?
Was he a handy lad with the mitts
　　　　Sidestepping beautifully

When a bigger lad charged at him,
                Expecting to knock him down?
Did Jesus trip him up
                Then go to town?

What was he like in the scrap
                When the dirt blinded his eyes?
Did he ever get a kick in the balls
                From some frigger twice his size?

When, in the streets of Nazareth,
                Did he first hear the name of God?
Did he know it was his own name
                When he first tasted blood?

Did he go in search of birds' nests
                In meadow, field and glen?
And if he found a thrush's nest
                Did he rob it then?

Did he ever fish for eels
                And watch them die at his feet
Wriggling like love in the dust?
                Gospels, you're incomplete.

What was he like at school?
                Was he fond of poetry?
Did he make the teacher feel like a fool
                Because he lacked divinity?

What did the teacher think of him
                Doing his father's business?
Did he wonder at times if Jesus
                Was out of his tree, or worse?

Did Jesus like to sing?
                Did he whistle and hum
As he walked the streets of Nazareth
                Going home to mum?

(I've heard it said he lacked
                A sense of humour,
That his mind was grim and grew grimmer
                And grimmer and grimmer).

What was his appetite like?
　　　　　What did he like to eat?
What did he see the first time he washed
　　　　　His hands and feet?

What were his fingers like? His mouth?
　　　　　His throat, toes, thighs, teeth, eyes?
Did he often cry? For what? And what
　　　　　Was the sound of his sighs

At night when he was alone
　　　　　And no one had ever been created
Except as shadowy strangers
　　　　　Who went their separate ways?

What did he think of his neighbours?
　　　　　His neighbours of him?
Was he a quiet little fella
　　　　　Fond of his home?

Or did he sometimes seem
　　　　　As if he were biding his time
Like a man with a job to do
　　　　　That took up all his mind?

At what moment did he know
　　　　　That home is not enough
And he must scour the darkness
　　　　　To give and find love

Among strangers waiting out there
　　　　　Full of need,
So full his heart inclined
　　　　　To bleed?

Did he break up his family?
　　　　　Did they resent him?
From the day he left did he ever
　　　　　Get in touch again?

Was he handsomely made
　　　　　Or humped, mis-shapen?
Was his life a preparation
　　　　　For what can never happen?

64

When he saw the sadness of sex
                Did he sit and think
Or slip down a Nazareth laneway
                For a happy wank?

Back in the Holy Family
                All hope and despair on the shelf
Did he look in the eyes of others
                Or smell himself?

Did he stand in a doorway of time
                Look at a street
Hear people bawl for his blood
                And then forget

He'd ever existed? Did he shudder
                To know the future now?
Did he know? How could he bear it?
                The sweat on the boy's brow

Turns to blood in my mind of questions,
                How foolish they are,
What do I know of anything,
                Even my own star?

My own star above all, perhaps?
                My own blood?
My own tracking, trackless, shapeless, restless,
                Sleepless head?

Pass the wine, please

The sixty-four thousand dollar question:
How will he be seen?
The foremost man of all creation
Who lifted his people from pits of obscene
Indifference, rescued generations of slaves from squalor,
Made them aware of who whey are?
Did he show them how a stranger is a brother?
Breed ideas of justice where no such ideas were?

                Or will they say

c

'The bastard went too far'?
Had a passionate nature but in the end became
An eccentric subjectivist, reckless adventurer,
Self-obsessed lunatic perpetrating war?
Will unborn judges revere or mock his name?
Pass the wine, please. Don't know the answer.
I am in other things, but not in this, a chancer.

Golden's Cross

Take off into the snow whenever he comes
Like a pompous wind down a humble road
Scattering the grasses with cosmic drums
Announcing the advent of a god

       Importing himself for pleasure
With a girl who's happy this should be so;
      Or visit the river in summer
And feel its invitation in the blood and smile

At warning-signs stuck into the earth
(They're fading already). Or take the boat to England
Or read a man's face for fun, assess the Boss
      Congratulate him on his inestimable worth.
          Whatever prisons clank in my head
I found my paradise at Golden's Cross.

I Am Resolved

Jesus, I said, I do not swear, I am resolved,
No matter what blinds my eyes or blocks my way
Or ordains that my whole purpose he halved,
Not to let the clichés get in my way.

The first cliché is love. I tore a strip of his skin.
Look at this cliché, I said, was it for this you died?
Was it for this you dumped yourself in the loony-bin of sin?
Yes, he replied.

66

Strip by strip I peeled the clichés, bits of flesh,
Slivers of bone, then the vital mucky stuff.
Clichés, I said, clichés, is this all you have to give?
Why try to hide the fact of human trash?
Why not Hitler the bastards? Cut up rough?
What am I to do with the clichés since
Every cliché is prepared to say what it means to live?

I'm not going to mention his reply.
You know it, anyway.

A Pleasant Evening

I drove Jesus out to Restaurant Merry Bó
In my snappy little Volkswagen (secondhand).
Starters were good: Jesus had avocado
With prawns while I chose courgette soup and
Bacon with croutons. For the main course
Jesus took vinegared cod, filleted by the Merry Bó
Boss himself, there at the table. Steak with butter and herb

Sauce was my melt-in-the-mouth choice. The
Dessert trolly brought chocolate mousse and
Lemon soufflé. We scoffed the lot, God help us.
The house wine was good, a real presence on our lips.
The bill was reasonable, a mere thousand. I
Paid. A pleasant evening, given our relationship.
Driving home, we agreed that eating is an art.
Jesus released the occasional fart.
Later on, I Merrion Squared and got laid.
All that womanthing. All that Volkswagen. All that food.

Saturday

On Friday, the nailing and cutting-down of the God.
On Sunday, the rising up.
What happened on Saturday?

Feeling a sudden brain-spasm
I sat down that Saturday to study
The Church of Ireland Historical Catechism
With a Foreword by the Most Rev. Arthur W. Barton, D.D.

I discovered Queen Elizabeth the First
Took lessons in Irish Grammar from a book
By Lord Devlin. Storing the Lord's Grammar in her head
She sent Irish type to Dublin
That Bibles and books be printed
To bring good Christian luck to all.
That was the most erudite Saturday of my life.
On Sunday, God rose from the dead.

Handclasp

The first time we met we shook hands,
He looked me in the eyes, I knew
He'd never patted anyone on the back,
My favourite odious gesture. No

Handclasp in my experience resembled this,
Unutterably different from all I'd known.
Handclasps teach more than Universities,
Are shocking revelations of men

And women. I know a politician whose clasp
Is like babyshit, a Civil Servant's
That makes me wish to vomit, bomb, let rip

But I don't, never; an academic's that suggests
A Ph.D. in spartan wanking. But this was different.
I loved that handclasp, that quick, visionary grip.

Open Your Hearts

Open your hearts to the Holy Spirit
For Christ's sake.
We'll be back to you in a moment
After this commercial break.

FOUR

Bunk

Wizened Boy

The dun cow opened herself then
And gave birth to a plastic bag
In the middle of the stable.
The bag contained a wizened boy
With slit eyes and a crooked mouth.
The farmer and the farmer's wife stared aghast
As the wizened boy freed himself from the bag.
'Who's my father?' he asked
The couple, the couple did not reply
But stood and stared, this was unnatural,
This was the dun cow's monster, a bad freaky mistake
That could be here to stay.
Terrified eyes focussed on the wizened boy.
He said 'I want a large hammer in my right hand,
There are things and people I have to break.'
The couple gave him a hammer. He set out.

From the Wall

Escape his death-breath now.
Get out of here.
His voice circles, circles
Around my fear.

I know he's going to come out with it
Soon. ''Twas a bad sight,'
His voice staggers, 'Eight riddled, but they
Had right on their side too, some small right.

Hadn't they? Hadn't they?'
He's pushing me now, hard, into the wall.
They had no damned right on their side,
No right at all.

'They had, they had,' my voice lies.
Death-breath's smile turns away
From the coward who crawls from the wall
With nothing to say.

Grey Ashes, Black Ashes

Death in Bellefeast, seagulls screaming,
I saw all the books ever written
Sprouting wings in the thoughtless morning,
All the writers long forgotten
Moving fingers done with moving.

Books flew to a darkness between two stars
The earth and I were the last spectators
One by one the books became fire
The darkness laughed as the flames leaped higher

And higher until only ashes
Drifted away:

     Grey ashes of thought, black ashes of feeling
Started to fall on the fields and cities
Where people had given words their allegiance
Till black and grey ashes began falling, falling.

I'm back where I started, the taste of nothing,
Death in Bellefeast, seagulls screaming.

No End to Style

Again and again, the generations
Come, workers from fields and meadows
To walk, talk, pass the salt, meet relations
And throw, in the August twilight, long shadows.

                             How should my heart
Ever begin to believe anything?
Even the wretched voices in my head
Lie like men who've perfected
A style of making money.
There must be a heaven for frauds
Since hell is too real.
Liars die peacefully in bed.
There's no end to style.
Self-insult is sharp as any.

I pass through birds' bones, weeds, stones
To kill my few perceptions.
What man, true man, is not a phoney?

When I Look

When I look south I see greed
And muck in their peasant eyes
When I look east I see creeps
And conmen and chatterboxes
When I look west I see bull-necked
Wanglers refusing to pay their way
When I look north I see murder
And money and cute hooks fishing the sea.
Now is the time to make east become west
South become north and so on until each
Curse-o'-God shagger becomes another.

     This should make the desert blush with interest
Open new sympathies for tadpole and cockroach
Unleash the mystical possibility that I am
Your sister and you are my brother.

Lough Derg

Lest anyone should think I am incapable
Of sorrow for sin, I cycled with all
Speed to a boat at a lakeside, a small
Fisherman oared me over to Lough Derg in Donegal

Where sorrow-for-sin goes to town
And remorseful sinners gather
In the parched weather
Calling on God and his colleagues to come down

And forgive them for doing whatever they've done
Or failed to do. I joined in
And whispered to God to forgive my sin
'Judas' said God, 'You're a gas man.

First, you betray me. Then you plead to be forgiven.
D'you think we're gone-in-the-head up here in heaven?
I'm not a God to bear grudges and yet
I think you should hang yourself, you treacherous get!'

This divine advice seemed to me a bit extreme.
I looked around at men and women on their knees.
What in the name of Jesus are they up to at all?
What are they afraid of? Who are they trying to please?
Am I the sole witness of some bad penitential dream?
Are these breastbeating people victims of some immeasurable fall?
Are they stooped in silence because they haven't the heart to scream?
Are the slapping waves the broken hopes of little souls?
Do the blind pretend to see? The deaf let on to hear a call?
Is a man half-happy only when creating his own pain?

What makes a man crave to be a God-licking slave?
What makes him mutter despair to the wind and rain?
Why can't he live with his own voice in this freezing cave?
Are these antics a parody of his preparation for the grave?
O piss into the wind, then piss into the wind again.

I've had some atrocious cups of tea in my time
But Lough Derg tea makes tinkers' piss taste like wine.
I've tasted bread that would scutter a cat
But Lough Derg bread would frighten a starving rat.

Now and then I've found it hard to sleep at night
But after Lough Derg I'll snooze an innocent snooze
While sorrow-for-sin befouls the world like shite
The morning after a monumental, gut-bursting booze.

One encouraging sight I saw, one sight alone:
At the back of the church, triumphant, gasping in joy,
Mr Daniel O'Connell was screwing Miss Molly Malone.
God bless you, Daniel, may she bear you a happy boy,
I prayed at O'Connell's every emancipated moan.

Then into the boat I got and rhythmed back to land.
Up on my bike I mounted and hit for Sligo town
Where I guzzled Ben Bulbens of fish and chips in grand
Style while hungry gods gaped enviously down.

The Colour of Doubt

Months of struggle in the sun and rain
Have come to this:
Croke Park; All-Ireland Final; half-time;
Sixty thousand men begin to piss.

It swells across eternal concrete
Down James's Avenue to Jones's Road.
A demon on the Hogan Stand brandishes his wand;
The piss is blood

Drowning Dublin now, out
Into provincial towns and cities,
Swamping every field, every waiting plain.

Slowly the blood assumes the colour of doubt.
All over Ireland sprout the fresh uncertainties
While sixty thousand howl their ancient pain.

The Toymakers

It was snowing when I reached the toymakers.
They said 'We want to listen to God speaking in our time,
We want to direct history, that is no crime,
We are servants of the Word, make toys, are all brothers.'

I spent three weeks wandering through the houses
Of their village. Time and space had gone on holiday,
Love was reasserting itself as the greatest of all forces,
I won many new friends, I learned how to milk a cow.

Beards were optional. A clean-shaven West
Corkonian who had not, despite the rigorous discipline,
Cut free from the traditions of childhood

Distressed the toymakers when he said there must
Be a Day of Coursing when greyhounds in fine
Fettle would thrill his brothers with spilling blood.

'No!' cried the toymakers 'That would mean betraying our God.'
The snow passed. Time to go, the toymakers waved goodbye. I hit the road.

Bags

The first bag of griefs he hoisted on his back
Was the griefs of children, a sound of playing
Mingled with cries. The second bag
Across his shoulders was the griefs

Of women. Sighs first, then screams flayed
The sacking, all was still for a while.
The third bag of griefs was the griefs of men
Or those who dreamed they were men, their style

Of suffering authentic through centuries.
This was a bag of pictures, including one
Of a man seeing himself in another's eyes before

Killing him, scurrying on into another picture,
Then another, heavy bags on the shoulders of one man
But voices from all the bags cried 'There are more! There are more!'

Radio Revisionist

Sit by me in the darkness, there's nothing more exciting
Than squatting here, naked and still,
A guilty Buddha out of a fat novel,
Pondering on my odd natural treacherous will.
Revision me if it makes you feel better.
They're hanging hostages this bargaining summer.

My Production Notebook

To get a proper understanding of the event
Which I foresaw would matter much to men
Though few among them grasped what it meant
I kept a production notebook on the crucifixion.

I wanted, above all, to get the details right.
For example, the precise structure and weight of the cross

Involved concentrated study late into the night.
I did several drawings of the nails, this was

Fascinating work, I chose samples of the mob's faces,
I noted exactly how the hammers fitted into
The honest fists of those who drove the nails home

For a pittance. To grasp the drama, my production notebook
Is vital. You may consult it at the University
Of Texas: they bought it for an undisclosed sum.

It Slipped Away

One day I saw a zebra
Accept a tiger's fangs.
I saw the tiger eat his fill
Though he didn't gorge himself as humans do.

And one day I saw a virgin
Accept a refusal of her invitation to love.
                        Her face turned grey,
She broke aside, into herself, wept a little
When her might-have-been lover went his way.

        And I too accepted something
Of which I find it difficult to speak.
For a moment, I accepted God's blessing
On my own calling as a traitor.
        I knew the meaning of happiness then
But it slipped away like a never-again-heard song
Beautiful to remember, beyond all right and wrong.

Hungers

I took the battered century in my arms
And kissed its lips and kissed its eyes and said
'Too well I know the Trojan Worms
Waiting for you, old son, bowed under blood,
Withered with loneliness, stupid with noise,

76

Your veins caked with politics.
    Near the top of that cliff-face
A seagull manages to feed her young
Ignoring the poison brownfoaming the shore,
Thickening the air. Everywhere
The greedy, elegant monsters grow strong,
Twisted children die or live as cripples
Sprawled like stricken birds in a pity of bridges,
The dead moan in our hearts but tell us nothing
Or we have forgotten how to listen.
Your belly is full of war and death and money.'

The sad battered century said, 'I wanted you to live
But killing is your way and then a rest from killing
And the killing again. Child, lies are your food
And lies will make your heart beat strong and proud
And prompt you to discover worlds
You scarcely dare to dream of now.
And still you will not learn from the seagull.'

The battered century sighed and seemed to sleep.
I covered it and left it there
And walked where squawking hungers ripped the air.

I was a face, the kind you know must care.

The Authentic Voice of Judas

Witnessing a young man with a black moustache
Dragged from his car, beaten up and shot
By a zestful mob (as a result of which
A million voices babbled in my heart about
Responsibility at home, church and school)

I wondered if I had an authentic voice
To speak against the mediaful
Murder causing the mob and others to rejoice.

At certain moments, silence is a sin.
I followed this voice down a starved laneway
And cornered it behind a large plastic bin.
'Are you my voice?' I asked, 'My own voice? My very own?'

'I am not' was the reply, 'You have no voice I
Can decipher, you are bits of shrapnel in dead skin,
A cider-boy dismantling Rose Morley's dress,
Mob-howls, dumped bodies, bullets making nothing of bones,
Priests' silken consolations, orgies of doom in the gutter press,
Molly Maguire, bride and groom planning the happiness
Pursued by a young man with black moustache
Before they crucified him. No, you have no voice I recognise as yours
Unless it be this laneway packed with shadows, hungers.'

One Awful Morning

The tolerance of cities is born of crowds
Gathered/rushing to ignore each other.
The most tolerant man in the world is one
Determined that he'll never know his brother.
My psychiatrist, a perceptive leggy brunette,
Knows how to attend and to ignore.
'Judas' she says, hazel eyes professional yet
Moving, 'Why does betrayal visit you more

Natively than other men? Do you consider it
An art, like verse? Are you worried by the suffering
You cause? The confusion? Humiliation? Pain?'

Usually I answer such questions with silence but
One awful morning I replied, looking
Skywards, 'Don't know, m'dear, must be the fuckin' rain.'

In This Respect

'I know the bloody man's a bishop
Don't I hear him in the pulpit every Sunday
Tellin' all the poor workers how to climb up
To heaven, to accept poor conditions an' slave's pay
An' why we should obey our bosses
'Cos work is so hard to come by these days
But why does he sack a priest who wants justice
For every man and woman in the diocese?

Father Harty is a fair man, loves the people,
Knows the bishop is weak to the strong, strong to the weak,
He speaks an' writes his mind, he's not afraid to strike

For common men like me. The bishop wants to shift him where he'll
Be silent. The bishop says Christ was a humble man
But in this respect Christ an' his lordship are not alike.'

Advice

I conjured the devil to ask him should I betray
My master and friend. The devil
Was hiding in the wax of my left ear
And seemed miffed that I thought him bent on evil

Advice. 'Beggars like you are responsible
For my bad reputation' he said testily,
'Besides, no matter what I say you will
Do what you will do while I stand aside

Plunging deeper and deeper into ill-repute,
Blamed for what goes on in heads like yours.
It's all Greek to me' he added plaintively,
'I've no power over the freedom of men
But since you ask me and since I hate the sight
Of your miracle-working carpenter's son who adores
Himself, I say yes, yes, you scheming thing, betray, betray.'

A Scattering of Hay

I go back to the stable this winter night.
The door coughs open, I edge into the darkness,
Stand still. Somewhere, an old woman
Is shouting in a drunken voice,

    'Every mother's son in this accursed place
Has to go to a foreign country to make a livin'.
This bloody hell is a curse-o'-God disgrace.'

She stops, whimpering. I hear a bottle smashing
Against a wall. My eyes search the darkness.
Opposite me, near a corner, lies a cow,
Sleeping, I think. Men's voices blur from the road.

I move slowly over to where the manger is,
I put my hand in the manger, there's only
A scattering of hay, I feel cold and sad,
The feeling passes, I stand in the dark a while.
Nothing, no sound but the cow's breathing, calm and even.
Men I have drunk and yarned with would smile
To see me here, standing, they'd say, on the floor of heaven.

Taste

Now that I know the taste I've longed for
All my days, I think of the first time
I tasted Marina's kiss in the ruin of the Nor-
man Keep. Honey is acrid by comparison.

I remember the first time I tasted blood,
My own, a sunny field, June day, a swinging
Right cross from Francis Ignatius Wade,
Self-taste flooded my being.

And then for years I thought of the taste of evil:
Would it be the flesh of an enemy on my tongue?
Would I eat my enemy? Make a meal of the curse?
Feel at home forever at table with the devil?
I tasted it last night. I must write you a long
Letter about it sometime. It was bad. I've known worse.

Trifle

I stood in a supermarket considering
Twenty-seven different kinds of ice cream
Thinking of a Vietnamese typhoon
At its work when I heard a scream

From the desserts department.
A woman with an automatic rifle
Was shooting men women kids in a demented
Fashion. I noticed blood in a strawberry trifle.

She killed nine people in all.
I counted them twisted in the débris
Of fruit salads, meringues, chocolate cake, pavlova, apple pie.

A young man grabbed the rifle, held the woman in control.
'Who are you?' I asked. 'A student' he said, 'I'm doing a Ph.D.
In ethics entitled *Man's Compulsion To Lie.*'

The woman was shivering, failing to cry.
I went on with my shopping, passed the ice cream by.

Lessons

When I teach the Catholic Catechism
Deep in the swallowing South
I'm ramming bloody testicles
In a Northern Protestant mouth.

When I teach the Protestant Catechism
Deep in the swallowing North
I'm hounding a Catholic emigrant
To the grimmest place on earth.

When I take both books and burn them
The ashes scatter and fall
On a hundred thousand rifles
In a bunker in Donegal.

A White, Empty Room

'I'm happy to be home, I can't believe
I'm back safe and sound with my wife and children.
I was walking along High Street
When they swept me into a car
        And drove to an outlying Station.
They locked me in a white, empty room
For seventy-two hours. You did it you did it
They repeated until I began to believe I was

Guilty. I'd never felt such guilt before.
You're a murderous thug, they said,
Shouting through every bone in my head,
You'll never see your family again
You'll get life you'll be hanged that's for sure.
Why did they suddenly release me then?
I was guilty no I'm not guilty now I know I'm not.
I've never even seen the place where Cassidy was shot.'

A Bloke Told Me

'They shut me up, they wouldn't let me speak,
Locked me in the cell of my own stink,
Tied me to this wheel grinding in a mill,
Banged my napper to ensure I'd never think,
Ripped the words from my mouth, turned them to stones,
Threw the stones in boghole, ditch and river,
Kept me from school, said I was a fool
And 'twas God's plan to keep me so forever.

They put me on the dole because work is for others,
Queue up, they said, if you want a bite to eat,
A sup to drink. I queued. The queue was a slum.

Half-thinking told me I had to nail the fuckers
So you'll appreciate how I felt when a bloke told me what
Can be achieved with a small home-made bomb.
I know what I think now. I explode; therefore I am.'

82

Better Than Bingo

I'd like to be divorced from old lady reality
But she insists she's married to me.
(I do believe she may deceive.) In summer
She adores six weeks by the sea
So the pair of us slip off to Mullaghmore
And book in at the Sacred Heart Boarding House
Run by Mrs Mary Rose MacMennimon
Forty years widowed yet mindful of her man.
In three weeks my old lady shows a miraculous
Return to lust. The old dear glows. Young men
Stand transfixed by her medieval bum
Wriggling in magical rhythm down Main Street.

Mrs MacMennimon says, 'You're a grand wee lass.'

My old lady gloats 'I'm enjoying my Second Com-
ing, it's better than Bingo. You're such a sweet
Boy, Judas, most traitors are a pain in the ass.'

A Woman Is Bleeding

A woman is bleeding in my sleep: up
To me now she flows and says 'Do you desire
The blood of my eyes to challenge your eyes
Or do you wish me to bleed into a cup,

Hand it to you to throw at the bully
Screw in Block Four?
If he has the right kind of break in his skin
This cup o' blood will hurt him for sure.

Or do you want to lie with me here,
Fly down with me now in my blood?
We'll be all one then like the homeless people
In the streets of ice, our blood will give them shelter,
Even the cold churches will offer heat and food,
Let me bleed into you, or live sly, dry and unbridgeable.'

Miracles

Styles of dying change from heart to heart.
Sylvester Daly went for a pee in the Feale
But instead of relieving, drowned himself
Swaying hide-and-seek among intriguing reeds.

My back excels at lying, so I'll lie
With whiskey and a Bible and a famous jerk's
                    Complete Works.
    I'll sip, I'll stare at God's cavortings,
                    I'll pretend I've read
The famouse jerk from first to last.
Could happen, too, like miracles in bed.

Initiation Rite

Whenever you find a group in society
Which feels that what it's doing
Is seriously different from any
Other group you get the kind of thing

I was subjected to when I joined
The apostles. My initiation rite:
I was hosed with cold water
And dumped in the street

In a babydoll nightdress, I was pelted
With stones and gassed with CS,
My private parts daubed with indelible ink

I was handcuffed to railings through a freezing night
And had my naked buttocks lashed with a baseball bat.

These humbling treatments did me some good, I think.

Despite Such Moments

A few weeks after sticking me in the earth
my intellectual friends
Decided to celebrate my worth and unworth
As they believed they knew such things.

They got a novelist to read something about beginnings and ends.
An abominable little prig
With a rat-trap gob and a smoggy mind
He celebrated me as the ultimate male

Chauvinist pig.

Right, in his way. A String Quartet found
Appalling music to remember me by,
An old whore from Berlin read *The Scholar Gipsy*
And a nameless apostle sang *The Salley Gardens*.

I saw and heard all from my earth-cell. Touched,
I cried a little as if I were slightly tipsy.
Then why, despite such moments, must the buried heart continue to harden?

The Prize

The Prize was for one who could get rid of a god
In the most effective way.
Getridders came from all quarters of the globe
And outlined their styles, each in his own way.
There were Civil Servants who advocated the twitching smile
Academics who professed la politesse
Poets who favoured a simple stab in the back
With the victim in a state of emotional undress.

An eminent Judge from a foreign country
Considered all styles with such passionate scruple
He was, for months after, a wreck.

At a Dinner attended by anybody/everybody
The Judge awarded the Prize to yours truly
For a simple peck.

Apparition

He stretched there ready to be nailed
But we couldn't find anyone to finish the job.
We put ads in all the national papers,
Radio and telly, looking for someone who'd

Grab the hammer and home the nails.
Nobody came forward. I thought
We'd have to let him stand up and walk away
Laughing at the plight
Of us who'd seen the light.

Then, when all seemed lost, Flanagan
Apparitioned. He asked about the fee,
Pondered, said 'I'll do it! Where's the hammer?'

Flanagan gave it all he had.
Afterwards, he vanished with the money
Eschewing all display of bravado or glamour.

Like Ourselves

Breeding can't keep pace with the level of slaughter.
Government allows twenty thousand killings a year.
This year alone, however,
Ninety thousand have been shot or
Hacked to death.

I approach the village.
The death-stink hits my nostrils
Like the smell of a traitor-friend.
I see them lying there
Waiting for the end.

Like ourselves, they're an endangered species.
The eggs are an aphrodisiac.
You can make beautiful handbags out of the skin.
The villagers are too busy killing
To take any notice of me
Photographing the river of blood
Pouring to the sea.

Reminds me...

I Never

I have a taste for Latin since I answered Kelch's Mass,
I loved the bell, the bread of God, I loved the words
Hic est enim calyx sanguinis mei.
The time is now, my head bends towards
White marble and whispers whispers whispers
Eternity breathes like a frosty morning
Kelch lifts the chalice up to heaven's windows
Nothing is stale and faded, all pictures bright and shining

Though Kelch's cough is rattling his throat,
He drinks the wine, wine rattles his Adam's apple,
He swallows God with phlegm, the day is blest,
The calming bell strokes demons out of blood,
I never died or cried or lost, betrayed or was betrayed
Till *Ite, missa est, Ite, missa est.*

The Wurrum

In the beginning, The Wurrum found it hard to exist.
He couldn't prove he was there.
He was grass, apples, wheat, nettles, almost
Everything that grew. Then, out of somewhere,
Came a gorgeous boy with eyes
Even a suspicious mandog might trust.
From the beginning this boy seemed wise
With an appetite to make a glutton burst.
He ate. He ate. Within him, The Wurrum grew.
One day in a meadow, from a Sunday shite
The Wurrum slipped and wriggled out of the boy
Who bled awhile, then felt all new.
The Wurrum bellied about, snaky sight,
Lisping 'Let me tempt you with my joy.'
Then The Wurrum turned on the boy
Wrapped itself around his toes
Imprisoned his ankles his shinbones
Roped itself about his knees
Thickbled itself into his thighs
Strappered his balls his prick
Chained his belly his chest
His shoulders his neck

Subdued his chin
Clamped his nose
Which bled
A little then more then torrentially.
The Wurrum drank it all
Then burrowed into his head.

Gralton

The priest was loud.
'Follow Gralton or follow Christ!' he roared,
'Good people of Drumsna, remember our Lord
And the way he died for all men.
Gralton is a socialist.
Socialism is another name for communism.
Is it Christ or Gralton in transcendent Leitrim?'

'Gralton, by Christ!' an old man said.

Gralton escaped to New York. One night
He found a beggar in the streets, took him home,
Gave him food and drink, a bed.

When Gralton woke the beggar was gone.
So were Gralton's money and clothes.
Not for the first time Gralton was naked.

Like Myself

A thousand years later, they stripped me naked,
Flung me face downwards on the floor.
In this position I was held by several men
While others flogged me with cords stiffened
In melted pitch. My flesh piecemealed
At every stroke until my back was one
Large ulcer. Believe me, it was no joke.
Also, my brothers, I was miserably afflicted
With a beastly plague of gnawing vermin
Crawling in lumps within, without, about my body,

Hanging in clusters from my beard, lips, nostrils
And previously stylish eyebrows, blinding me.
Areta, the silver platekeeper, true to his cruel ways,
Gathered and swept the vermin upon me twice in eight days.
Spirited exercise of intelligence was my only crime
But that's how aspiring heretics were treated at the time.

After Such Knowledge

One evening, chatting with the damned, I noticed
How satisfied they were.
For every question concerning the living and dead
They had the answer.
The damned are an expert lot
The damned are convincing and urbane
The damned are so erudite
They flush your bewilderment down the drain.

The damned are burning with insight
Into time and eternity, mystery and art
And the mind of God.

I saw my brothers there, I saw the light
Of learning illumine the dark places of my heart
And the secret prisons in my blood.

After such knowledge I am paralysed with gratitude.

A Former Particular Friend

Sir,
   I spent the whole of this day watching Costigan.
At one he went out, I followed him closely as I dare.
He stopped at Madden's in Cork Street,
Returned in one hour, went out no more.

This week the people have an air of mystery about them,
Two houses in particular: Connolly's and Healy's in Meath Street.
In the former there is a particular dim room.
I have watched several men go in and out

Who bore a bad character in the First Rebellion.
There is a meeting in Healy's tonight,
Of what kind I cannot tell but no trouble or pain
Shall be spared until I draw the picture right.

Duncan, I am informed, is gone to the country
But is due back in town today.
He resorts Floyd's Public House at the Harbour.
I shall take the pulsebeat of the place in my own way.
A former particular friend is housemaid there.
I long to renew my friendship with her.
In prime girlhood she was helpful, I remember,
Telling me all she knew of the world about her.

Beyond Suspicion

Sir,
    I continued the whole day between James's Gate and Dirty Lane.
I saw Costigan several times, he looked busy and undressed
By chance. I got in company with an old man
Named Twomey, a great drunkard, open in his speech, the best

Drunken company I've had, he's living in Thomas Street
This forty years, knows everyone, especially the Rebel Party.
I humoured him well, he told me he'd bring me acquainted
With Costigan's men who drink at Patrick Harty's.

I will use every opportunity in my power
To make myself useful; so will my friend.

I have taken a lodging nearby, opposite Costigan.
I pass for a clerk, a humble clerk, nothing more,
Four hours of business each day, then work's at an end.

I stand beyond suspicion at my front door,
Mine is an innocent stance, no gesture out of turn.

You will know, dear Sir, whatever I may learn.

Worth Watching

Sir,
   First to Clintons the Trunk Makers
Then to Corrs in Brides Alley
Then to Warrens the Pawn Broker in Capel Street
Where he'd a long discourse near the yard-gate:

From there to the Commonwealth Coffee House
He stayed for an hour until
He left for Fleet Market, Porter's Snack House,
Number 144 Lazor's Hill:

From that to the Front Square of the College:
I hovered, being slow to enter;
He came out with a young man in a dark Surtout,
Went to Hastings the Copper Plate Printer
In George's Street, from that to New Jail, Green Street,
From that through the Castle Yard to Corrs in Brides Alley.

I left him there in the dying light.

The man is worth watching. His name is Halliday.
Tomorrow, I shall watch him all day,
Every step he takes, every place I see him go,
Every road, street, lane, house, all people met, you, Sir, shall know.

Mr Watson

Sir,
   Mr Watson absconded from Liverpool on Sunday morning
Came by Holyhead to Dublin
Arrived on the Tuesday afternoon following
Was in Kelly's hotel four hours with a florid man

Is of a clumsy clownish appearance
Five foot ten, fair complexion, clipped whiskers,
Has a remarkable large mouth, cropped hair,
Is mightily round in the shoulders

Has on a light drab hat, a blue Dress Coat
With yellow buttons, a striped Swandown
Waistcoat, a yellow silk handkerchief about his neck,

Speaks with a passion, casting quick
Glances about him, protecting what he has to say.
Watch him, watch him, night and day.

A Country Gentleman

Sir,
    Duncan was in the flagyard from 12 till 4
A man sat with him in earnest discourse
Costigan has a deal of gentlemanlike visitors
In and out of his office.

A young woman was three hours looking through the blinds of Costigan's house.
There was a bustle among them, the house was all alive,
Several looked sharp at me, nervous-suspicious,
I went home, changed my dress, returned at five.

At six, a Country Gentleman left the house,
I followed, by his walk he was in Liquor,
He stopped to admire the hardware shop in Dame Street,
I did the same, he entered the College at his Liquor-pace,
Stopped in the Second Square, third door from the corner,
I stayed at the gate till midnight, he did not come out.

The College is dangerous, of that I have no doubt.
Students sing seditious songs, are drunk and flippant.
Porters at the gate of hell are not more vigilant.

An Incoming Tide

Sir,
    Thursday, late, I shall give you a call.
You asked me a question last night.
You will recollect I told you I have not the small-
est doubt in my mind there are Gentlemen at

The head of affairs of both Talent and Property,
Certain Gentlemen who…but this is my answer,
Unless I am sure, I think it uncharitable to mention any
Gentleman's name for my own suspicion, Sir.

I have my silence, my eyes, mind, watchful air

And cannot deny, in honest thought, I do suspect,
Yet I must wait till I am satisfied
Which I shall seek with all my power to ascertain

And I am every day your devoted servant
Coming nearer the point like an incoming tide
To know what I cover, drown all guilty men.

The Transaction

Sir,
    Please send information about Thomas Archdeacon.
I interrogated him again concerning the transaction
Between himself and the Nailer from Dublin.
He admitted a number of lives were lost in
The streets, he'd unleashed a spate
Of riotous conduct in the environs of Donabate
With the hope of turning attention
From the transaction.

I am desired to represent this matter to you,
That you will be pleased to return me
The best account of Archdeacon you can procure.
The man is well-versed in landscape-painting
Which he executes with taste and judgment.
Discriminating women allow his manner is charming.
He learned to play the fiddle in Mountjoy Prison,
        I have heard, though I am not sure.
He fiddles with a light touch, patient as any prisoner.
This is the picture I draw: a talented man
Capable of the transaction.

Let Me Survive

Your Honour,
    It is in your power to liberate me
Or cause me to be liberated. I
Was not in Dublin on 23rd July, 1803,
I am the victim of some treachery,
I did not aid, abet or in the smallest degree
Promote the Insurrection of that day.
I am betrayed; I cannot say why men betray.
It is not my wish to see the sword come reeking
From a brother's breast and next moment
Expect the same for myself. I am seeking

Mercy, Honoured Sir, that I may live to protect
The grey hairs of a wretched father far gone in age
And a fragile wife who'll perish, for perish she must
Without my help. May the Supreme Being keep your heart
From harm, forgive this scrap of paper, turn your rage
To mercy, let me survive that others may exist.
I swear to heaven I did not betray you or my King.
Please give the blessing I crave, Sir. You will be blessed.

A Man Named Clarke

Sir,
    There is a man named Clarke in Manchester.
By his discourse to his neighbours he is guilty of a crime.
He has a home but dare not go there.
Anywhere on earth is now his home.

His father keeps a Brewery near Smithfield in Dublin.
I am informed by two Irishmen they recollect
A man named Clarke being in prison
In 1798. He may have been in Dublin, they suggest,

On 23rd July, 1803.
Inspect your books, you may find his name.
If this be so, please note the truth of my intent,
Write by return, mention the reward due me
For apprehending him, I know where to find him,
Make no delay, I am a friend to Government.

Minding His Own Business

Sir,
   You were once the object of my hatred.
Your very name was terror, a snake's poisoned hiss.
I was too fond of company-keeping and talk of politics
To mind my own business.

Hearing you had information of me, I quit Ireland,
Came to England. I left all my old disgrace
At home, found employment, worked with honest hands
And minded my own business.

I am now, Honoured Sir, getting deep in years.
You are, in the Hands of Providence, the cause
Of my welfare. And still good fortune grows.

I send ten pounds to you to dispose of for any char-
ity you think proper, a small compliment because
You gave one unfortunate Irishman all the happiness he knows,
For which his heart gives thanks, glad that God still blesses
Him, far from the land of traitors, minding his own business.

A Very Improper Sign

Sir,
   Lord Dufferin hopes to acquaint Major Sirr
Of a very improper sign,
Obscene gazebo of a traitorous mind
Put up at a Booth in Donnybrook Fair.
It is a kind of painting, the offensive
Creation of a Rebelly judas-cur
Spawned, bred, instructed in the gutter.

     His Majesty lies in his coffin,
     On his breast a bottle.
     The Queen stands with little
     Or none of the dignity we love in her,
     In an odd posture, scarcely human,
     And one I dare not associate with Woman.
     She seems to weep over the dead.

How can even a stab-in-the-back go low as this?
Inscribed on the coffin, in red, white and blue lettering,
The words, 'Stop, traveller, bow your head
Touch your heart, meditate, and piss.'

The Protestant Boy

Sir,
    I wish to let you know of one Jack Hanly
Residing at 4, Fleece Alley, Fishamble Street,
A bitter Rebel, muscled with villainy,
Talks fair to your face, at the same time cuts

Your throat if you are a Loyalist.
You have his name in your book for the First Rebellion.
He received pistols stolen by a nephew of his
Out of the Ordnance, whose name is Peter Flinn.

Flinn works for Hanly at above place.
Hanly had an apprentice, a young Protestant,
Hanly made him go to Mass, the lad was
Let into Hanly's secrets, pikes concealed in his house,

When the Insurrection was discovered, he threw
The pikes over the coal-yard wall
From a yard at the back of a shed
Next door to his house, the shed is his own,

Was let by him to a Smith supposed to
Forge pikes, he absconded on that day,
Not seen since, Hanly was privy, for he
And his son and Rosenburg the Protestant boy

And Flinn and Flinn's mother carried something away
In their aprons the morning the pikes were found
In the coal-yard, all which they brought from the shed.
Several other moments young Rosenburg kept in mind.

Jack Hanly led him such a pauper's life
On account of his bearing a Protestant name
The lad threatened to bring him to justice
As soon as he would be out of his time.

96

To prevent this, Hanly has hurried him
Away this week, I believe has sent him Aboard,
If you find this lad you will not find him dumb,
There is gold for you in his every word.

A few words from him would hang Hanly, I'm sure.
This lad slept above Stairs, his Master below,
Last Saturday night, the lad went to bed, slipped downstairs
Again for something, Hanly heard him and knew

This was his chance to be rid of him, said
He was a thief intending to rob, brought him off
No one knows where, Hanly sent a bad
Rebel named Cleary who told the lad in rough

Words his Master would swear Robbery against him
If he'd not consent to venture Aboard.
Cleary and Hanly kept him two days confined
With only hard scraps of bread, they stirred

Such fear in him he went Aboard, or somewhere else away,
Hanly swore to his neighbours he heard a thief on the stairs,
The thief was Rosenburg, the Protestant Boy.
That's all the proof he had for sending the lad where-

ever he sent him, or maybe he murdered him
For Hanly's a desperate fellow, attends
Meetings somewhere every Wednesday evening.
This keeps him fixed to his Rebelly friends.

He has two English soldiers working for him,
Has been picking out of one whose name is John
What strength of Army there is in Dublin,
How many Duty Places there are in the town,

How many outposts, how many sentries out at a time,
How often relieved. Hanly's thick in what goes on,
A swelling, widening, deepening crime.
His house is easily known

By a Black Wooden Figure of a Boy
Fastened out of the Garret Window
Such as Tobacconists have
Which he fastens a Green Bough to

On a Loyal Rejoicing Day, this Bough
He dubs the Tree of Liberty,
He works in said Garret on the left as you
Enter, or else at a Wheel in the

Back of the Shop, he makes it a point
To fire shots each fourteenth of July
To honour the French Revolution.
I am persuaded Jack Hanly must die.

He is five foot six inches tall, lusty,
Marked with the Smallpox, in bullish mid-age,
Wears a wig with a strutting vanity
And awakens in me a heart-scalding rage.
I burn to see this traitor walk free.

I would know what has happened the Protestant Boy,
Young Rosenburg, ten years old, five foot one,
A thin spare lad, has a cast of the eye,
Is knock-kneed, and somebody's Loyal Son.
I pray you act, Sir, on this information.

False Bottom

Sir,
    Elijah Guttery of the county of Dublin
Being sworn on the Holy Evangelists
And fully examined, gave this information
To the four interrogating purists:

        In pursuance of orders from his officer
        Guttery searched the house of James West last night
        And there found a False Bottom under
        The bed of said West. There came to light

A Plated Goblet with a Crest engraved thereon,
A Powder Pouch, a French Musket Lock,
Cartridges, Straps, Breastplates, Bridles, Stirrup Irons, Spurs,
Seven Bottles of Whiskey, the names of six men,
John Reilly, Frank Devine, Ted Gorman, Simon Drake,
Vincent Lawless, Martin Cullen: known robbers.
This False Bottom, say the purists, was West's only mistake.

The Wrong Man

Sir,
   It was decided Lynam should not go.
Lynam said nothing, bowed his head,
Stared a long time at the floor.
Hickey said Conway should go instead.

Keenan, wishing to go, objected to this,
Left the meeting-room, stepped out into the lane.
He appears to have vanished without trace.
There has been a bitter dispute among the men.

Delaney and Kane wanted Keenan not to go on his own.
Redmond and Hughes thought good might come of it.
Dargan said they should be patient and wait.
Kiely and Wallace said Keenan was his own man.
Goggin and Carey thought him a slithery rat.
No one can say where Keenan has gone,
If he went at all, or with others, or alone.
All we know for certain is that
Lynam didn't go. That's good. He is the wrong man.
He cannot do firmly what must be firmly done.

The Desired Point

Sir,
   I was in company with Tarrant on Saturday night.
We talked much on the desired point,
Tarrant chewing wisdom and spitting wit,
A lawyer by trade, words never out of joint.
The night before, until three o'clock,
He was in company with Lawlor, Semple and Glynn.
A man by the name of Gill from Blackrock
Joined them, said little, killed a bottle of gin,
Dozed, woke, left, went to a house in Grattan Lane,
Met a dragoon of the 12th Light Horse,
Stayed an hour, came out, shook hands with the dragoon,
Walked to Brides Alley, then to Fishamble Street where
I lost him in a maze of dirty places.
I see Tarrant again tonight, this will prove a boon,

The stinking lanes of Dublin contain the secrets of the earth
And, I could swear, of the sun and moon.
The desired point will be clarified here, and soon.

Coming Soon

Sir,
    We moved among the Brewer's men in Dirty Lane,
Made friends of some, as you suggested,
Thursday night we were brought to a New Street wake,
A Drayman's wife laid out in a Rebelly bed,
Young woman, wasted. Ten children in ten years, the Drayman said.
The most detestable songs were sung, the most
Treasonable words flew wild around the room.
The Drayman swore his wife was a happy ghost
And the men to smash the Despots are coming soon.

The Servant Girl I had the honour to inform you of
Tells me every Saturday night numbers of men
Drink in her master's house, for what purpose she can't tell.
She's a watchful girl, countrycute in matters of love,
Will open a door next Sunday, let me slip in,
The house has many rooms, she says. I'll examine them well.
If these rooms have secrets, Sir, you'll possess them all.

Inadvertent

Sir,
    A relation of mine in the First Rebellion
And knew the Second came to town this week.
He lives in Wicklow, fifteen miles off,
He came to my room where I took stock

Of his words. Certain men from Dublin go there,
Keep their spirits up by all means in their power
But no meetings have as yet taken place.
My cousin will call every time he's in town.

The people are beginning to wear yellow handkerchiefs
And yellow waistcoats; growing saucy,
They care not what they say or sing.

Cash and Boyd, two Captains in the Second,
Have invited me to Wicklow. They may
Provide some guide, some inadvertent little thing
Which you'll hear on my return. God save the King.

The Common People

Sir,

Saturday, in Tallow,
Talked with the common people.
They speak of The Cause,
Rebellion, battle.

Porters on the quays
Desire to unite.
Their talk grows bolder
They're shaping to fight.

The people are worse than the King's Speech said they are.
They are brazen-daring, I keep a watchful Eye
On the Company at Dawson's place, I suspect that man
And believe he was acquainted with the Second Rebellion.
I will enquire the names of those that gather in his house
And have the honour, I trust, to find out their conversation.
If the common people believe in themselves, what comes of that notion?
The seed of Judas thrives among them. It must be kept down.

City of Knockers

Let us now praise the city of knockers
In the streets of sneer and the pubs of mock;
These are the artists, my vicious brothers
Whose dreams have come unstuck.

This Civil Servant had a poem published
In *The Squirish Mimes* twenty years ago;
McGinty, pissed, tells how he relished
Corpsing a painter in his studio.
Jones tells how he shat on an editor,
Noonan outdoes him with how he clipped
The wings of a runt who thought he wrote plays;
Smith shredded a girl then quickly bedded her,
Adair knew the greats so he withers the living;

O city of knockers, you deserve my praise.

Bagatelle

Jesus was divine, I felt diviner
Especially after I'd composed
My Judas Bagatelle in B Minor.
I noticed how my colleagues dozed

While he went aside to pray
To his father who is himself and someone else as well,
Who, I dare not say.

Knowing that sleeping can be hell
And criminally irresponsible
I embarked on my Bagatelle,
Finished it without an error.

I play it now for friends who sleep
When their creator kneels to pray and weep
For them, himself, and other victims of the terror.

The Ultimate Rat

Hosting a TV Chat Show
I interviewed God.
'Why did you create me?' I asked.
God's buttocks squirmed. 'I had to' He said
'I wanted the world to see the most

102

Treacherous get it has ever known.'
'Were you pleased with the result?' I probed.
'Yes' answered God 'As men
Go, you are, you must admit, the ultimate rat
With a face like a bucketful of mortal sin.
You'd betray your own mother,
                              wouldn't you, my son?'

'I suppose I would' I mused as I flashed that
Winning Judasgrin. Viewers adored my honesty.
My tam-ratings soared high as heaven.

What's That?

It's one thing to kill a man
But quite another to break him up and down
As if all the circus animals went mad
And trampled the clown,
Trampled his unforgettable face,
His concocted head, child-beguiling smile,
Arms askew like demented branches,
Belly a mud-puddle,
Legs dry twigs in summer dust.

Broken? Bloody sure the corpse is broken!

But what's that crawling towards it, touching the brow,
Touching the flesh as if some precious lost
Thing were found? Am I deluded? Madly mistaken?
Christ, what are they going to make of the corpse now?

A Maligned Saint

At a gathering of the Christian churches
It was decided after long discussion
To conduct intensive research
Into my character, where I went wrong,
My special position in the human family.

In a comprehensive Gallup poll
Fifty million people were asked
'If you were judging Judas now
Would you show him any mercy?'

The result, excluding don't knows,
Showed I was not popular; but one person
Out of fifty million thought I was blessed,

A maligned saint. All the others said
I should be damned again and again.
Someone, somewhere, believed in me. Fuck the rest.

Sorr-ee

Even if you're constipated or heavily in debt
Or elephant-headed after a rake of beer
You'll apppreciate my delight when I heard that
I'd won first place in the BBC Competition
For The Outstanding Amateur Prophet Of The Year.

I was sitting alone
In my vatic bedsit when the news
Electrified my phone. I got sozzled on elation,
I hopped over the moon, from that cool perspective
I began to doubt the voice on the phone.

I rang the BBC.

They said I'd not been placed in the first five
Thousand. Sorr-ee. I sat and meditated on the man
Who'd done me the honour of trying to hoax me.
He might have been my friend,
I here, he at the other end.

The Club

I did my damned best to get into the club,
Tried the front door, was chucked out,
Went for a window, got the boot,

A side door, was smashed against the railings,
Wrote letters, nobody listened,
Raged on radio and telly, nobody budged,
Well fuck them and their club, I said
And turned to my life of crime.

Crime? Imagination, I'd call it,
Enterprise, initiative, the name of the game,
There was a scandal, someone had to pay.
When things go wrong you need to be in
The club, close to those who make things happen.
What happened me could happen anyone, I'd say.

Tea

All of a May morning I strolled out with my inferiority complex.
It whimpered, pointing 'These people think I'm trash.'
I said 'Don't be such a touchy little bollocks,
Your flesh is as respectable as any other flesh.'

'O I know it is' snivelled my complex, 'But what about my soul?
What do the brash masters of ridicule think of that?'
'The problem' I said 'Is painfully metaphysical
And is, if I may venture a consoling cliché, old hat.'

'My soul' serviled my complex, 'Is causing me hell,
The corpses of my teeniest hopes are piled in a mass-grave;
Others, respecting themselves, pour mockery on me.'

'Others' I replied, 'Don't matter a spider's testicle,
A fiddler's fart or a whore's boot. Now, by your leave,
Slouch home with me for a cup of unbeatable tea.'

The Prize

I was awarded the Nobel Prize for Treachery
Just when I was beginning to feel
All my work had gone for nothing.
I'd begun to be slightly unreal

And could scarcely believe the tepid
Response to my adjustment of history
Though I know men are ignorant of what's happening
In them, about them. You can imagine my
Relief when the Great Minds dropped recognition
In my lap. I received fifty thousand pieces of silver
And an inscribed cup to commemorate my winning

The Prize. I bought a hideous Spanish Bungalow outside Skibbereen
Where I continue to meditate on the matter
Convinced, despite the éclat, my real work is only beginning.

Traps

'He lived and died like a soldier.
He had no emotion about anything,
A politically aware young man.'

We grow traps like potatoes here.
Dedicated minds see to that.
Do you want a rapist? Murderer?
Badger? Fox? Ferret? Mad dog? Rat?

Do you want a woman wanting something
Can't be had without a trap?
Be honest, so much depends on an honest reply.

I can invent kisses to begin with, bring
Fingertips to the biblical radiance of a lip,
Conjure hitmen from the labyrinth of a sigh.

But what do you want? Do you know what you want? Do I?

Boom

'Know what I like, man? I like that big bomb
Some enlightened blighter will soon finger off
For the hell of it, just 'cos the bum
Feels his balls tickled by the notion of

An exploding world
Like the way I break
Plates in the kitchen for old crime's sake.
And it'll get us all off the rack
Of each other's company, we'll just have one
Final fuck
That won't get into the history-books –
No forests, no paper, d'you understand?
To hell with forecasts, their measured gloom,
Spruce oracles of Government doom
In the box in the corner of the living-room,
I want that bomb
So the world shakes
And vanishes like a man into a woman
Going boom coming boom bloody boom boy boom.'

An Expert Lot

Dozens of international journalists
Attended the crucifixion.
An expert lot, they moved through the mob
Doing the job, doing the job,
Collecting every scrap of the mob's reaction.
One whizzkid thought it might be a zippy idea
To interview Jesus on the cross
But Christ declined.
This was a tragic journalistic loss
Because the whizzkid had ready some very real
Questions, starting with 'Jesus, how do you feel?'
The television crews excelled themselves,
Slaves to the truth, sweated night and day
That every detail be revealed, the whole story told.
Even when the heavens darkened and the mountains coughed
And drops of blood became boiling rivers
The cameras rolled.
Although the whizzkid failed to get an interview
With the Son of Man, he was undaunted
And managed to patch together
A programme that haunted the minds
Of millions who saw it on colour TV.
Some critics, however,
Protested at the silence of the central character.

What, they wanted to know,
Was his point of view?
Luckily for the whizzkid, he had a pal
On the staff of the Leading National Newspaper.
Pal, knowing sensitive whizzkid was shattered
By cruel reviews, arranged to set things right.
Discriminating viewers were quick to see the light
When they read The Only Review That Mattered.

Wellingtons

Blood and muck attend on crucifixion.
All that morning the camp followers, well breakfasted,
Crapped howled mullocked for miles around
Horny for the shaming of the Son of Man.

The bloody muck rucked higher and higher.
The mob waded ankledeep in its own shitself, and stuck.
The sun went black, stank like a battlefield corpse on fire,
Spectators copulated in the shite, moaning 'Fuck! Fuck!'

In the midst of this unedifying scene
A Church of Ireland Bishop in wellingtons
Picked his way fastidiously through filth.

'Sir' I said, 'It is unusual to see wellingtons
In these parts.' 'Yes' he replied, 'I'm convinced that on
Days like this they're good for the health.'

Over the rutting hordes he strode, he strode,
Stepping on bodies like a health-freak god
Muttering to himself the while 'Dear! Dear!
Good Lord! What *is* happening round here?'

Light as a dancer's were this gentleman's
Steps, though gruesome were his wellingtons –
Footwear I associate with bloody pain
And do not wish to see again.

The Crossword Man

Bombs have a tricky habit of betraying
The intentions of the bomber despite the purest
Patriotic intentions. This one
Had quite a reputation as a boy
For solving knotty crosswords
In the posh English papers

        But now he's betrayed
By his own home-made creation
    Up to its wicked capers.

Look at Lucy Willowes o no you can't
For she's in pieces in a plastic bag
And the crossword man is gone home

To plan a weekend cooling off in a mountain shack
Clean air clean food clean water he'll be glad he came
To ponder Five Across Seven Down: shake, shade, shape, or shame?

Zone

No matter where I travel in my own little holy land
The buggers are after me, trying to prove
I changed forever the history of mankind
And flung in the gutter that immortal love
My master gave to every knacker scabbing the road,
Every robber leper killer pimp bandit whore thief
Insulting the face of heavenly god
With crimes I can hardly believe.

I'm the one who's wanted most. And now they intend
To set up The Hot Pursuit Of Judas Zone
For ten miles on either side of the border

Dividing me from my redeemer; but the bond
Between that man and me will go on and on
Despite church, state, stories of betrayal and murder.

I Was There

Sculpted columns, high ceiling,
Noon on Monday he'll be
Brought handcuffed to the court
When nine members of the jury
Are selected by lottery
From a group of thirty-five.
The court-clerk will take three hours
To read out the charges.

Joined the Movement at eighteen
Advised Latin-American dictators
On methods of interrogation.
Something of old Hollywood in his riding-crop.

Looks gentle as Saint Francis,
Benign old man, thin grey hair,
Sick from nervous disease
And a recent operation.

He will say
Certain national heroes were traitors
He will say
Moulin committed suicide
When he learned he'd been betrayed
By famous Resistance workers.
He will not apologise for his role as an officer.

He will say
He was a soldier doing dirty work
For the collaborationist government of the time
He will say
He is not guilty of a single crime.

He will ask
Why should he be tried
By those whose atrocities elsewhere
Have gone untried, unpunished?

He will play the tape
Again and again.

The Prime Minister is calling
For special lessons in schools
To trace the irresponsibilities of our fathers.

Other old men are gathering
In the shadow of the temporary monument
To speak of horrors more unspeakable
Than those at court.

The wizened butcher will listen to every word
His thin hands touching his thin hair.

He will say
That is not the whole story
That is not the whole story
I know
I asked questions of men and women
I organised the children
I followed instructions
I am your killer
I was there.

A Womb of Skulls

Out of nowhere there lit upon my mind
This vision of myself, eternity's prize dunce.
Illumined, I plunged underground
In the company of an old priest and a local
Historian of the National Schoolteacher kind.

Down we went,
        down, down,
                till we came to the skulls
Ranged in a cave.
               'They were here, waiting to be found,
Killed by their brothers and sisters in Christ,'
The priest said. The historian nodded.
                    I touched
Each skull, the historian told the tale
From beginning to end, the priest nodded,
We climbed back into the light,
Helicopters snarled at us.

        I stood still and watched.
'The killings last night,' the priest said,
'Don't move, just stand, talk to each other.'
We did. The sky snarled, the helicopters

Complained out of sight, across another gulf.
The earth is a womb of skulls. I like it.
I see it all
Through a crack in myself.

A Bag Like Everest

The way she turned what I said to her
Into something I wouldn't dream of saying!
She has a gift for changing a harmless murmur
Into a policy of betrayal.

                              The phone then –
'Wasn't it funny in print?'
Skibbereen Eagle, Squirish Mimes, Bethlehem News,
I'd read anything, looking for a hint,
A clue to the compulsive lies in language.

How many millions of lies are told every minute?
Child to father, man to woman, woman to man,
Lover to lover, friend to friend, worker to boss,
Boss to wife, wife to child, child to...?
                              My ambition is to get
A bag like Everest, collect all the lies in
The world and, packed bag on my back, walk
Through my brain beyond all treachery of talk
Until I find a cosy corner where
I can set my Everestbag on fire,
Brood on the blaze, see the pile of ashes grow
Like bonfires made by children long ago.

        Suddenly the wind works, the ashes rise
And scatter, self-born, spawning, countless clouds of lies.

Statistics

I'm terrified of people who give me advice.
History, says he, will judge you harshly
If you go ahead with this.
Seventy per cent in a recent survey
Said you are a force for evil
And should be put down.
Eighty per cent said hanged; twenty, electrocuted.
Do you not find this a cause for concern?

Confronted with the truth of statistics
I revert to my boyhood shyness, avert my eyes,
Hide my hands, they're sweating, bury my head.

I'm not a witty sort, clever gets make me sick
Yet, mouthing my words as if I were Solomonwise
On mountaintop, 'Fuck history' I said.

Baby

In a nation where people are afraid
To go out at night
We must vote for men and women
Who're not afraid of an acceptable level of carnage.

It's time to clear Death Row.
Two hundred and forty prisoners are waiting to die.
If we kill twenty a month
We can relax, baby.

Baby, you know well that the best
Governments are those not afraid to kill
Those who make us afraid to go out at night.

Baby, when I kiss your Death Row breasts
I know why I must kill the killers
Who must kill in the dark and die in the light.

You gotta vote right, baby, you gotta vote right.

The Knife and I

It wasn't the first time I saw the sky become
A sheath, the sun a knife contained therein,
But never before had I seen the knife climb
Among accommodating stars, flick down
At mythical speed to strike at a tribe
In a part of Africa till then unknown to me.
The maniacal knife butchered left and right,
Insatiable, I hope never to see
Such carnage again. When the tribe had been
Exterminated like the Incas or the Latin Mass
Among simple people who adored that language,
Needing burial on the bloody plain
Abandoned but for bodies, predators, opportunist flies
And a horde of newsfolk asking questions
Because the world loves the truth or colourful versions
Of same, the knife and I had a conversation:
I asked the knife for help
To bring about some changes.
The knife's reply encouraged me.
Startling is the state that I foresee.

Modest Enough

Not many men have seen the gods' faces.
I'm proud of the fact
That Jesus and I were on first-names basis
Right from the start.

There was none of Your Reverence, Father,
Right Honourable, Mister, Sir,
Your Grace, Your Lordship, Your Most High,
Your Holiness, Your Majesty, Imperial or

Otherwise. Just plain
Jesus as we tramped the roads
Bulging with sick and dying

Stopping now and again
For what must have been food fit for gods
Though we sometimes ate to the sound of souls crying.

Photograph

I took this natty coloured photograph
Of Lazarus as he emerged from the tomb.
That, in my view, was a miracle and a half.
I doubt if I shall see its like again.

Lazarus had been extinct for several days.
When he was summoned into the light
There was no sign of him awhile, then to our amaze-
ment, looking a bit dazed and underweight,

Lazarus came forth, blinked, gazed around
And said 'I'm dying for a cup of tea
And a slice of Bewley's coarse-brown.' As he drank
And ate, I colour-photographed him, quietly.

Now, when I consider how flesh rots,
I study that photograph. One of my better shots.

The Original Is Lost

'For days after being called back to life I was fine
Apart from a slight dizziness
And a wee pain in my back. Then I began
To miss the comfort of my tomb, tranquil place

Such as might delight a poet in search of solitude
Where the verses can be polished like silver.
I realised I'd lost the death I'd been brooding over
And working towards for decades, in however crude
And blundering a style. I felt this loss most keenly,
So keenly indeed that I placed an advertisement
In the *Lost and Found* section of the *Squirish Mimes*,
"Lost: one death. Small reward offered to finder. Lazarus."

I received a single reply signed *Bargain Basement*.
It said, "I can sell you a second-hand death for 30p.
The original is lost. At a push, this second-hand will suffice."

I didn't answer Bargain Basement. I'll just go on like this.'

Modern Music

'Dying lived down to my lowest expectations.
My death-rattles resembled much modern music
Prompted by a symphony of bloody eructations
And other symptoms of being grievously sick.

Life, I spasm-reflected, is not something I have chosen.
My brain fails, my sight dims, my breathing is farcical,
My balls are frozen.
Thanks be to Christ the tomb is the end of all.

It is in me arse. "Lazarus, come forth!" he said.
Like a schoolboy suffering his first day at school
I came forth, and back to the world of men.

My wife remarked I was looking well after being dead.
I felt, as my friends nudged each other, a bit of a fool
And now I must endure that modern music all over again.'

Golden Age

A Golden Age is the creation
Of idiot years identified by some idiot event.
In that pusillanimous Roman Administration
Not a Civil Servant knew what was meant
By the miracle of loaves and fishes
Or saw John the Baptist's head
One of history's most succulent dishes.
I applaud the Resurrection of the Dead
Because I am constantly resurrecting
Myself when I should have the sense to lie
Down and die. Only this morning I heard
A hitlervoiced reporter say it's been too long
Since Judas mocked the apocalyptic sky.
Bring back the Golden Age, he said,
Let Judas be restored.

116

Cup

I stuck my tongue into the cup when
it was passing round the table and I knew
I drank a heart
because I tasted the blood starting to flow
backwards into the village on a June
afternoon with the old mill grinding its teeth
in the heat and I tasted the blood
in the future among rushes on a roadside

      where Anto Macauley is lying
      shot through the head,
      the right material for
      a fiery ballad

      sung at the wedding of Mary and Joe
      by whole-hearted Danny McGroome
      whose babysitter has fallen asleep
      like his three children in their upstairs room
      with a bad electrical fault
      starting to take effect:
      the cup is a burning house
      in a screaming wilderness
      suddenly childless.

Snack

Silverville House; early Georgian; my choice
Because it has been lovingly restored;
All the resources of my inmost voice
Concentrate in one adoring gasp 'Good Lord!'

I began my snack with slices of hot pigeon breasts
Accompanied by a chilled Beaujolais '82.
Two bottles merely tingled my head.

Salmon then, a bottle of fruity Sancerre
From Comte Bernard Lafond, now dead:
Strawberries next, exotic Muscat de Beaumes
From an old pal, Jean-Louis Raboulet,

Rich flavour, long but not cloying, lullaby in a glass.
After this twilight snack had come to pass
I belched and bellied home to bed.
I did not dream, or can't remember if I did.
Dreams live in hunger. I like my food.

A Religious Occasion

I was there for a purpose, not a lark.
I shall long remember
That Sunday afternoon, one mild September,
Standing with 89,374 Catholics in Croke Park

Hearing the Artane Boys' Band play with verve and spark
The National Anthem and *Faith of Our Fathers.*
The Christian faces of the spectators
Were proof of the hard spiritual work

That goes to make true lovers of sport.
I was part of that crowd, one with the electric feeling
That turns a rigid stranger into an instant brother.

It was, dare I say it, a religious occasion.
The ball was thrown in and those two great teams
Proceeded to kick the shit out of each other.

Miracles

They may be at the top of your agenda
But they're far down in mine.
Impressed you are by instant healing of lepers,
Rousing the dead, turning water into wine,
Feeding a starving mob on a few scraps,
Making the weak strong, the strong weak,
The crippled walk, the blind see,
Deaf hear, dumb speak –

And to what end? Augustine Clancy,
National Teacher, despairing of my religious knowledge and my spelling,

118

Yanks me out in front of the First Communion class,
Slips down my trousers first, then my fancy
Underpants, lashes my bum till my yelling
Splits the parish. Miracles, my ass!

Before My Time

I'm a terrorist before my time
Conscious of the value of plasticbag blood
The good vibes of creative crime
In the hearts of those turning their backs on God.

There's only one way to treat God:
Walk up to Him and kiss Him.
He appreciates the direct approach.
Mess around, you'll miss Him.

God is a Bomb.
To get the best results, handle carefully,
Time properly, choose a fruitful place
Where you can turn murder into martyrdom.

Follow these instructions or it's likely
Godbomb will blow up in your face.

Who'll clean up the mess then? Bloody disgrace!

Towards Dawn

Heroism had abandoned the earth.
I met and persuaded a young scholar
(The kind of absorbent, precise mind of which
There is a distressing dearth in our
Centres of learning) that my infamous kiss
Was the measured effort of an enlightened man
To escape from what does not exist.
I spent an eloquent evening in an
Out-of-the-way Tropical Fish Restaurant
Exercising my most fruitful forms of analysis

And explication, making the erudite boy able
To grasp the savage clarity of the fact
That men are damned or saved according to their
Capacity to believe any aspect of the most outrageous fable.
Towards dawn, his eyes closed, his will parted, his brain burned,
My fabulous concept of heroism had returned.

Experiment

Speaking as one who from an early age
Discarded the musical illusions of hope
In favour of a more sustaining rage
At the prospect of a deft neck-stretching rope,
Knowing I was a manipulative schemer
Among dog-faithful men who told no lies,
I once experimented with disguise
And was in the eyes of all The True Redeemer.

Crowds followed me like debts.
I did a crash-course in miracles,
Healed the sick, raised the dead, normalised the insane

But soon tired of the multitudes of wets
Boring me with their fucked-up bodies and souls.
Undisguised, it was nice to be myself again.

Iago, bless his heart

Nothing quick about crucifixion. Most .
Audiences like a bit of a spectacle
Before the body parts company with the ghost
Which rockets away to heaven or hell
Or some outer sanctum in inner space.
Before that, however, screams, cries, groans.
    First things first.

The thief on the right with the villainous face
Is dying of thirst, and says so.

Iago Letts, master of the Galway Blazers,
Is mooching home after a hunt and a kill.
Seeing the thirsty bloody thief, Iago draws
From his hip-pocket a flask of Jameson.
The thief goes to town, swill after crucified swill.
Iago, bless his heart, would do the same for any of us.

Lovers of the Genuine

Lovers of the genuine will warm to Semtex,
My Czechoslovak explosive
Which, packed in a tin can and flung,
Will not encourage targets to live.
        It comes with wooden handle attached,
May be thrown at patrols or dropped from a height
On armoured tanks, using a plastic
Dustbin liner as a parachute.

Semtex is more powerful than disruptive prose
Or detonating verse, so genuine
It must do what it was created to do.
If you're compelled to polite your way through lies
And live the death of average non-man
        Semtex is the line for you,
The only line your heart will know is true.

Office of Enquiry

Outside the Office of Enquiry the dog-lovers
Discuss the effects of the judges' decisions
On the minds of foreign visitors
Interested in the best native breeds.

Inside the Office of Enquiry a decent
Englishman is sorting the evidence
Gathered from army, police, ordinary citizens.
Whatever the Englishman makes, he must make sense.

Whatever the Englishman decides
Someone will be betrayed.
It is simply not enough to be decent.

Was it the result of an old feud?
Was it just Morris? Was he helped by McQuaid?
Was it cold-blooded? Was it an accident?

Dog-lovers sniff the air. Keen that justice be done?
The Englishman considers the machine-gun.

This New Theory

Historical revisionists are now convinced
'Judas is the only Irishman among the Twelve Apostles'.
Certain local historians are incensed
Yet this new theory has a large following.
Some revisionists say Judas was born in Cork
Others say he was a Dublinman
Others still insist he came from Kerry,
A cute hoor who'd steal the salt out of the holy water.

After all that, I ask myself, who am I?
And then I wonder, does it matter a tinker's curse?
Am I you or Uncle Ted or Carney pilgrimming to Knock?
I know this morning I shall never die
Because like God I'm everywhere although
I think that I may settle in Foxrock.

Back from the Verge

Strong is the urge to go over the top
Like a muddy Cockney, patriotic with murder.
Once again, dear friends, I'm back from the verge
Savouring a shaky sense of order

After sniffing my own sweetfoul dissolution,
About to spend eternity
In a damp rusty horse-drawn caravan
Clattering the roads of Waterford and Tipperary

122

Condemned never to halt at a roadside bungalow
Opulent, tasteless, yet offering the milk and bread
Without which my anorexic spirit would cease to be.

Back from the verge, outlook varied as a rainbow,
I'm ready for tea and toast, nursing the small talent
God in his odd way concentrated in me.

Nowhere

The camp is nowhere, yet a hundred
Starving stragglers drag in here every day.

This Legendary Coastline

This legendary coastline is vulnerable.
Force 9 gales, forty-foot high waves,
Regina Coeli has a crack in her hull,
The drowned are turning in their graves,
The Italian skipper admits
He has 90,000 gallons of my crude on board.
Regina Coeli is drifting towards the rocks.
Good Lord!

Even the Son of Man
Might hesitate to walk on the water tonight.
It is time for the National Emergency Pollution Plan.

Regina Coeli is breaking up. You never can tell
When the sea turns traitor. The oil pukes free.
Begin another slick chapter of hell.

Acid

They sprayed the air with acid
Breathed it like the first promise of love
Heard long ago in the corner of a garden.
They drank non-stop for a week
Sang songs of faith and fatherland
Then from basements and bunkers drew forth
Effigies of me, grotesque and vivid,
'The worst human being ever to walk the earth',

And erected them in public places
Tearing and kicking me
Howling and mocking me
Spitting and jeering me
Screaming for my blood.
I study their faces, not unlike my own.
When I'm in shreds they feel exhausted and good.
I want that mob
To trample me alive
Because every day my interest grows
In the bright lies of perspective,
In the faith of those who think
They constitute the truth in ink.
I'm an effigy, in any case,
Bunting fluttering in the breeze.
Being kicked in the stomach, whipped in the face,
Barbed in various inventive ways
Helps me to see my kind, superior
To me in every way, in an odd light.

It's their words I can't forget.

Words reach me as I'm shredded, words fierce
And simple, knife-edged, obscene, not without wit,
Poetry of course, concise and murderous, you may taste it yet.

Riot

My third visit to that seaside city
Which I adored in cold and heat
Coincided with a prison riot
One icy morning in late January.
I'd always been attracted to the spot
And was upset to hear five hundred
Prisoners who'd called an end
To their part in the riot were shot dead
In the prison yard.
               The President, a friend
Of mine, said he'd ordered the executions
Because democracy must prevail at no matter what
Cost. He gave me permission
To celebrate Mass where the blood of the dead
Stained the ground around the altar. I felt quite
Apocalyptic as I offered sacrifice to God.

Gobblegasp

I happened on the old century, his back
To a blackened wall, eyes jailed in pain.
'What's wrong?' I asked the old hack.
The jacked century gobblegasped, 'My main
Artery is clogged with lies, no air, no air,
Or so my old carcase feels.'
               'What kind of lies
Make you suffer so?'
               'Normal' came
The gobblegasp, 'The kind one hears and sees
Everywhere, decent lies, know what I mean?'

'Can I do anything to relieve your pain?'

'Yes, show me a city where the air is clean
And poison doesn't cancerise the rain
And the light's not bruised with hungry crying
And breath is evidence of more than men half-dying.'

'Sorry, old thing' I smiled, 'That dream is dead.
You've been awake too long. It's time for bed.'

The Experiment

I'm not sure where the experiment began.
Some say it was the brainchild of a traffic-cop
Who developed ideas on the nature of man.
Flanagan says it started in a small room behind a breadshop
Where connoisseurs gathered to sample the baker's best
And measure ways in which bread kept them alive
As much, at least, as milk from a mother's breast.
Hitler, who holds all culture springs from people's fear of the grave,
Believes, if I understand him, the experiment started
At an undertaker's party in an Austrian village
Resonant, on that occasion, with music and song.
    Theories of origins vary, yet all are agreed
Somewhere along the line, for reasons hard to grasp,
The experiment went wrong.

FIVE

The chosen few
in the heavenly know

Interview

When I was being interviewed for my job as an apostle
I thought Jesus's questions were rather prickly,
Like sitting on thistles.
Yet I answered intelligently

As I could, giving the exact names and numbers
Of persons in the Blessed Trinity,
The birthplace of Joseph the carpenter
And the tricky problem of Mary's virginity.

I answered reasonably well on miracles,
Moses, Abraham, Isaac. I cut
The balls off the false gods. I made a case for whores,

Murderers and sundry criminal misfortunates.
At the end, Jesus nodded. He looked me in the eyes.
'Congrats, Judas' he said, 'The job is yours.'

The Secret

To think that I, the one man for the job,
Easy in my skills as absolute schemer,
Should have helped to birth that murderous mob
Lusting for the blood of its redeemer,

Appals me, or nearly does.
So it continues, this helpless treachery of men
In churches beds governments colleges.
I live again, again

Well-dressed as ever, plausible and good,
A friend of children who will suffer,
Hating fatigue, determined to let it rip

Like bombs hatched in Hitler's blood.
He passes on the secret to his condemners.
He becomes his judges. World explodes. The rest is gossip.

E

In at the Kill

From my vantage-point as traitor
I see what's true.
Truth's face is an alligator's,
Ugly as sin, but it'll have to do.

Or it's a camel's carcase in the desert sun
Rotting at an ungodly rate.
Ants work overtime, a busy hum,
Efficient as plague, inevitable as fate.

Soon enough, the bones appear,
Prone in the sun. They change too,
Shrink, splinter, belittle themselves. And still

There are men would assemble, disentangle the puzzle,
Call it truth-seeking till they're blue
In the spirit. I was in at the kill.

Necessary

Consider the scene.
Who's necessary here?
Cut off that man's right hand, this one's left ear,
Things will be as they have been.

You can do without Peter,
Slap another in his place.
You needn't break your back to find
Another face like John's face.

Nothing irreplaceable about Andrew and James.
Look at that Mary, one whore is much like another.
Shuffle the deck, pick your cards, what do you see?

Men and women with appropriate names,
Disposable.
                    But who can replace that other?
Or me?

A Potholed Version

Obstacles to conversion are many.
Bringing souls to God is a canny art.
A dedicated lad, I put my heart
Into the job in many's the rough country.

When we were converting Ireland
There was small pleasure, much pain.
Frankly, despite my prayers, fasting, good deeds,
Pilgrimages to bleak centres of penance,
I never grew accustomed to the fuckin' rain.

But worse than that, dear brothers in Christ,
Scattered like mini-abysses throughout the land
Were the Grand Canyon potholes in every road
Gaping like hell's mouths in that boggy sod.

After many broken ankles, cracked shinbones, sprained backs,
We lost
All trust in the inhabitants of the island
And got out fast
To trail elsewhere with the Word of God.

God knows what we left behind.
A potholed version of The Message comes to mind.

So Lost

I will sit here in the dark and name their names
To see if they ever lived in me,
These men I knew and travelled with,
Images in memory

So lost they lack even the power to accuse
Me of what I know I must accuse myself:
Someone was betrayed, that was the bad news,
The rumour multiplied like dust on a shelf,

Multiplied, burying itself under itself, layer
Upon layer, cities, families, griefs, governments, lies,

Until all I have is this darkness calm and deep
Like a parable enlightening the air
Or the same air bearing prayers and sighs
Or an uncontrollable desire to weep

Breaking my eyes
Like tomorrow's traveller
Rocketing through poisoned skies.

I Like Smiles

There's one poor apostle whom
They are killing with prominence.
I'd like to save him from this doom
But he's a bit of a bollocks

Chirping towards damnation
A machine smile on his face
Plus a lust for gusty acclaim
No applauding gods can satisfy.

I am in a position to say this
And despite today's plague of horseflies
I pray, dear God of style, I say it well:

I like smiles, could be a sign of happiness,
But there's one smile wrings from me deep sighs:
That of the eminent victim prominent as hell.

Iggy Squelch

Iggy Squelch of Our Cross and Passion University
Did a Ph.D.
On the role of the kiss
In myth and history.

He interviewed me.

Did you kiss him?
Kiss? Yes. There was a kiss.

Did you cause it to happen?
I never kiss anyone
Unless I mean the kiss to mean something.

What was the meaning of that kiss?
The strange thing about kissing is
You never know till afterwards.

You kissed him in the garden?
Yes, yes, I did, I was
Trying to say something,
Whenever I say something
I try to mean what I say,
Unless I mean what I say
I know I don't say what I mean.
Know what I mean?

Were you giving a sign?
I was giving a kiss.

Who was watching?
Whoever was there.

Who was there?
Other people. The whole fuckin' party.

What did they do?
They moved in.

What happened?
Sin.

We continued thus, for hours, if I remember right.
Iggy Squelch was a cute questioner.
There was no escape.
O and I nearly forgot to mention –
Iggy got the whole thing on tape.

Tough Mission

One of the country's most noble sons
Eager that freedom be achieved as soon as possible
Assembled a dozen choice killers
And christened them The Twelve Apostles.
Skilful they were when he found them and yet
He drillskilled them further in the Glen of Aherlow.
One morning he called them together and said
'My dear Apostles, it is time to go.'

Up to the bad capital of the land they came,
Twelve men for twelve jobs, tough mission,
Twelve enemies died when the Apostles struck.
It was glorious work, it won proper fame
Like poems executed with skill and passion
And having nothing to do with good or bad luck
On either side:
Those who lived, those who died.

Slander

They said our god was an epileptic
Whose revelations were only fits;
Most of the time he was a feverish
Babbler rattled out of his wits;
He was a horny sensual god
Who tried to satisfy his randiness
By perfume-drenching his body
And smearing lipstick over his dress;
He was called pretender, deceiver,
Apostate, idolator
And other names you might fling at one
Locked in a drunken stupor.

In spite of that he was all we had.
We cling fiercely to our slandered god.

Badun

Making a living may unmake a man.
Everywhere I look I see
Victims of responsibility.
They write the lines but the lines don't scan
They write the songs but they're out of tune
With music that is theirs alone;
The dreamed harmony becomes the groan
Of a sick man cursing the moon.

        Not once has the moon given a sign
That it hears the curse of an unmade man
Self-betrayed by doing what's right
But I know a badun walking the line
Between should and won't and must and can.
Irresponsible darkness is the light
By which he plies his trade,
Re-making what making a living had unmade.

Slices

Two handsome waiters wheeled in
This heart-melting cake at the Last Supper.
Just looking at it was enough
To prompt me to commit the sin

Of gluttony. What a cake! It tasted even better
Than it looked. Nearly everyone there
Stared at this heavenly fare
And began to feel fatter.

Peter got a slice, Paul got a slice,
Andrew got a slice, Simon got a slice,
Zebedee got a slice, I was quick to take

My slice, a Bishop dropped in for a slice,
Then a Cardinal, a Pope, infinite priests,
All got slices. Where's the cake? Poor, poor cake!

A Happy Smile

Word about the marvellous wine
At the Wedding-Feast of Cana
Spread quickly through the universe
And reached Brendan Behan in Dublin.

He jetted out to the Feast.
Downing glass after fabulous glass
He looked around for Jesus.
'Congratulations!' he said to the boy, 'This

Is the best drop I've had in me natural.
Your blood is worth bottlin'. I've never
Tasted the like o' this, any place I've been.'

Jesus gave Behan a happy smile.
Joseph and Mary looked at him in wonder.
'Thanks be to Jesus,' sighed Behan, 'Wine! Infinite wine!'

Unauthorised Version

Would you blame me for thinking the entire
Event was going to come a cropper
When Brendan Behan splattered through the door
Of the room where we were having the Last Supper?

The man was pissed out of his borstal mind,
His trousers at half-mast, blood bubbling his face.
'Where's the fuckin' drink?' he shouted at Jesus.
'Come in, Brendan' Jesus replied, 'Take your place.'

Behan sat down, started swigging the wine
And guzzling the odd lump of bread.
                    After a while
He sang *Tonight is our last night together*
And his own unauthorised version of *Molly Malone*.
                    Jesus smiled.

The Twelve Apostlettes

'How is it?' I asked Jesus, 'You haven't even
A single woman among your twelve apostles?
I mean, aren't you a prejudiced son-of-a-bitch?
Bit of a male chauvinist pig? I'd like to suggest

A dozen women – to be known as the Twelve Apostlettes
Who will constitute an alternative to your men,
Introduce another notion of salvation,
An alternative hell and heaven.

I wish to nominate Sally Noggin, Dolly Mount, Nell Flynn,
Biddy Mulligan, Valerie Valera, myself, Tosser Conner,
Molly Malone, Bonny Bell, Paula Foll, Vinnie Greene

And bearing in mind inevitable sin
As well as necessary concepts of virtue and honour
I nominate, lastly, Mary Magdalene.'

'Thank you,' Jesus smiled (the smile was fleeting)
'I'll bring the matter up at our next meeting.'

Now We Are Seven

We come now to the Seven Deadly Sins,
A fair collection of begrudgers
That would set up house in a bishop's foreskin
And hop in and out like flybynight dodgers
Up to their pranks in the ranks of the innocent.

And yet, well, let's look. Pride? Yes, I'm proud,
And proud of my pride. I covet much that I see
And lust when I can. That's how they measure a man.
Anger, you bastard, how often you've robbed me
Of the best in the world and gave me the worst.
Gluttony, I know, is the belly's ambition
And envy the eunuch's shriek to possess.
Sloth is the essence of Irish dynamics.
Seven? I'm guilty of all. And more. And perish perdition!

A Lambasting

Brendan Behan lambasted me at the Last Supper.
For starters, he told me with a grin
I was a spiritual Jack the Ripper
With a face like a plateful of mortal sin.

Then he said as he dared my eyes
I had the cut of a slithery get
And the innocent Jesus would find in me
What he'd live to regret.

I was, he added, the kind of man
Who gave a divine beauty
To your average rat.

'Finally' he rasped as he downed more wine,
'You're the prison bully and you're hangman-smelly.
And that, Judas, is fuckin' that!'

A Dream of Yellow Rain

If I were a psychologist I might view
What appears to have happened through analysing eyes;
If I were a nuclear scientist I might know
Why certain stars are fiery, icy and wise;
If I were the one I kissed and betrayed
I fancy I'd find it hard to forgive me
        But I am none of these, I am my own
Man, yours, the Good Book's prince of treachery.

Rivers whisper my name, my name smears the sun,
The sun protests, my name rips outcast through space,
Lost planet, shredded effigy, withered bone.
Nameless planets spin to praise his face
And the pained depths of God's unsleeping heart
Harbour a lonely truth: Judas plays his part.
Play me home to the ticking of a clock
Thought of eternity betrayed by time
Where Christ is water and Peter a rock
And yours truly an unruly patron of crime.

138

I'm still not sure what I did or said
Don't know the meaning of one unblooming thing
Begin in a garden, end with the dead,
Begrudge no man his crust of bread
But doubt your ears when the love-choirs sing.
It happened, I insist it happened, the lads played
Their parts, I wonder did I get them wrong,
What is a prayer, a sin, the magic of money,
A name chosen-created to bear all the blame,
A man-made judgment premature or delayed
Voices whining in beggary or angelised in song,
A world gorged with poisoned milk, poisoned honey?
My sleep tonight is a place of pain.
I am a dream of yellow rain.

Joker

One of the apostles, he shall be nameless,
Was a bit of a joker. Oft, when the chosen
Were blitzed by collective depression
And their souls and balls were frozen
By gloom-icicles, the joker upped with
A yarn to bring the melting laughter in.
'On my way home from the wedding-feast
Of Cana' says he, 'I shot through the windscreen
Of my Morris Minor, was rushed to hospital,
Operated on, bandaged all over with the exception
Of my balls and prick, which I gazed on with some feeling.

A roving fly alighted on my pricktop.
A nurse rushed in, screamed "Shall I swat the bastard now?"

"No" I replied "Tickle my balls and I'll stick him to the ceiling."'

A Sweet Event

Fred Edselshit and Sons handled the auction
Of the Last Supper Memorabilia.
Fred, whose heart and soul are in the game,
Took personal responsibilty for the publicity

Which went like a neutron bomb. Speculators
Perfumed from all corners of the globe.
It was a sweet event, nostalgic at times,
Prices skyhigh. A touchy Buddha bought Christ's robe,

Tried it on, didn't fit, kept it all the same.
Paul Getty paid fifty million for my napkin
The Pope spent a similar sum on Peter's fork

The Ayatollah Khomeini bought a leftover bottle of wine
Jack the Ripper purchased a knife for a price you might find in a dream
And the chalice was snapped up by some anonymous body on the phone
        from New York.

Fred Edselshit said he was happy with the day's work.

Strangers Are Strangers

Decades later I met one of the apostles.
His face had emptied itself of the world's frantic traffic.
He'd abandoned the work nine years earlier
And taken to walking on his own
Through towns and cities in different countries.
He never spoke a word to anyone.
Strangers are strangers and should be left alone, he said.
What difference can my words make?

There's no lessening of pain and humiliation,
Money and money's children are kings,
I knew one moment of knowing, ice in the mind,
I desire not to intrude on anyone ever again,
I live in a world, I know people and things
Die and endure, I wish you, Judas, whatever is good
For you, you are strange to me as loved, lost God.
You were of us, in us, one, though now I hear you are bad,
Bad lad, bad lad, bad lad, bad lad.

140

Dingle

I mate occasionally but am damnably single.
Still, I love a frolic now and then
On holidays in Ballyferriter or Dingle.
I have a penchant for Irish-speaking women
And get on well with The Church who
Has a sweet blas and loves holidays in the South-West.
I think The Church is a bit of a bitch
But I like to pretend I place my trust

In her pronouncements. Once in Dingle we
Went out drinking together. 'What have we
In common?' I asked. 'Nothing that I can

See' smiled The Church. 'That's where you're wrong'
I replied. 'How so?' inquired The Church.
I smiled 'We both betrayed an innocent man.'

'Dear Judas' smiled The Church, 'That's where you're wrong.
But it's not too late. Finish
Your pint. We'll go for a walk.
I'll set you straight.'

The First Time

The first time I kissed The Church
Was at a party in Clonmacnoise.
We were both slightly pissed and lurched
Towards the base of a Celtic Cross
Where the kiss took place. It was a French one,
Sloppy, germful, yet dexterous and long.
'That was refreshing' smiled The Church 'You're a gas man.
Now do sing an Irish song.'

I obliged with *The Rose of Tralee*,
A harmonious rendering of that difficult air
So frequently murdered by drunken women and men.

'That was beautiful' smiled The Church 'I see
No singer in Ireland who can compare
With you. You're pure music, Judas. Kiss me again.'

Redundancy Plan

I put forward a Redundancy Plan
For The Church. The terms were good
Including a month's holidays in Bundoran
For all who'd exploited the Mystical Blood.

The Church went into herself and came out
Sprightly saying 'No, I've decided to continue.
In spite of the prospects I have no doubt
I'll survive.' I said, 'I am in you

And you are in me.' 'That is a matter'
Smiled The Church 'For my theologians to debate.
So tell me a story, Judas, or do sing an Irish song.'

I gave The Church a rendering of *Mulligan's Daughter*.
Then I asked 'How do you always manage
To be so authentically wrong?'

'Man' smiled The Church 'It's a matter of knowing man
And who is likely to benefit most
From a thoughtful Redundancy Plan.'

Guilty But Insane

The Church was hauled up before the Judge
And charged with keeping the people down
Using the Sacraments and the Ten Commandments
As the major instruments of oppression.
(The Eleventh Commandment 'Thou shalt not be found out'
The Judge dismissed as a frivolous addition
To the Literature of Hortatory Prohibition
Though he conceded this was the Commandment
Most religiously observed by Irishmen.)

The Church pleaded Not Guilty.
              'I am the people'
The Church said, 'Not merely Popes Bishops Priests
Holy Etceteras. I'm waiting for Christ to come again.'

142

'Something' the Judge concluded 'Is wrong on a universal
Scale. I should sentence you to two thousand years, at least.
Instead, I find you guilty but insane.'

The Church smiled at The Judge. He blessed himself.

The Catechism Said

The catechism said God is everywhere.
There are times when, not wishing to steal
One ray of his limelight or take the shine
Off his bliss, that, in a gutshell, is how I feel.
                O there are mornings
     I wake up in paradise
     Not in my sweaty bedsit
Nights when before an audience of fifty million
I unleash rockets of immortal wit
To brighten space and entertain the stars
Staring back at me,
               stars' eyes desperate and dumb
     As shivering tinkers
         Squatting
    In uncharitable ice
That will not thaw for the hell of a long time to come.

As I Splashed and Swam

The apostles and I were having our daily
Dip in the Forty-Foot for the good of our health.
Peter enjoyed it because it was truly
Electrifying, made him feel like a wealthy

Man. The others liked it too
Even when winter chilled their apostolic balls.
Dalkey! Killiney! Good! Beautiful! True!
And yet, now and then, a strange thing befalls

Even innocent men frolicking in the sea.
To be precise, a strange thing happened to me.
As I splashed and swam I swallowed a lump of shit,

A raw, untreated, solid, calorie-conscious,
Middle-class lump of shit.
It spoiled my day, made me greensick among happy men.

Heavens, shall I ever be unpolluted again?

Under the Table

There was a bomb-scare at the Last Supper.
We were tucking into the bread and wine
When the phone rang in an abrasive manner
And someone said in a Cork accent at th'other end of the line

Dat dere was a big hoor of a bomb in de room, boy.
Unpardonable, I thought. Nothing excused it.
Zebedee found the bomb in a bag under the table.
Jesus defused it.

After that opening shock the evening went well.
Peter got sloshed and showed his old
Tendency to pull rank.

I told him, in the vaults of my mind, to go to hell
And brooded on my tentative efforts to open
An account in a Swiss Bank.

Where Is Little Nell?

You'd never dream, looking at the various paintings,
There was a woman at the Last Supper.
Afterwards, over a few whiskeys, chatting,
She told me it had been her life's ambition
To be present at the final fling because
Male clubs were damaging to men and women alike.
Her name was Little Nell, she gave me pause,
I relished the way she threw the whiskey back,
She was glad the Church was founded on a rock
But feared the rock might sometime become sand
If a woman weren't included in the paintings

Reminding future times of that revealing night
In all its drama and complex trappings.

I examine, in vain, the Great Masters. Where is
Little Nell? Her radiant face? Her sparking yappings?
Her sweeping-away of all male chauvinist shite?
Who ousted Little Nell? Who quenched her cheeky light?
If I could, would I paint her into the scene? I might.

Dazzling Variety

Moving tensely or at ease through temples and office-blocks
In the company of High Priests and Bank Managers
I was always prepared to pull up my socks
And so enjoyed a dazzling variety of careers.
Once, unemployed, finding myself on the rocks,
Unable to afford even the vilest wine or beer,
I became a male prostitute but shucks!
I was a lousy queer.

After this fling I grew respectable again,
Ran a high-class brothel in Berlin
For top-rank Nazi officers on the town.

Yet, after all, I am pig-ignorant of men.
I seem to have lost that consciousness of sin
I once considered uniquely my own.
The soul snores when sin sleeps in the bone.

The Job

I survive in a city of boiling envy.
When Peter got the job of First Pope and Bishop of Rome
Certain of the apostles got apoplexy
Because they felt the job was theirs, and theirs alone.
It was a tough job too, with the aim
Of preventing the whole show going to the bad;
Peter was the man for it, gallant and game,
And he gave it everything he had.

Peter was a canny fisherman,
He knew the moods of land and sea
And he didn't let the job go to his head.

When I hinted he was watched on every side
By envious gets who'd gut him in a tick,
'Ah, fuck the begrudgers!' Peter said.

Enter, Smiling

OK for you leaning lazily over the bridge there
Watching the water greenblackpoisoning along,
Bright boy, one more slack-minded questioner;
'What went wrong?'

I gave it my all, same as the rest
Slogging away night and day to drive the message home.
For what? Pompous bastards with a lust
For power. Gangsters in Rome.

Pity. Possibilities blossomed there.
The one joy of my life was seeing men
Give all their hearts. Then certain hearts grew sick.

Eyes charged with passion assumed a calculating stare.
Enter, smiling, chairman, secretary, polite assassins.
I should have led them. I could have made them tick.

Event

'Please, please address us on the stupidity
Of the Women's Movement, we know you're one
Of the genuine male chauvinist pigs in the city,
Convinced of the natural superiority of man

Over and under woman, we want you to do
A Norman Mailer on those intellectual
Girls who're only aching for it anyway,
We want you to call a cunt a cunt, let it all

146

Hang out, that'll get them coming, show them
How atrocious their prose is,
We'll guarantee a fee, give you bite and sup,

Just be yourself, grunt at the bitches, you know them,
We've spent months organising this event,
It'll be fun when you fuck it up.'

Fishing

One morning I went out fishing with Peter,
A hot-headed sort, and obstinate
So when he told me to pitch my line in the river
I quickly obeyed. I caught a trout.

'Bravo, Judas!' said Peter, enthusiastic flames
Zipping through his eyes into his beard.
He proceeded to coin affectionate names
For me: Flyboy, Mackerelman, Troutscout, Sharklord.

'Further' he went on, mimicking the master
Whose style of expression is divinely precise,
'I shall make you a fisher of men.'

'Does that mean' I asked, looking through the water,
'I must stick this hook into men's mouths and eyes?'
'O Judas' laughed Peter, 'You're such a clever, foolish man.'

To Work

Suppose I have nothing
But a swift's broken wing
A swift's terrified eye,

                        Is that enough
To keep me strong
When accusers and interpreters
Define my wrong?

Has my enthusiasm cooled?
Am I disappointed because
Enemies that should be cut down
Are not cut down?
Do I smell a false messiah, one who according
To law must be done away with
That yobboes suck authority from myth?
Am I one of many disillusioned men,
One of many, yet the only one
To do what must be done?
Should not this power proclaim itself,
                    arise and sing
To hearten people whose hearts are low?
Must noble blood be spilled to breed a cosmic lie?
Will yuppies thrive because one knew how to die?
Accusers, interpreters, to work, for I
            Have a swift's broken wing,
A swift's terrified eye.

A Minor Rôle

I could have organised the ship from stem to stern,
Sidestepped the crucifying mess.
Had they listened, I'd have made them learn
Ways to bridle chaos.

I could make a Buddhist and a Hindu chat together
Discussing Protestaant and Catholic views
On the changing state of atheistical weather.
I could make the Arabs love the Jews.

Instead, my organising genius was ignored,
I played a different part in that vast
Redemptive plan,

Mere cheeky kisser of my prayerful Lord.
A minor rôle, you'd say. Why must
Gods always pick the wrong man?

148

The Dark Night of the Hole

I was cycling home from a disco in Nazareth
Under the luminous vacuity of a harvest moon
Which tempted me for a moment to take my eyes
Off the road, o giddy-treacherous man!

Failing to spot the warning blink
Of the local Corporation lamp
I cycled straight into a hole, sink-
ing without trace, apart from the damned

Screams I somehow hurled at the moon
Like a mob's insults at a crucifixion.
My bike was in smithereens. So was I
In that profound hole, stinkydeep like my mind

Which proceeded to release imbeciles and demons
To tell me Irish/Jewish jokes through all eternity.
Workers found me in the morning. I'm glad I was found.

The dark night of the hole returns now and then
Like the bad jokes told and relished by passing men.
Who the hell makes up these jokes? Did you hear this one...?

Whatever I Am

Whenever I run into the other apostles nowadays
They glance the other way.
Peter is the only one to halt for a moment
Turn on me his fierce eye
As if he's going to unleash one
Of those enraged tirades I find so endearing
But even Peter manages to keep the lid on.

I'm out in the cold, all on my ownio.

Theological types argue I'm lost
My psychological friends speak sadly of alienation
Whatever I am, it's not nice.

How could it be? My brain is packed in frost
My blood, a poisoned tributary of the Shannon
My heart, a regular thump of ice

Though I saw miracles once, miracles, you realise.

Alive and Well

To judge by the numbers of letters arriving
On my silver plate every blessed morning
The Judas Conservation Society is thriving
In its aim to keep me strong and flourishing
Despite approved rumours that I'm hanged, dead
And buried in some corner of the Holy Land.
Members of the Society give their lifeblood
To me, they have been lobbying all Family
Planning Clinics to use my special judassperm
So that goo-goo Judases will pop up
Like morning milkbottles on your doorstep
To emulate my style from here to hell.
Also, with the help of every snake and worm,
Every palpitating rat sniffing a trap,
The Great Religions of the world elect me alive and well.
I'm in a buying mood today. What have you to sell?
Thank you for helping me stay indefatigable.

About As High

I took a year off from my aggressive
Messianism to raise my consciousness.
I tried the Eastern Caribbean Islands
Overwhelmed by American Cable TV
– No use. Off to South Africa
Where I supported revolt of the black masses
Against white pornography.
Repelled, however, by black and white excesses,
The savage dominion of right wings everywhere
And an average of three death-threats a week,
I sought a spot where nobody could destroy

The grain of freedom I've learned to treasure
Plus those private vital pleasures of the flesh,
So happily transient, I've come to enjoy.
Did I raise my consciousness? About as high
I'd say, as your average expert's eye.

Laureate

For ages the apostles toiling in silence
Kept no chronicle of their affairs
Content to spend their days working for love
Seeking no praise.

Then one said 'Judas, you have a way with words,
Write a poem, a song
To celebrate the fortitude of these good men
Who've laboured long.

Be our poet Laureate!
In verse that trips, tinkles, resounds,
Remind the crass world that we are here.
We'll give you silver and beer.

Sing of Herod's birthday, Hitler's enterprise,
The Pope's decision to dress in white
When black despair envelopes the hearts of men
To left and right.'

I accepted the offer. I wrote a verse praising
TIME MAGAZINE for choosing Hitler
1938 Man Of The Year.
Everyone said my poem was amazing.
I deserved my silver and beer.

Beer and silver, silver and beer –
I still compose the occasional celebratory titbit
Lacking in passion, perhaps, by with my special tricky skill.
I make startling use of the hortatory cliché –
Honour thy father, Love thy neighbour, Thou shalt not kill.

I do not expect my verse to be collected,
Enough for me the plaudits of the moment.

Ignoring slanderous chit-chat, envious jeer,
I celebrate the official apostles
In my own style, modest and transient
Amid beer and silver, silver and beer.

The Job

Why didn't I get the job? The thought
Is something of an obsession.
If I'd been appointed I'd have changed
The image of the Apostolic Succession.

With my special talent who knows
What might have happened?
Would the Church be facing
Its present state of spiritual collapse?

Peter was first choice.
Judas the traitor, Peter the rock:
Perish the labels; we soldiered together once.
Peter was able-bodied, quick-tempered, strong-voiced,
Good-hearted. But did he do the trick?
Or is the rock self-smashed into smithereens?
Why do the most living hearts
Attract the deadest has-beens?
How did that passionate adventure
Become a bad theological lecture?
How did the agony of loving eyes
Become a sordid political enterprise?
Although my soul is helplessly adrift
I have a few questions left.
There'll be no answers till the polished men
Get the smell of blood from the hill again.

The Question

Whenever I see the apostles getting bored
Or about to grow
Pissed-off with the responsibility placed on them by the Lord
I ask the question 'Who killed Marilyn Monroe?'

Two weeks before she died she sang 'Don't be
Uptight on a Saturday night' over the phone
To John F. Kennedy on his birthday.
Stilled is that voice. Dead naked alone

The ravishing innocent was found in her bed.
Who did it? The Mafia? The Kennedys? The CIA?
The Pope? The UDF? The Anti-Abortion Society of Crossmaglen?

Two thousand years have fled since this matter came to a head.
It dies away for decades. Then, prompted by moralists like me,
It surfaces. We talk. The apostles sparkle like lovers born again.

Peter's Seminars

Why, attending one of Peter's seminars
On ways to spread the Word
In West Cork Wounded Knee Madagascar
And other spots by which the heart is stirred,

Do I see, not hordes of aboriginals
Waiting to be transfixed by the primal glow
Of language in the mouths of the apostles,
The chosen few in the heavenly know,

But a rat-eyed, bearded veteran
Of some war ambiguosly chronicled,
Waiting by a third-floor window, patient,
With an irregular cough
Four cheese sandwiches
Crisps
A large can of Dutch applejuice
A Barbara Cartland
A rifle on his knee for the young man

Whose head he'll soon blow off?

Mouths of continents gape when the thing is done.
I like Peter's seminars; they turn me on.

The Heads

Look at the heads.
Consider what a night's carousing will reveal:
Grey hair at the temples, mouth half-open
Chest out like a boy's full of pride
Strong fingers caressing a glass into warmth
Legs outstretched, all pain gone for the moment
But it'll be back and that's for certain,
Lips laughing now as they haven't laughed for years.
There will be talk of this night, such talk
It'll scorch the packed wax in their ears.
Look at those eyes, jewels beautifully alone,
That one's right hand under his chin, the light
Quietly fingering his jawbone.
Such a night! All together! Yet each one keeps his place
Including me, there, at the corner, near the end.
You can't define me as enemy or friend.
I've never seen such a determined look on a man's face.

SIX

You

Carlotta

I think, Carlotta said, there's nobody as crude as
You though I admire-abhor the skill
With which you move, dear Judas,
To the kill.
If you, most treacherously accomplished blighter,
Should in a sudden patriotic burst
Become a freedom fighter
Whose attitude to blood is like a guinnessthirst

     You'll wait halfway down a lane for him.
He walks into your trap, you shoot him in both legs,
He'll live chastised, you walk away from every hatepain cry,
Forty steps, you stop, ponder, here's a problem,
Turn, walk back along the crying lane,
Halt over him, look, two bullets, one in either eye.
That's skilful-crude, Carlotta said, wonder how you'll die.

If I, If You

If I had not betrayed you
How would you have accomplished the miracle
In the unspeakable cities
Where children develop a killing style

Early? Would men have been so brave
Or women so given up to your memory?
Who would have dreamed it possible to save
Vanishing humanity from the hard-earned grave?

     And if you had not betrayed me
How could I ever have begun to know
The sad heart of man? How could I,
Watching seas of greed lick the shores of the
World and vanity all the human show,
Have found the courage to die?

If we swapped questions, o my brother,
Would we know why we betrayed each other?

Voice

The voice began, a scrape of nails over flesh,
Became the sound of rutting badgers, then
Was that drunk dung-faced fire-eyed cursing foul-
Smelling man who staggered to the frying-pan
On the Stanley range, lifted the sausages,
Stuffed them into his gob,
Savaged the brown loaf, looked at me,
Closed his eyes, moaned, started to sob
But checked himself. What he said next
I did not understand at the time. Nor do I now.
It's his voice I remember. For thirty years

I forgot all, the curses, remorse, bewilderment,
Blind oaths of revenge. Last night, the voice cut me
In two. I wanted to kill it, but froze in fear.
I don't know what it said but my heart
Cringed, a beaten dog. I got the long knife
And waited. Stab the voice, I thought, stab the curse.
Even as I knew it didn't exist, it grew worse,
I was split and maddened by what
Was not,
Growing more vile and foul in me. I had to kill it, kill
Nothing. It's gone, it raves and threatens still.
Did you arrange this? Am I accomplishing your will?
Are you nothing too? Nothing? Pretending to be all?

Design

In search of a new design I
Considered hanging myself from the door of my bedsit
With melting elegies by a fiddler from Athy.
But I decided this was not right.

The old castle loomed in my mind.
All my affection for maimed ruins was there
Plus a leap from the top down vertigoing air.
Then I thought of the muck beneath; and I declined.

It had to be the tree
It had to be the rope
Swingin' like a doll in a child's whirling hand
Swingin' like a sign in the wind.
     Before the Word sparkled this plan was mine.

Consider me
       At the butt-end of hope
Twisted.
       If I were you
I'd sketch this new design
'Cos twisted humans swing nearer the divine
Though not all the time, I must insist, not all the time.

A Casual Masterpiece

I am sitting here in my silence
Listening to your silence
Away from the streets of poison
And the cocksure minds
Blackleathering it across the pages.
I know now I can never be lost enough
In the silence, the only gift to survive the rages
And pains of a heart waiting to trip over love
In this tedious crazy place
That hates itself more than Hitler the Jews
And is better equipped to destroy
A glimpse of heaven in a turning-away face,
A casual masterpiece
Of this winter afternoon's eruptive joy.

For You

In these green and leafy days of May
I love to sketch
Guts of brothels, noses luminous with decay,
Avaricious brats, old bags on crutches,
Chubb Alarms, Interest Deposit Rates,
The divine design of a bishop's fart,

158

Mechanical faces of the poor, profiteering rats
And Experts on European Art.

I sketch the fiery spirits
Of the Seven Deadly Sins,
Schweitzer among the lepers, a politician's smile,

Bitches playing with men, men nailing bitches,
Hitler picnicking among the Sussex Downs.
These sketches are for you, wispy things, intended to beguile.

You Can

If I can imagine you I may well be you
Or it may be that you are me.
Come, let's trip through the Judaic-Christian dew
For a Last Supper by the Dead Sea.

If these men have their way, all the seas will be dead soon,
Poisoned by their thoughts and heartsblood.
O my brothers, you live in a rat's nose,
I see you sniff the corpse of God,

The joyous old creator you befouled,
He tried his best, put his shoulder to the wheel
But couldn't cope with you, you darling man,

Rutting and ratting through the world
Believing you can think, believing you can feel.
Of course you can, of course, of course you can.

A Sweet Jig

I sat under a palm-tree watching the sun
Doing a sweet jig on the water
And thought for all I was worth
(Not much) about the matter:

I imagined you were at my side
Listening with that patience unknown to other men.
'I did it' I said, 'Not from greed, vanity or pride
But because I believed it was the right plan.

May I ask did you suspect me from the start?
Did you know everything living in my mind?
Did you smile to mine the pits in my heart?
Was I a bright man? Or was I stupid and blind?'

We sat under the palm tree, I talking, you listening.
I waited. You looked at me, through me, said nothing.

Two Shadows

I'm opposed to all forms of death-penalty
Save that which one imposes on oneself.
As a member of Amnesty International I
Believe capital punishment should be left on the shelf

Of the judges' loo in the Supreme Court,
Packed neatly in a small, black box.
I abhor cruelty, a popular sport
Among those for whom law means no one rocks

The yacht. I have in mind disorientation,
Systematic rapings of the victim's sleep
And rhythmical interjections of fear.

Primitive men create emerging nations.
Over all such places two shadows creep.
One is mine. The other sheds real tears.

A Sudden Wave of Loneliness

All that tittle-tattle about thinking and feeling
And friends never again gathered in the one place
Because the merciless world is waiting
To make them step and work to a new pace.

You said Peter had betrayed you
And you could kill him without blinking.
You cried a little, put on your coat and left.
I sat there, thinking.

Thoughts of you stabbed me, I took the pain
And sat there, feeling you with me, into the night.
A sudden wave of loneliness swept over me then,
I was a drowning man, a calm drowning man
Becoming torn paper a boy might set alight
For fun to hold awhile and watch,
       drifting in ashy pieces anywhere through the town.

Lonelier

Something lonelier far than you or me...

Down here
In the heart's hell, the crumbling skin,
The trembling hand,

There are small moments when all I care to do
Is praise the loneliness
I cannot understand.

Accusations

Accusations come and go like the days of the week.

You were too fond of money.
Isn't everybody?

You acted alone, consulted nobody.
What about my turtle-computer?

You wanted control over your own God.
That was in both our interests.

You struck people as a cold bastard.
Detached? Yes. Illegitimate? No.

You were the Ultimate Male Chauvinist Pig.
I had a beautiful grunt.

You hadn't a clue about love.
What does that mean?

You hadn't a single friend in the world.
I had myself, occasionally.

You couldn't connect.
Preferred to dissect.

You were always too bloody smart.
Among apes, that's an art.

It's impossible to speak to you.
Then shut your mouth and give your arse a chance.

The whole world sees you as a symbol of the bad.
May they continue to do so, till worse can be had.

name

how we make your name punctuate our prattlings
like the slave-boy slipping
among his goats and sheep in the bold light
of a northern hill

or the prime minister at the conference
outlining reasons for having to kill
or not having to kill depending
on oil or hostages or terrorist interference

        he makes names for bushes and stones
for trees bending in the wind
he finds names at night for his friends
the shepherding stars

and he makes names for his unborn children
making a crust in Boston or Camden Town
or shrivelling into pygmies at home
behind respectable walls

or making love or war or stumbling on fame

o where would we be without your name?

162

A Bird

I am haunted by a name.
If I battered my head against a wall
The blood would form into the name's letters at my feet,
If I prayed to a god who eats men's brains
To stimulate his drowsy intelligence
He'd send the name in the wind and rain
Like a never-before-heard bird out of the sun,
A bird whose bones are made from the longings of the dead,
A bird with one song
Repeated with a keen, unsatisfied passion
Claiming my heart and my head
   and far beyond
Whatever I think I know of right and wrong.

I Was There

If, at any time in the future,
You enter this garden, drunk
Out of your puny mind,
And submit another man
To the evil scrutiny
Of your inquisitional glare,
Try not to drown the poor creature
In the foul boghole of your breath.
Last time you reeked in, I was there.

Child of the Sword

I dreamed we were waiting for a train
To go where there was a chance to be happy.
Somebody stabbed somebody up the line,
I ran to the victim, his neck was bloody.

There beside him lay Saint Bridget's Peace Cross.
It said, 'One day, a beggar called to her
Asking for alms. Bridget looked in the man's eyes
And seeing whatever she saw there

Gave him her father's sword. Today, right here,
A child of that sword stabbed a man in the neck,
He's quiet in his blood now, tonight he'll be raving,

Tomorrow a corpse.'

                    The Cross is polluted air,
The train roars goodbye at my back,
You lean from a window, smiling, waving.

The Trick

The first time I saw the trick I couldn't believe my eyes.
As a rule, my eyes do not betray me
But on this occasion they told me lies
Or so I thought. There it was, so true,
So undeniable, yet I knew this must be
Lies, all lies, but where's the proof?
Calm yourself, I said, this is a trick, the
Truth is a tricky business, learn the trick, bloom full of
Truth, others will call it style in time.
I learned, as God is my maker and judge, the trick
And in return the trick learned me.

We became each other, one and the same.
I can do it now, produce it with shock-
ing ease, it's there, you see it, nobody

Dreams of calling it a bag of lies.
What can you believe if you can't believe your eyes?

The Hell of an Effort

If you haven't been there, you don't know it.
If you have, you don't speak of it.
Isn't it fierce weather for the time o' year?
Thanks be to Jesus Flanagan isn't here.

A day at a time, that's how you manage.
You know you'll never undo the damage

You did to Kitty, Pete and Albert Lou.
Fact is you've made them sicker than you.

Two hotels, a family, part of your brain,
The whole kaboosh flushed down the drain,
The hell of an effort is needed now
Keep telling yourself that you know how
To live with demons living in your ear
And thanks be to Jesus Flanagan isn't here.

Where You Come From

Hell is not where you go to, it's where you come from.
You come from here, this place, this black hour.
It's bad here at the moment
With a lunatic in power
Children dying off like decency
Flogging torture starvation mockery
Black magic witchcraft poisoning of wells
The air packed with agonised cries
Our women vanishing leaving no traces
Our city besieged with a new disease
Old devils wearing new faces

And all the bad out there thriving here at your side.

        But don't worry, I have keys
To unlock your prison, compensation awaits
You, heaven, I tell you that, when have I ever lied?

The Madness of Football

Beautiful country, driven-out people –
Yakuntya, yahoorya, yabollocksya,
And the boys and the girls studying
For jobs in another country:
        Beautiful country, driven-out people –
I remember Mad Sweeney,
District Inspector Sweeney, to be exact,

Issuing guns in the Phoenix Park
And telling the RIC men
To open fire on the crowds in Croke Park.
Was there a Final feeling that Sunday
Or a totally different kind of sport,
A breakthrough in virile craft and art?
The papers forecast a battle royal.
I stewed in the crowd, I saw men fall.
Beautiful country, driven-out people –
I'm shot through with the madness of football.
Run, hit, kick, score, win. Win. That's all.

Teabags

I too have seen God in teabags, heard
Him lisping in the ticking of my clock
Tocking Sinai interpretations of the Word
Intended to improve my luck

        but I end up
Smelling my neighbours in church shop theatre
Damp creatures preparing for the long drop
From mortgages and babies and those peculiar
Forms of concern that cause this pimpled youngster
To spittle me in the street with
'I hate the bastard! I hate my bloody father,
Trying to live my life for me, shape me
Into his own fascist narcissistic middle-aged myth.
What can you say to me? What can you do for me?
This is bad, Judas. This is really bad!'

I'm perplexed-profound. 'Teabags' I mutter 'Study each feature
Of teabags. Be mystical. You'll understand your dad.
Place teabag in cup, pour boiling water, let it steep,
Extract teabag, throw it away, then drink, my son,
      drink deep of love and hope.'

Deep

Now and then throughout my career, let me
Call it career, I've tried in my grisly solitude
To open a dialogue with God.
'Good morning, God' I say, 'And how are things with you today?'

Silence. I wait a while before pursuing the matter
Then, hoping a cultural topic might prompt a reply,
Murmur, 'I'm getting interested in Nazareth folklore,
I bet you have fond memories of that, eh?'

Devil a word. But I don't give up easily.
I probe. 'Are you happy with the way things have turned out?
Does your favourite creature love the good, the beautiful, the true?'

Dumber than the dead. Silence deep as eternity.
I used to be disappointed but now that I think of it
If I'd made the world I'd keep my mouth shut too.
Especially if I'd made me, I imagine
Dialogue with me would not be my prime concern.

Honest

'My husband, chairman of the group that
Revolutionised the toothbrush in this
Age of rampant dental rot
Suffers from executive stress
Especially on journeys to East Africa.
Urbane, educated, ambitious, honest,
He tells me of his nights with prostitutes,
The only way he can find rest.
He's honest, he may have AIDS, he told me so
But he refuses to go to a doctor.
I refuse to sleep with him. I'm afraid. Myself. The children.
What do you, my friend, think of this matter?'

'Your husband's honest, dear, but sick;
An honest man with a dishonest prick.
I too shall be as candid as I can;
Your tragedy is you chose an honest man.'

Twist

You'll meet me at a twist in yourself
Which you must not confuse with a bend in the road
Where any longing man might meet
Another man and follow him for good
Or God or the hope of a cure for boredom
From woman or child or enough said enough done.
God blast it! Is there any end to this grim
Trivial round, chaining one dumb man
To another dumb man?
                              That's where I come in,
Interesting factor, new slant, fresh programme.
Can't you see, baby, I'm gonna be a hit
Because there, at that twist in yourself, sin
Is born again, the days can bless and damn,
You will swallow the old dark, the old light,
Meeting me in yourself, soon; but not yet.

No Symbol

Draw back a little, do not invest me
With your lack of...no end to that catalogue,
You are sole proprietor of your own misery
And ecstasy, picking white flowers in an autumn bog,
Counting the sins on your soul, innocent rogue,
Solitary ten-year old witness
Of Adam Gandon making love to a sheepdog,
Sniffer of womanblood at the centre of a mattress
In a hotel bedroom, she cried, she still drags
Your mind for her drowned love, you will not
Yield your secrets, you do not know if you
Betrayed or were betrayed, what does that mean?
Words are labels in chaos, bedlam and rout,
Someone is taking revenge on you, no doubt
About that, call off your mind's dogs, I am no
Symbol of anything, I am not known, heard, smelt, touched, seen
By anyone but myself in my own
Prison of flesh and bone,
Another ordinary appalled man.

168

Since, therefore, some distinctions have been made
Draw back a little. Betray, if you will; or be betrayed.
Someone will pin words on what you are and did and said.
Words for such a task, indeed, are gathering in my head.

This, I Said

'I walked up to him and I said did you
Steal my fishin'-rod?
Fuck off he said or I'll get the guards
An' they'll quieten you begod.

You stole it I said you mean bastard
Knowin' 'twas the only livin' I had.
I stole it he said an' what can you do about it?

This, I said.

I lifted him up over me head
Let go Jesus let go he screamed
I'll confess I'll swear I stole it I'll sign forms

I threw him into the river I threw
His coat and cap in after him
And last but not least his can o' worms.'

Bed

They wrote me down! The watchers wrote me down!
What sneaking watcher had the gall to write me down?
There are more versions of me than there are judging men.
When the master spoke, he said he was one,
Or three-in-one, or one-in-three, some such drivel.
A few who use words speak heart and soul,
Speak the blood's black skies as far as they're able.
Eat soulwords, heartwords, bloodwords. Or go to the devil.
The devil may not have you, of course, he's very pernickety
About those he's willing to use his words on.
He told me he once spent seven eternities,

Including an eternity chez God, struggling to find his own
Voice. When he did, it surprised even himself
With its infinite range of infernal effect.
His accent is bland, posh, with the occasional
Descent into crude if colourful peasant dialect.
He loathes vulgarity, he suspects it's good for the soul,
He has a liking for Sanskrit and official forms
Of Irish, he gives the nod to Anglo-Saxon's rutting edge,
Milton is his favourite poet, he thinks the Bible is crap,
Forbids his kids to read it, might keep them free from harm
And harm teaches kids the nature of the storm.
Such is the devil's word-mastery, he's turned hell into a college
Where choice language is really on the map.
        The Map of Ireland is what girls making beds in hotels
Dub semen-stains of sleepers on the sheets.
I leave it to you to imagine who makes the devils' beds in hell
And what they call the sheetstains of the devilsleep,
If sleep there be. Who lies in a devil's bed?
Who lies in yours? In yours? Lies, lies, lies,
Who knows the cosy hole where Cain was chosen to be bad?
What was your hot spawning-spot? Or mine?
I flatter myself, a castellated Victorian double-poster,
I'm just joking, y'know, I must, and yet I speculate
(You must too) on the warmth of that populating stink.
Every cretin among us has to come from somewhere,
Trouble starts in bleedin' bed, some usual stupo night,
In the beginning was the word and the word was – well, what do you think?
Think! Think until you are a pain-thorned head.
What then? Your favourite pills. Fall into bed.

Whatever You Want

Not to the living but to the dead do I grant sincerity.
I listen closely to those who have nothing to say.
Throw yourself on the bed, darling, weep fiercely
And between vast heart-racking sobs tell
Why priceless Simon went away.
My floor is covered with tears and snot
I'm being swept into your lachrymose hell
Where sincere devils cry in their chains and rot
And wish me well.

Give me that old cold-hearted loonypuss moon
Shining on its icy own
Hanging there to charm aspiring eyes
Being whatever you want it to be:

Clownmug, angel's harp, last loverword,
Heaven's magnetic turd,
Yellow bucket full of human lies.
Is the yellow bucket sincere? Do you think it tries?
Or are you deaf and dumb
And caged in your own sighs?

In the Wings

Many died that I might exist.
Either that or they were rough drafts
For me, the finished poem you read in your lost
Youth one day you saw a hawk culling sparrows.
Only your eyes saw this. Otherwise, it didn't exist.
You kept it to yourself, a small
Fierce parable of the order you believed in.
Let others call it murder. You knew it was mercy.

So victims arrange themselves into neat rows
To accommodate their executioners. In the wings,
Moralists buzz like flies over shite,
You are coming into being, nothing can stop you,
One witness complains, another sneers, another sings
Of the role you play in the birth of the immortal light.

Heavy Footsteps

You cross my mind when I hear footsteps
On iron gratings above my head.
I climb stone steps into the light
And eat my heart out for the dead –
    My liars, I love my liars, gargling
Their hearts out, foam on their lips
Cursing this world's sober ways
Before they stagger home to wife and right abuse.

I love you, bad scarred liars, who have all the cop-on
To let things happen, madden men, strike
For solitude, knowing you won't be missed.
Heavy footsteps. Yarns. Whispers. Someone I kissed.
Jamesie Horgan praises the Quakers' charitable dive:
'Thanks be to Jesus I'm hungry, drunk and alive.'

doorway

why, in that moment
of heart's darkness, of
severance without end,
did you turn to me
in the freezing doorway,
smile and say 'I'll always
be your friend'?

SEVEN

High on silver

The Bribe

So much, so little, no more, that's it, what is it?
What do you want for that?
Do you think you can buy me for that?
All of me? My heart? Mind? Body? Soul?

Why do you smile when you make the offer?
Do you know something about me I don't know?
Are you so confident I'll take the bait?
The bribe? That's what it is, isn't it? The bribe?

And I am to change the world for that!
And you'll get what you want and so will I
And this is the moment we both know something true.

Wipe that smile off your face, you pious respectable rat,
Someone who can't be bought is about to die.
Give me the money, here's what I'm going to do.

Get the Horror of It Hot

Take a pain. Rough. Deep. Slouch through Amber Street
Where crutches are begging for paper
Money as if coins would block a cripple's gut
And involve him, publicly, in an agonised caper

He'd be hard put to explain to a benefactor.
The pain corkscrews through you like a bad style.
Even the promptings of a divine instructor
Won't help, you're stuck with it, it is your sole

Hope, source, muse, honeycunt, unborn poem.
Take the pain, write it, get the horror of it hot,
Swoonfeed the world with melody of hell
Translated by apt chaps in Paris Berlin Rome.
Invest in pain. Pain pays. Interest grows like rot.
I'll review the lot in the *Squirish Mimes*. You'll sell.

Summertime

Waiting is the garden of impatience, she says,
Then her friend turns up and I leave.
Put the clocks forward an hour, it's summertime,
And what is there to see?

A few stragglers hungover from yesterday's game
Smooth newspapers loud with old lies
A wedding perfuming a packed chapel
Bourgeois ladies with satisfying thighs.

And I hear a biographer professing his belief
That in the queer seas of human experience
There is one bucket of perfect honey.

And I see, padding along College Street,
A priest steered by a mystical sense
Of direction into a bank, with a bag of money.

Query

I asked my turtle-computer about the nature of money.
'Love' said the turtle, 'money is love
Of money. Money is blood, is not feeding starving
Brats in the Kurd world, money is Europe,

Saturday nights, new hats, menus, copious fucking
Among the lower, middle and upper classes
Who steam into each other like buses in Fleet Street
Or monkeys rats elephants rabbits asses.

Money is what the dead leave to the living
And the living expect from the dead.
Money is family church school our ancient nation
Set in the polluted sea. Money is for takers
Though I understand a few givers
Exist.'

'Christ' I replied 'Your thoughts are stock-exchanging my head.
Is there anything I can give you to show my appreciation?'

'Yes' gluttoned my turtle 'Feed me a thick buttered slice
Of stupid human information.
Then ask me another question.'

A Subtle Relationship

My computer is shaped like a turtle
And shows all the nutty tendencies
Of a genuine intellectual. We have a subtle
Relationship characterised by courtesy
And counsel; an old-fashioned couple. When, for example,
I was agonising over what to do
In the final stages of my apostolic debacle
I consulted my turtle to find the true
Shape and direction of my future.
Chewing the data of my overwrought mind
The turtle advised me to consider the notion of hope.

'Betray, by all means' whispered my turtle-computer,
'But please, dear master, please remember, if you find
Yourself in some despair, put no hope in rope.'

Little Jewel

In that nasty Wall Street crash
I lost fifteen of my thirty pieces of silver.
My heart will not recover those missed beats
Nor my spine forget the shiver
Twanging my brain for days.
Did I allow the disaster to throw me?
No. I counted the fifteen pieces that remained
And bought six bottles of Black Bush whiskey.

I said to myself, silver is only silver
And there's more where the thirty pieces came from.
That high-priest thought helped me to survive.

The old question, what is money? is fascinating as ever.
The fact that silver is inseparable from my name

176

Is a little jewel that makes me glad I'm alive.
Let planets crash and smash, I hoard my shame
As a miser hoards every shilling.
When the moment comes to invest, I'll make a killing.

In the Stock Exchange

'Holy Jesus my whole neighbourhood is upset
Not a body can sleep at night
Because this red setter bitch is in heat
And scatters of dogs from Dublin and Meath

Smell her in the air and get
Randy as bejasus for the ride and set
Out to find her, sweaty bitch, you know what
I mean, pure female, drives males mad with

Her smell, Christ Almighty, the silky wet
Little bitch brings twenty dogs all hot
And panting into, Holy Jesus, the Stock

Exchange where they all try to screw her,
The little punter full of the readies takes the lot, ups
And outs into the streets. What's next, mate? Pups!'

Hunger and Thirst

The priest lifts God out of the tabernacle
Lays His body on a silver plate
Pours His blood in a silver cup

The priest has not breakfasted yet

When he eats God's flesh
Drinks God's blood
He does so out of such hunger and thirst
He might surprise even God

In the body of the church
Augustine Joyce goes from pew to pew
Collecting money from me and you

The priest's words mingle with the money-tinkle

Augustine Joyce's eyes are pleased and vigilant
When the priest locks God back in the tabernacle.

Circulating Bags

Whenever I go to Mass
I am impressed by the sound of money
Dropping into circulating bags
Handled by the most faithful of the faithful.

And I think of that angry afternoon
When the dreamer, having released the doves from their cages
Fell into one of his rare, scattering rages
And booted the moneymen

Out of the temple into the street.
Then I see the necessity for cash
And wonder would heaven, or what seems
Like heaven, endure without it?
I once cashed a cheque in the Bank of the Holy Spirit,
I know what it means to buy and sell dreams
And cannot say, therefore, who will inherit
The earth or any part of it.
Circulating bags suggest money is the heart of it.

Coins

You'd be surprised at the ruthless demands
Put on a coin.
With thirty pieces of silver in my hands
I was a rich burdened liberated man,

The future tucked neatly away
In my mind's wallet.
What did these coins feel like in my
Fingers? Back in my bedsit

I mixed the coins with others of a baser sort,
(As conquering folk are wont to do
Who doubt the lines 'twixt false and true)
Blindfolded myself, tried, by touching,
To tell the coins apart.

I could not. All coins were all
The same to me. What, had I been blind,
Might have been the nature and fulfilment of my art?

Thirty Pieces of Silver

1.

Looking for me, son accepted father,
Father's gift of a name
That had sufficed
Generation spawning generation.
Father tendered me to son
The morning the boy became
A soldier of Christ,
Sweat of self-begetting greed
Holy oil in his fist.
I confirmed his every word and deed.
I am lord of his heart and head.

2.

I was lost in earth-loosening rain,
Slipped underground.
        Passers-by trample on treasure.
        Will I ever be found?

3.

Sitting at the driver's wheel, he questions her
Standing sexy-perfect by the red Vauxhall.
He gives me to her, she slips me into her purse

From which dark sanctuary I can hear him
Fucking her against the hospital wall.
In the distance, an ambulance brays,
A dog begins to howl. The man is getting small,
Smaller and (o pricey night!) smaller again.
Fulfilment shrivels the best of men.
I lie in the darkness, the price of their pain.

4.

John Collendar pushes me across the counter
To the man with the rat's eyes.
'I want it! I want it!' Collendar pleads.
'You'll get it' the rat hisses.

5.

Eve Lynch stands at the door of her pub,
Her last customer leaves, blind with bliss.
She mutters, watching him reek into the night,
'I have your money, handsome, and you have your piss.'

6.

Dreaming of me, Nell Whalen bows her head
Murmuring 'My God! My God!'
Am I the kind of God Who seems to care?
Do I squirm at being adored?
Shall I answer the lady's prayer?
Shall I ignore her passion or
Inflate her with my answer?
When you pray to me, darling Nell,
Shall I reply with heaven or hell?

7.

Nancy Wright, though shy, begins to feel me.
Steal me, Nancy, steal me!

8.

The young millionaire
Hands me to the old teacher,
Smiles with a grace beyond compare

And says:
    'It is sad, after twenty years,
Veronica has left you.
She had the most divinely assuring smile
Played the fiddle damnably well
Turned meals-on-wheels into a fun event.
My blind uncle grows eloquent with gratitude
Every time he mentions your name.
He still sees more than most men
And chuckles when he remembers your illuminating banter.
It is typically magnanimous of you
To call this, your crowning project,
The Veronica Communication Centre.'

I am a different kind of teacher.

9.

The priest lays the crossword aside
    (Even Christ has a bride)
Turns out the light
Sleeps.

    His breathing is even.
In the puzzling dark
I lead him towards heaven.
When I permit him to forget
The clues fit.
Whatever it is
There's only one word for it.
The crossword sleeps on the quilt
That smothers duty and guilt.

10.

Staunton has two days to find me.
If he succeeds
The family will stay together.
If he fails
Nora will solve herself in the river.
Which way will Staunton turn
To celebrate or mourn?
Black-white, love-hate, big-small, virtue-vice;
Families are dice; gambling is fun.
Staunton's heart is chosen and thrown.

11.

I made the rifle available to the boy.
Newspapers christen him a terrorist.
When he has killed three men and a woman
He'll have earned the bosses' trust.
He'll be shot dead one September evening
Having dinner in a hotel in another town.
The newspapers will speculate for a day or two.
Then the killers will admit the killing over the phone.
Communication thrives; I flourish; some hopes begin to sink.
What would happen if the guns began to think?

12.

Blessèd be the sad poet who introduced
The woman to a brighter kind of lie.
She giggles at the price the pig pays
For lessons in how to fly.

Blessèd be the woman who introduced
The sad poet to a bit of fun.
I made festooned bosthoonery of her work,
I, the prizes he won.

Come to me, ye poets and women
        Afraid to fly;
We'll spin together over sun and moon
        With a new ferocity.

13.

A tourist drops me into a tinker's cap
On a sleety bridge. Poverty! Poverty!
The tinker hoists his arse from the ancient blanket
And hobbles off for a hot whiskey.

14.

I have watched you grow to love me
In the sick prison where I made you free.
I am the way the truth and the life.
No one cometh to the Manager but by me.

15.

I know three men, born on the rocks.
I inspire the first with greed
The second with envy
The third with style, a key
To open formidable locks.

The first and second will scatter their bad seed everywhere.
The third will endure, skilfully fragile.

Each, in his way, causes me to smile.

16.

I built a university,
Dedicated it to learning's fastidious god.
There, I said to a young man who saw through books,
Is where the best things are scrupulously misunderstood.

17.

I fit in the slot.
He presses Button B.
I plunge in ecstasy.
He says 'Who do you tut-tut-think you are?'
She replies 'Who d'you want, dear?
        Wife? Mistress? Daughter?
        Take your pick!'

His silence is raging pain; it's all he's got
Though some would say he searches blindly for love
And is no thisway-thatway fish in muddy water.
Still, I understand the contempt of women
        For men who stammer,
Dead when they falter.

18.

I'm a priceless trinket
Blood of war
Goodbargain bad Spanish wine
        in your local supermarket
Slave-labour
Reason for Junkie Jordan to drown or not drown
Stinking digs in Camden Town.

19.

The stolen car in which Flash Williams is travelling
Crashes on the Malahide Road.
A harvest moon is the sole witness.
I sink temporarily in a pool of blood.
Crude accidents make possible such moments
Of instructive solitude.
Whoever sweeps the blood away
Will find me lying there, fair pay.

20.

Educate Jack, Adolf, Jill. This will be
To your credit. Use me
To tell them why you have cried and laughed
        And refused to be spirit-shredded.
Teach them why bicycles must be paid for,
Be delicate-stern when you bequeath them
        The end of skill and craft.

Mammy! Mammy! How's me overdraft?

21.

In this wizening country there's a massive gap
        Between rich and poor.

Melt me
Make a silver bridge of me
Let the poor mooch over me to the rich
The rich poise over me to the poor.
Let them hold hands in mid-silver.
        I would say
That's the best joke you heard today.
My favourite International Banker flips me in the air,
Heads up he'll keep his Butter Mountain for another year.
Enough there to grease the seized souls of the poor.

22.

The old saint's body turns ecstatically sick
When he sees heaven flowing
From the eye of the bright boy's prick.
Though my nature resists total knowing
My interest is growing all the time

At home in law, at home in crime.
With me, without me, hearts learn to quake.
I'm the best teacher of heaven and sex the world has known.
Money talks, they say. Wrong. I'm silent, I don't even
Have a mind of my own. All the other minds
Pour into my no-mind. Some will surface, many drown.
My no-mind knows heaven is a night on the town
With gods and goddesses letting their hair down.
The bright boy is beginning to know his price.
The old saint is breaking the holy ice.

23.

I know I'm not happiness, I'm just a slight
Down-payment on that real estate.
I'd travel anywhere but feel most
At home in the Bank of the Holy Ghost.
The Manager, wearing shoes of gold,
Jigs and reels on the poor and old
Till their flesh is trash and their bones are sold
And they're fit for admission to the Fold.
I doubt not churches are built on rocks
But who is the man with the greedy box?
Does Martha Hannon, kneeling there,
Know the price of her shyest prayer?
If she prayed to me instead
Would I prove a loving God?
That's enough questioning for now.
Be happy, Martha. Want to know how?

24.

Rachel sparkles in the parking-lot with Daddy
        Who receives me from Davison
Like a rustling eucharist from the Age of Gold.
        Davison was born to buy Rachel.
        Rachel was born to be sold.
A mystical poet who swears he cannot be bought
        In this or any other city
Might lilt her cries are silver
        Her tears gold,
Unpollutable river of pity
        Flowing through heartless lands.
Daddy and Davison shake on the deal.
        Rachel changes hands.

25.

I vanish into the hole
Wander lucrative and lost
Until I come to rest on Society Hill,
Philadelphia. In a pseudo-Georgian mansion
I am gold.
This evening at dinner, glittering amid chat,
I decorate a beautiful throat.
I shine for her, being part of her plan.
Ted Weiner's eyes caress me a moment,
Return to his duck.
I like the feel of her neck, sound of her heart beating,
Velvet pulse of her intent.
Out of the hole I came, and may return,
Love's instrument.
When her fingers touch me, I am all astonishment.

26.

Little poem is all but written.
What to do with the singing thing
That already is assuming the look of a lived-in
Dutiful shabbypolished old shoe?
Mr Editor, how much do you pay
For a moment of durable insight
Into this perishing day?
Enough for last month's fire? Next month's light?
What price a modest spot, a garden flat
On a hillock in the shade of Parnassus
          With hot
          And cold
And ever-expanding realms of gold?
          God bless us!
Is that all? Finito? Caput? Nothing more?
          Send the poor poem
          To a Stray Dogs' Home
Where it can snore away its days
Rousing itself odd times to gnaw an old bone
Shaped like someone's notion of inspiration.

27.

Eyes globe in wonder when I rustle my head.
This morning, sixty-six million of me
Winked at Sheila Pine.
That's a lot of bread

186

And considerable goblets of wine.
Let me be your miracle, Sheila,
Let me make you wise,
Wink when I wink, Sheila,
And I will be your eyes.

28.

I facilitate starwars and the training of fleas.
I put you on your knees and take you off your knees.
I transfer your pain from your elbow to your head
And then, for a lark, to your heart.
I change pain to fun, fun to pain.
I am snoozing in gravel warmed by the sun.
Pick me up on your lonely stroll through the city.
I was never lost so I cannot be found
Though I may become your dumb companion.
       I'd a friend once,
            went underground,
                   never seen again.

29.

I have not chronicled the wars fought for me,
       Rarely in my name.
I sponsor conferences on the nature of happiness
       When I have buried the young men
Who died to order, by mistake.
I purify the water sipped by arthritic professors
In the rebuilt hotel by the fabricated lake.
I publish the precise, inane theories that lead nowhere
       Or back to themselves, nowhere.
I nourish the gutsy ambitions of the escapees
And hear their prayers for a renovating month in Greece
Along with me, away from me, away from the stones
       Over the heads of the young men
       Resting and rotting in peace,
Pennies fallen from their eyes, flesh from their bones.
I turn young men into innocent skeletons.

30.

Caught!
You cannot hold.
A slot, thank God, a slot.
I fit, copper is silver is gold,
You empty yourself into thankGod the sea,

The sea
Filthy and free.
Your flesh blood bones could disintegrate and vanish like that
But you pick yourself up
Brace yourself
Like sad Adam equipped only
With the consciousness of his mistake
And speculate into the light, looking for me
Using my language with such well-coined skill
It stamps your heart, and lives there, as poetry never will.

Limits

Stepping outside limits has always been
A remarkable feature of my character
Though at times I fear I'm a cautious knacker.
Given the prevalence of greed among men
I might have asked for three thousand pieces of silver
But I stepped beyond the limits of greed
By limiting myself. I sometimes see, as in a trance,
Paradox is my natural element, my soul needs
The stimulus of an intricate metaphysical dance
Though my assassin's patience permits me to see
Good fortune is a quickly taken chance.

With my thirty pieces I am content to be
A modest investor in the stock market.
A small profit affords me maximum delight
A shy gesture suggests cosmic mystery
A timely silence bristles with killing wit
And limits, properly used, beget the infinite.

Relax

Let me relax now into my hatred of judges
And the menbeasts for whom law is money.
This is a beautiful hatred, a hellhoney
Soaking the sky, I taste it on roads and hedges,

In every corner of my bedsit,
In the ticking of a clock
And the humming of my second-hand fridge.
I note its colours in the wasp perched on a rock

Near the river where my hatred flows
Through the dreams of judges and menbeasts
Guzzling blood and money from stacked-up criminals.

I dream of a worldfire made of judges
And judgments, the fire is fanned by the foulest
Curses of condemned men rotting in prisons where
Hearts are not deluded about the future.

Some Creature

The night I got Businessman of the Year Award
I spoke with charm and some rhetorical skill
On why one must be always on one's guard,
How imagination and will
Should guide the hand turning the wheel of money.
I told three judasjokes, they went down well.
One, in particular, was queer but funny
As hell. This was one joke I had to sell.
They bought it, beaming, told it to their wives
Who laughed amid cosmetic blushes.
They bought it too, big deal, I do not lie.

Later, strolling by dark rebellious waves,
I heard some creature, in the chill reaches
Of the night, emit a piteous, heart-scalding cry.

Favourite Things

When I consider favourite things
I think of snooping around foreign
Cities looking for War Monuments
In great Squares with pigeons shitting
Acidly as they have done for God knows

How long. Tasting each delicious moment
I draw nearer, nearer, until I see the rows
And rows of names. There they are, the brave dead
Apostles of peace on either fighting side,
Gutted in muck or blasted out of the air,
Corpses collected, when possible, and returned to clay.

I meditate on men of money in their pride
Sadly nodding at the death of every soldier
Who was never trained to think or to betray
Muslim Hindu Buddhist Christian Jew.
That's one of my favourite things. I have others too.

Free Barmbracks

Why, when it's clear as the lines on your face
My life is entangled with treachery
And most folk know I'm a choice disgrace,
Do some have a sneaking regard for me

As they do for young men and women
Making their point through the exercise of terror,
Who may or may not apologise when
They explode some unfortunate in error?

The sad mistake may be the assiduous
Assistant-manager of a supermarket planning
Free barmbracks for customers on Hallowe'en.

At his dispersal, indignant voices scorch the shelves,
Terrorists experiment with methods while customers
Murder free barmbracks as though
The assistant-manager had never been
Within an ass's roar of the supermarket scene.

Head

This greedy head belongs to the landlord
Of the Last Supper Inn:

He's a long, thin slieveen of a mick
From somewhere in Leitrim,

He owns houses from Nazareth to Donegal,
He's a moneylender, a bailiff,
An auctioneer committed to smiling:

Goes to mass every morning
Pays Christmas and Easter dues
Picks wives and husbands for his daughters and sons.

When a Bishop dies he slides into mourning
Profitable tears stockexchange his eyes
Which, could you see them, are soft as stones.

Number One

The Pinstripe Pig, good friend, much given
To farting in public and private
Knows his flatulence is perfume from heaven.
He will sit

For long, meditative hours
Loving the smell of his own farts
Though other humans may feel sick.
Inspired by love of that heavenly smell

Pinstripe decides to preserve the music,
Bowls off in his Rolls to his Personal Studio
Records his farts for several days
Edits that music till the work is done,

The record made. Light of his eyes rivals the sun.
Pinstripe enjoys a cult following now
In Russia Asia The Ganges The Himalayas.
Here in the West, he's Number One.

That Pinstripe Air

The Pinstripe Pig loves works of art
Pays gigantic sums to adorn his office.
Gigantic sums? Squeaky financial farts
From that art-loving orifice.

Pinstripe loves Victorian scenes,
Family gatherings, Sunday afternoons,
Garden frolics, Fathers advising sons,
Sensitive clouds touching Autumn moons.

How oft have I spied him there
Alone
Contemplating pictures with that Pinstripe air

Well-known to ladies rich and debonair,
Well-known to lovers
Of art and cash, everywhere.

Money in Love

My good friend, the Pinstripe Pig, says
There's money in love
Especially in shining teenage eyes.
Pinstripe's mind, all bonny-bladed edge,
Hires me to write songs
That shiver their little fannies
While they pour out tears and screams
And tidal monies.

Pinstripe sits in his office all day
Breaking record after record.
'Thanks be to God' he sighs 'for the fucking young,
The fucking young.'

                    Child, if you're lucky,
Pinstripe will blow you a kiss, he's music-lord
Thrilling your days with love's old sweet song.

Listen to Pinstripe, child, and you can't go wrong.

Pal

Jesus and I have but few true friends,
The kind who'll lay down their lives or savage
Their bank-accounts on behalf of a racked mind,
A beleaguered body. I've a pal of that vintage.

Though brutish sottish perspiringly big
There's nothing he won't do for me,
He'll go to the ends of all his hells for me
Will my buddy, the Pinstripe Pig.

If they dump me in prison for not paying my debts
If they revive the old torturing style
To make me sensitive responsive aware,
All I need do is scribble a note
To the Pinstripe Pig. He'll
Flam the bastards out of my hair.

Experiment

I have been short of silver in my time.

Strolling dolefully along High Street, Killarney,
I met an Englishman with a catchy name.
He asked me if I'd like to make some money.

Soon to a London clinic we were bound.
Packed with healthy types (but broke) the place was big
And opulent. Imagine my surprise when I found
I was chosen as a human guinea pig.

I have no bone to pluck with radioactivity
But for years following my experiment
I was sudden fits, blackouts, migraine.

The things a hard-up man will do for money!
I have a sense of self-betrayal. Be assured I shan't
Endanger my health if I'm stuck for cash again

For in my wisdom now I know a pig is not a man
Although (let me whisper this to you)
The reverse is sometimes true.

Like All

Certain parties, eager for the details
Of my deal with the High Priest,
A man who in the depths of his entrails
Knows the value of a penny, often ask me

G

Why at the moment of bargaining
I specified thirty pieces of silver.
These queries do not set me fuming
Nor does indignation weasel me all over.

I have no desire to shuffle or evade,
Lead a fervent enquirer astray, pull
The wool over his optics or adjust his leg:

I consider the question, brood a bit and say
I was specific about pieces because like al-
most all men I fancied a little nest-egg.

Not Rich

I am not a rich man and yet I was hauled up
Before the Chief Tax Commissioner whose rigour
Has robbed many a man of bite and sup
Because I failed to declare my thirty pieces of silver.

I found the Commissioner's questions rather unnerving
And yet I answered succinctly as I could:
How did you earn this not inconsiderable sum, sir?
Kissing.
And who, may I enquire, did you manage to kiss?
God.
I see.
I knew you'd see, your Honour.
Are your expenses heavy?
Like a cross.
Will they grow heavier?
Yes, forever on the increase.
Do you intend to make more silver out of kissing?
No, your Honour, as a business it's a dead loss.
You're an honest man, Judas. Live tax-free. Go in peace.

Pawn

Determined, from the start, to be nobody's fool
I launched into my scrutiny of money with the kind
Of disciplined fury that frightens a weaker mind,
Continued my research at Harvard Business School

Where Yankee genius burned me hot under the collar.
I steadied my nerves sufficiently
To produce my globally-applauded study
On the Origins and Development of the Dollar.

Money is amazing when you come to think of it.
It absorbed me as I sipped Common Room Sherry
And drank the sun on my favourite New England lawn.

My academic intensity deepened. Yet when I visited
The High Priest, I heard him muttering to himself:
'Here comes a king-sized pawn.'

Something By Michelangelo

Among the bad problems facing man
Is how to cope with sinister moneysounds.
Last year, the budget deficit of the Vatican
Reached six hundred and fifty million pounds.

The Holy Father, knowing my financial skill
Was subtly mingled with my original sin,
Took one look at his accounts, despatched Cardinal Kill
To call me in.

The Pope suggested flogging something by Michelangelo.
I quashed that. I said 'Summon the faithful Irish Catholics,
Ask them for their infinite natural gas

And sell it to the Young Nazi Party.' So
It was accomplished. The budget blossomed in a few weeks.
Knighting me, the Pope smiled. Strange things come to pass.

One Liquid Evening

The Pope and I, having solved the problem
Of his recalcitrant cashflow, at least temporarily,
Aware that hopes of medieval opulence were slim
Yet conscious of the need for long-term security,

Sat down together one liquid evening in Rome
And scrutinised the past with academic objectivity.

'I recall' ruminated the Pontiff, 'I got a large sum
Of money from my friend Mussolini

In return for certain tracts of land near here.
Mussolini came of peasant stock and had a strong
Pastoral streak in his belligerent make-up.'

'And what did you do with the cash?' I enquired.
'Invested it in America' smiled the Pope. 'Leave it there'
I said, 'Don't touch it. While there's America, there's hope.'

Brother James

Short of cash one morning
Feeling spiritually out of breath
I raised my drooping heart by purchasing
James Joyce's death-mask at an auction in Nazareth

For forty pence.
I took it to my Traitor's Pad
And studied it for hours.
No trace there of magical poetic powers.
James Aloysius Joyce looked sad,

Puzzled, constipated, waxed, hungover, blind,
Exiled, cunning, silent as the Liffeybed.
Has it, I whispered to the death-mask, come to this?

It has, you know it has, you prick, the mask replied,
You'd feel the same if you were auctioned dead.
O brother James, I sobbed, and gave the mask a kiss.

Quicksilver

They are torturing me because of my skill
In the Stock Exchange. They think it uncanny
That I grasp the elusive nature of money.
For such knowledge, smiling men would kill

196

Succulent virgins on the pill
From Cahersiveen to Castleblayney.
My torturers are mad because I am not phoney.
My silence tells them simply to go to hell.

When I meet men who think reality is cash
I say nothing to dispel the lie
But speculate to show my sense of fun,

Delighting in their faces when I crush
Their itsy-bitsy dreams. My torturers die.
My chipped quicksilver heart outspeculates the sun.

If I'd a Heart

I sit appalled at savage yuppie inanity
And shiny moneyboys snaking into power,
I smile as converts to Judasanity
Increase in numbers hour by hour.
Welcome, my daughters! Welcome, my sons!
Welcome, my aspiring hearts!
I cock my ear to hear your orisons
But can't steer clear of your neurotic farts.

Not shrinking from the stink, I think of you
And gazing on your faces now my mind
Transforms my thirty pieces into a special drink.

I pour this in a silver cup, offer it to
You to taste. You taste. How do you find
It? Good? Good. If I'd a heart, I think that it might sink.

A Devoted Celibate

After my kissing act in the garden, an event noted
By writers who love to set such matters down,
I acquired, though I remained a devoted
Celibate, a growing reputation in town

As a bit of a fast thing. Various gays
Gave me the come-on, including an Irish-speaking
Stone-breaker from the Knock Airport area.
I declined all invitations. Once, when working

As a butcher's messenger-boy in Inchicore,
The butcher, an insolent pig, asked me for a kiss
Several times a day. He said he adored me.

I charged him with sexual harrassment at work. The Labour Court
Awarded me thirty thousand pounds damages. The judge whis-
pered, 'I hope it's enough, Judas. Yours is the first case
　　　　　of its kind to be brought before me.'

Thank You, Silver

It was good to get the silver in my hand.
When the priest gave me the pieces I put them
Into my purse and went home.
I drank several glasses of wine, my mind
Excited as it always was when
I found something comprehensible and real,
Something I could see was beautiful
And untainted by men.

O radiant and resonant silver, I see you now
As once I saw the light of faith at my window,
The light of love at my door,
The light of hope on a dirty worker's brow.

In years to come, people will debase you,
Murder your light with their acquiring eyes
Forgetting what you were created for,
Not to pass from hand to hand
But to startle darkness underground,
Caged music there, truly, purely there,
To hear if you were lost enough to hear.
I hear it everywhere. Thank you, silver.

EIGHT

All the same in the dark

For Lack of Love

If somebody had loved me then
Kissed me in the street
Would I have done what I have done?
For lack of love a man will up and out

And maim or kill;
For lack of love he'll poison the sea
And sky, cripple the innocent trees;
For lack of love a man won't recognise

Whoever wants to bless and cherish him,
Bring gifts to his door, kind words
To his heart, open that heart when it closes

Like a purpose concentrating to a bullet
Or a knife plunged into a conversation.
For lack of love a man is blighted more than he supposes.

Outside, in the leafy pathway

Just then I knew that loneliness
Was the truedeep thing in my life
(But nothing I'd write home about)
And as I turned away from the faces
Full of untold stories
I knew that I must laugh or die.
I opened my jaws, I laughed and laughed
Till the tears ran down my spirit
And the black rain of memory and misfortune
Was bearable, bearable. I had no need to ask
Where are you now, you passionate
People of dust and love, where are you now
You dreamers chancers drinkers killers thieves clowns?
I stood alone in the black rain and laughed
At what had happened, had still to happen.
Something that had been imprisoned forever
Began to open.
Something that had never dared listen to love
Began to listen.

Your Little Button

Sit, look, pick, press your little button, guess which
Channel I'm on tonight, frolicking
With a steamy blaspheming bitch.
God, will I give the lulu a bollicking!

Don't stir, darling, don't budge from your chair,
Never again uncross your legs, just feel
Comfort paddling in the roots of your hair,
Warm honey in your centrally-heated skull.

Skull! Here's a green tennis ball
I found sad as a dried jellyfish on a beach,
I picked it up, brought it home to you.

Press your little button with olympian skill,
See me in colour, gape, squint, suss, don't touch,
I'll pop at your bidding,
Be your private priest kneeling to obey
Or your sucking toyboy or your prince pleased to betray
Or your very own bomb on its missionary way.

This Man

There is this man I meet who spittles me stories of sex
As if it were going out of passion.
He's a small badger-headed gobshite with mean eyes
And a hideous jollity in his voice.
I would like to slice him into grim little pieces
And distribute these pieces to dogs
Prowling in ravenous packs both night and day
Through our valium suburbs.

That's what I would like to do. Instead, of course,
I swallow like a disciple his lewd gospel.
Sometimes I enjoy it, sometimes I do not

Because I have this vision of the world as a man
With mean eyes and a hideous jollity in his voice.
I smell his heart, his guts, I absorb his rot.

In spite of that, on certain days I see
This odious contraption is preferable to me.

Prisoners

I'll let you into something though you're busy
Sweating for the Checkout Girl of the Year
Award, and will win it: I'm a lousy
Thinker, a stick-in-the-mud half-assed philosopher,

Then why do I continue struggling to understand
Myself clad in black jeans, yellow shirt,
A soccer goalkeeper's glove on either hand
And a conviction that someone intends to hurt

Me sooner or later, so deeply I may not
Recover or if I do, be maimed for life? Don't answer, check out
The politician with the Jeyes Fluid, whiskey, wine and cheese.

You made a prisoner of me, I got
Rid of you, I made a prisoner of myself, I doubt
I shall get rid of myself with equal ease.
Consider the faces in the queue. Not even Judas
In all his creepycrawlery was servile as one of these.

War

'And did you see the Coolun
           Taking a stroll
                      For the good of her health?'

'I did, she chose a street
With four lights on one side, none on the other,
Deserted except for a drunk
Muttering as he pissed, pissing as he muttered.

           And she took
A deodorant spray, penknife, scissors, iron bar
Because she knows that going for a walk
In that place at that time of night
           Is going to war.

Every night the Coolun goes to war.
Why not stay at home? What's she trying to find?
           Beautiful body, frightened mind,
Menacing shadows, abuse spat from the dark,
           Footsteps from behind.'

Everywhere a Woman Bleeds

I spit on my needs
She adores my smile
Says so with guile
Even as she bleeds like an old religion

Speared by new creeds
Hellbent on establishing a fresh style
For future randies while
I burn exhausted flowers and plant young seeds.

Everywhere a woman bleeds

I sneer at my own hunger
Mock my own craving
Know how to deny
Myself when I open sesame to her desire.
Constipated souls know shitting is believing.
One need alone I need to satisfy.

The Coolun

'And did you see the Coolun
Going down the road?'

'I did, she was going into a field
To have a baby all on her own
And there was a statue of Mary
The Virgin Mother of God
Staring down on the Coolun
Twisting in her blood

And then the Coolun died in the field
And her child died at her side
And the grass was the colour of wrong
O the Coolun was immature
And we whispered together and lied
How we wanted her to belong.'

She Muttered

'And when did you last see the Coolun?'

       'About ten days ago.
Her belly was out like a pup's
       And she was going

To England for an abortion.
       She hadn't combed her hair
And she was in a bit of a quandary
       Looking for the fare.

And the Coolun doesn't like sailing
But here was a boat she had to take
To lose the child she had to lose.

She had sad eyes but crying had no meaning,
She muttered something about a random fuck
       And the right to choose.'

A Small Price

'And Jesus there I was on the Irish Sea
And the wind like a father's anger
A rage of questions in my mind
       I grasped the railings
The wind ripped into me
A million fists
Became one fist

O Christ the wind

Sucking me out into the night
Sucking sucking
A man gone mad for the moment's body
He'll have it no matter what I say
The wind sucks me, sucks my flesh and blood,
I hold, my scarf and gloves are gone,
A small price to pay.'

She Knows the Smell

'And did you see the Coolun lately?'

'I did. She's on the dole
And trying to stop a thousand drunken Irishmen
Getting up her hole.'

'And is she still the same bright girl,
The shining one, heart's pulse, a joy to greet?'

'As a matter of fact, the Coolun is finding it
Hard to make ends meet
On twenty-nine quid a week.'

'But is she not made of riches
Beyond the dreams of men living and dead?'

'What the Coolun is made of, I dare not speak.
I only know, in this land of bastards and bitches,
She knows the smell of many a bed.'

Waiting for the Finger

'I'm glad I married a nice Jewish Girl
She'll need exterminating in time,
They all do, cry out for it,
Rehearsing their versions of The Bomb,
('Fifteen nuclear states. The world trembles.')
Everyone is rehearsing The Bomb,
My true friend lying in wait
For a friendly finger such as you might find
Manipulating a cunt on a Saturday night,
The week's work done, the lolly earned,
The letters answered, the kids in bed,
The dog fed, the flowers watered, the poem written,
The critic seduced, the Prize in the bag, the Bomb waiting,
A lump of patience getting in nobody's way
Waiting for the finger like the world for the Son of Man,
Waiting for what I try to imagine but never can.'

Where Dreams Begin

The man's head blossomed into a phallus.
The woman bent again
To kiss the lips, to hear
Submarine dreams in his brain.

A handsome head.
Never before
Had she known the fierce soulbody
Impulse to adore.

She had all, all. She craved more.

She lay there
Where dreams begin.
She rose and sank and rose and sank
Forever. She trapped
The godhead in her mouth
And drank.

Hiss

I find myself listening to the sound of a hiss.
The clean snake stirring the nest of love
Raises his mouth, his lips wet mine,
I sting the world, snakemagic my kiss,
I slide through your eyes, my heart starts to rave
Like the heart of a man who knows he's divine.

Mannerly Cows

Why do men go on like that about women's breasts?
Why do they call them stars? Say they're milk-white,
Snow-white, every white under the sun and moon?
Why do they compare them to God's own light,

Such as it is, struggling to break through clouds
Into the house or heart of some stupo?
Your average tit is structurally unremarkable,
Some are absurd, too small or too

Large, frozen billiard-balls or balloons
Full of pee, nipples aggressive or retarded
As morons on a day's outing to the sea.

I look at men looking at breasts, goo-goo fools,
They should keep goats or mannerly cows
More silent than women dare to be.

A naked, breastless woman once smiled at me.

A Brainy Lady

The lady is a scented wench who would
Intellectualise a simple fuck,
Analyse my sperm, I declare to God.
Here in my modest chalet at the edge
Of the Dead Sea, she throws me a brainy look
And suggests a study of my envious heart.
Our precarious relationship may come unstuck
If I don't comply with her analytic art.
I ponder, moodbrood, philosophyfart,
Suggest with Aristotelian cop-on
The mind betrays what it analyses overmuch.

She analyses this. I wait, sensitively hurt,
Misunderstood by a brilliant woman.
She relents. We fuck. She analyses such and such...

Topping an Egg

'She was one of these quiet Irish girls,
You'd swear butter wouldn't melt in her mouth
Or in any other imaginable orifice
With her hands guarding her legs
And her legs protecting each other

But Jesus in heaven when she started to come
I thought she was going to bite lumps
Out o' me. That same tame little girl

Was a fuckin' maniac, she tore strips
Outa my back, she gartered my hands,
The blood of her cunt stamped my left leg.

Next morning, her chaste lips
Expressed exquisite bafflement at the problem
Of which end she was expected to top her egg.'

The Old Days

'Fred Moody is obsessed with treachery' she said,
Making love to a large gin;
'And now he's obsessed with being obsessed.
How, I ask myself, did it all begin?
        Fred was one o' the boys, a careless sort,
Liked his pint, the girls, nights on the town.
Something happened, Fred cooled, no more sport,
The smile deserted his face, he became a frown,
He's weird, he says treachery is necessary
If people insist on living with each other,
He speaks little, just listens to what the next man says,
The poor gook is a million miles away,
Out of it, can't get his act together
Or stick his nose in a pint like he did in the old days.'

Little Budd

There were twenty nuns in the darkened room.
Sister Budd, like all the others, took down her pants
And whipped her bottom.
Swish! Swish! flicked the whips. The women panted

And thought of God.
That night, in bed, Sister Budd lay on her back.
There were bruises, cuts, a little blood.
She crossed her hands on her breasts and shook

With pleasure at the thought-touch.
If she died tonight she could be lifted
Straight into the coffin.

Years later, married, her husband loved to watch
Her in that position. 'Budd' he whispered, 'Little Budd,
Lights on, close your eyes, open your legs, I'm fuckin' laughin'.'

Little Budd giggled: 'Where would you be, my love, without my discipline?'

Whitewash

I was whitewashing the walls of my bedsit.
Felicity, dear neighbour who'd thrown me many a look
Of, I think, encouragement, looked in and said
'Judas, any chance of a fuck?'

No beating about the flowers for Felicity
Who sports an awe-stirring bush,
Heart-warming, prick-raising, crisp, aggressive, passive, hot, free,
Cultivated, odorous and quite inexpressibly lush.

Although I was spattered with whitewash
And the walls of my bedsit seemed to protest
I complied.

'Are you guilty, Judas?' 'Felicity, do you blush?'
Amid such banterings, long hours we passed,
Belly on belly, side by side.

Afterwards, she passed three remarks, one of them snide.

Peck

A single kiss can lessen your life
Expectancy by three minutes. Doctors believe
Increased pulse rates during kissing
Strain the heart. Yet kisses have

Advantages, they're good for the teeth because
The saliva produced reduces plaque.
Kissing's a slimming aid too, every kiss
Consumes three calories.

The commonest kind of social kiss
Is the well-known peck on the cheek
In theatre college Stock Exchange club pub street.

Be warned, however, about this
Seemingly innocuous peck.
Some see it as the kiss of deceit.

And you may be pecked
By any bollocks you happen to meet.

Next Room

She's stirring in the next room.
It's three in the morning.
I've never seen her though I've heard her
Cry out in the night, her body moaning
In the bed. 'John!' she cries, 'John! John!'
She rises early, I think she's an old woman,
She shuffles, I hear her slicing bread,
I wonder how the knife feels in her hand.
Who is John? Where is he? Is he alive or dead?
           I'll never set eyes on her.
I'll be leaving soon to return
To my work as an opportunistic hack
In a world that's not even worth betraying.
I saw a purposeful blonde foreigner
Leave the house just now, a knapsack on her back.

Here Is Monica Now

Monica Ivors came up from the country
To make a living in town.
Disappointment made her realise
Anything is on.

So here is Monica now, nude
On a spotlit revolving stage,
Spreading her thighs for well-dressed men
Middle-aged.

She lashes herself with a whip,
Is lashed by a man with glasses
Who works all day in a bank.
Monica sucks him off.
Then in the darkened room
She lets two lit candles blaze from her cunt.
Extracting the candles, Monica
Lifts them high, the melted
Tallow jewelling her skin, shuddering
At each hot drop.
Taking three white balls
She stuffs them up her cunt.
Revolving-writhing for well-dressed men
Monica does not stint.

The first ball pops, Snow White,
The second, the Milky Way,
The third is streaked with blood.

Monica wipes that ball in a hurry,
Bows to the men and leaves the stage.
The money is good.
Good.

No Recovering

God knows I could whisper it too, and have.
Was it a silken bed or a corpsecold ditch?
Was I master of the moment or its slave?
Who was the bitch?
Who was I amid ecstatic whispers?
Was I fullmad moon or the moon's eclipse?
The frayed thread of a tinker's jumper
Or a plateful of Bewley's chips

Lewd with tomato-sauce, victim of the fork
Of crunching Josie, fifteen stone weight

Intent, sweet Jesus, intent on devouring
The whole damned plate? Let memory work
Like MacAlpine Paddy, there's no recovering that night
Of breedy whispers and hot deflowering.

A Long Black Hair

'I wanted him.
I wanted an afternoon session
So I arranged for him to want me
In the glory of his passion.

I showered. I lay there.
He showered. He came in,
Lay at my side. O that skin!
I glanced at his vest on the chair –

A long black hair
Which could never be confused with mine
Stretched from neck to tail –

"Get out, you tramp, you bastard!" I screamed,
"How dare you enter my bed when
You've been fucking some Mary Magdalene!"'

Wants

'I want to plan the wedding all by myself.
I want music from Bach and The Chieftains.
I want a poem from Shakespeare
Or Spenser, he's good on marriage.
          The poem should be a song,
Sweet Liffey, run softly, like a tale of wrong.
          I want a Jesuit to do it.
Actually, I've met the priest I want,
He's no Manley Hopkins, no saintly poet
But he'll do the job without hypocrisy or cant.
          It takes a Jesuit to cut the crap.
          Jesus owes a lot to the Jays.
Somehow they make things come out right.

If a Jay's there there's no need to worry.
    I quite like the man
    I'm going to marry.
He wants me all in white.'

Lip-Service

That evening, having paid lip-service to my God,
I met a woman sniffing her husband's infidelity.
'Do you suffer' I asked 'from grief and rage in the blood?'
'I can cope' she replied 'so long as he doesn't tell me.'

Us

'While he was riding me he kept gasping
Jesus Jesus as if he were praying
In the middle of it all, his breath rasping
My skin and hair, all his voices pouring

Jesus Jesus till he came into me
With one wild final sigh of Jesus
Then he fell away and lay
Like a child at my side. Jesus. Us.

A pair of people in a breathing room
Woman full of man
Man empty of woman

He asleep
She awake
Jesus gone.'

I Am the Music Now

'He was a pure disruptive music
Alive in me when I was with him
Drinking his mouth drinking his prick
Breathing his name his name his name

Like the refrain of a poem I could hear
But would never understand
Except in glimpses between my thighs
Touched by his dark electric hand.

He vanished out of himself and became
The music living in me, I listened to him
In myself till I knew I could say me

And say all the Big Puzzles simplified when he came
Into me and left me when his game
Was over. I am the music now. Play me.'

Stains

James Joyce gave up fucking for Lent,
Taking upon himself instead
Sole responsibility for washing
Nora Barnacle's bloomers clean of those red

And brown stains that so fascinated
Him. Joyce was into stains. Sin was a stain.
Shit was a stain. Piss was a stain. He felt elated
Every year when Lent came round again,

Giving him the chance to get rid of
All the stains of fucking, making Nora
Sleep with her head at the other end of the bed.

Then slowly, gravely, the old craving to love
Returned and Joyce spent Saint Patrick's Day
Fucking till he was nearly fucking well dead.

That Smile

'The first time I went to see her, there she was
Sitting at the kitchen table. They'd told me
She was the most beautiful girl in the place.
Sure enough there was a... a... nobility

In her head, her features. Her red–gold hair
Had a life of its own, but her face set
When I approached. When I spoke to her
She looked at me as if I were rotten.

I continued as best I could.
Went away, three weeks later I returned.
When I spoke she smiled. I have never seen

Anyone so changed as she was by that smile.
She became the woman for whom so many yearned
In vain. Without that smile, who had she been?'

Jesus I Mean

'Ah well Jesus I mean when the Assistant Principal
Started having an affair with the Principal's wife
It was all right you know fair enough for a while
But Jesus I mean the time came when the whole life

Of the school was affected by the affair
And even the children in the classes were
Laughing at the Assistant Principal right there
In front of his eyes but he didn't seem to care.

We did, though. Six members of the Committee
Approached him, laid it on the line –
Quit the affair or leave the school.

He left the school. Then she left him and she
Went back to the Principal just in time.
Your man lost everything. Jesus I mean what a fool!'

All the Magic Language

What was her death to him if not money?
He refused to ask himself the question
As he accepted neighbours' words of sympathy
Standing at the door opening on the garden:

A neat enough garden, her work on it,
Gnomic rockery, pathways like suggestions
Of a life he'd never been too intimate
With, flowers collaborating with stones.

He had the money now, the well-kept house,
The books, pictures, her delicate bric-à-brac.
A young man home from England said
She was the beautiful woman on the pound-note.
Was that Dark Rosaleen or some pagan goddess
With all the magic language round her head?
She was none of these, she was herself, dead,
And her death cost more and less
Than he had thought it would.

Prudent

She thought she'd be broken-hearted after him
But she got forty thousand of a lump sum
And three-quarters of his salary as a pension.
Only when he was gone

Did she find him such a thick lump of a man
Running the family in a killingly strict way.
'Come in, Judas,' she says to me,
'And have a drop o' whiskey.'

'What you need,' I said, 'is a young student
With a handsome knob on his prick.
He might quickshoot his load the first time
But you could educate him to the job.'

'I wonder about that,' she smiled, 'I'm very happy
Since himself died. I enjoy being prudent.'

No Solutions

Corner table, Deirdre of the Fashionable Sorrows,
Black-hatted, literate paradigm of
Middle-class prosperity:
                              'And how are you?'

'Actually, to be brutally true,
I've just been having a ferocious tête-à-tête
With Emer on the subject of estranged husbands.
Three years now, I miss him and the children
And though I've done quite well as secretary
To a rich arthritic German businessman
I sometimes think of trying the old home routine again,
Letting my liberated ulcers go to blazes.

But I'm not quite ready at the moment.
Another year, perhaps. Perhaps I'll nibble then.
There are no solutions, only compromises.'

Cross of the Wood

Blood is the mother of thought
And thought the shadow of blood
Where Sebastian Conner is screwing
Sheila Noone at the Cross of the Wood.
In praise of her cunt his prick
Is a tremulous hymn,
Jesus is watching and listening
Thrown out of home
Condemned to wander the roads of the parish
Where Sebastian Conner
Would screw the moon
If the night was right
And Father Ignatius Flood
Is locked in a lush
Prayer-book fat as a Christmas goose
Waiting the knife.

The Way at the Time

'Are you surprised at the infant in the bag
Floating down the river in moonlight or daylight?
It was a servant-girl, you see, born in the bog,
Sent out at thirteen to work for a farmer,

Every penny of her sad wages went home
And she slaved away from dawn to dark.
When the farmer said "Come here girl" she came
And when he said "Go back to work now" she went back to work.

And when he said "Lie down in the hay" she lay in the hay
And she said nothing when he emptied himself into her
And put a child making in her almost-child's body.

I saw many's the tied bag floating that way
In the river. She gave the best years of her life
To the farmer, her family. That was the way at the time, d'you see?'

Weekend

'Up for the weekend from Cork
To cheer on his heroes in red
He dropped in with two six-packs last night
Commandeered me for my bed.
We fucked, that is he fucked me,
And then, tipsy and bored,
He rolled off me like a bag o' wet spuds
And snored O dear Lord how he snored.
Erect Sunday morning at ten
He fucked me again and soon after
Downed rashers and sossies and eggs
Then left in a fat shower of laughter.
I'm a churned damp field, he's a plough:
Where is the spiritfuck now?'

Party-Snacks

Astride a democratic slut
Feeling for my age most randy-hearty
I pondered on the gin and halibut
I'd consumed at Abigail's party.
That fare had made me rather farty
Yet I pursued my fucking
With a vigour both shocking
And inspiring in such a warty

Judas. This was the spiritual
Adventure at its most thrilling
And as my treacherous seed came spilling
Like futuristic pop into my lady
I wondered would there be a baby
To munch the party-snacks of good and evil
Or would there, after all that zap, be nothing, nothing at all.
I have this cosmic sense of waste whenever I have a ball.

I Suggest Joan Flood

'The main thing is to find someone to blame.
If we do that we'll put people at their ease.
I suggest Joan Flood, make her the focus of shame,
That'll quieten the tongues wagging in the cities,
Towns and villages of the land.
                              She's well known
As the best little ride in her own parish
Ready to open her legs for any man,
Cute little thing, shrewd, young, whorish,
Hated by married women, they'd love to see her nabbed
And put away for twenty years or so
Where she cannot lure a hubby to bed.
A whore in prison is as good as dead.
So get to work, lads. This case must be cracked
Within a month. Joan Flood is waiting to be
Convicted. Remember, an innocent child of God was murdered.'

Of All People

Though I'd rather be a tomcat than a theologian
(A tomcat spots a victim, knows how to waylay him)
I often ask myself why in the name of heaven
God created me in order to betray him.

I have no special art. There are times I think
I'm a simple turf-accountant at heart.

With his talent for absolute foreknowledge
And his position at the summit of immortal bliss

Why give me, of all people, the privilege
Of sending him up the river with a kiss?

Why not pick a woman, call her Judasena,
Cute little redhead with an iambic bum,
Man-conquering tits and a priceless smile
Fresh as Eve in yon garden of Eden, a
Gifted kisser of gods in kingdom come?
But no, it had to be me. I guess he liked my style.

No Exit

You would think, were you given to thought, that
A man on the brink of immortal shame
Might, shocked, falter. I did not.
Instead, as I kissed, I had a quick vision
Of a bungalow two miles the Dublin side
Of Clonmel. There was something Spanish about it,
But parodied, so vulgar it shrieked of the new-moneyed.
I couldn't explain my presence there, I didn't know what
Neighbours I had, or if I had any,
There was no trace of car or bicycle,
Carrots blushed in the garden, I wouldn't starve
Though famine is the least I might be said to deserve,
That bungalow was the ugliest thing ever visual-
ised by the bungalowblissful genius of man,
I would live there forever, no exit, on my own,
My big picture windows facing the road,
A vegetarian recluse with a special knowledge of God,
Planning, on brain-chilling mornings, a beautiful suicide.

My Loss

I too have been belted with the hammers of loss
Or some such rhetorical devices that caused me pain
Around the heart and other secret places
(Who has seen his heart?) while I queued for buses
In the no-sympathy rain

220

Or devoured a sniffy lamb chop
In one of our gurgling tatty hotels,
Jocund dives, gleeful unhygienic kips
That offer the citizen a nose-blitzing squadron of smells.

My favourite waitress, Aggie-Aggie from Mayo,
Sniffs my loss. 'By Jesus, Judas' says she,
Exquisite dimples heavening her cheeks,
'Finish your chop and together we'll go
Where you can forget one thing in the grip of another.'
'Thanks, Aggie-Aggie' say I 'You know what a stricken man seeks.'
Do I rise and go? Heaven beckons. Hell shrieks.

Spiritfuck

'So many churches' she said, 'Such power, such polish
Because one man lived his conscious life.
Words are walls – Aramaic Greek Latin English French Polish
Etcetera; and my own anger freezing me stiff
In barren rooms of European and American
Cities. The day I heard that prayer
Means trapping the mind of God –
I a cage, he a bird of the air –
I understood the origins of my anger.

I sat alone and knew I had to open
Myself as I had never opened before.
I must be more open than any wound
Or any door
Anywhere.

I know spring water and polluted water
I know legends of love and loss
And the meaning of eat my body drink my blood.
I know the heart of the woman who yearned
For one true ultimate spiritfuck
Because I too long to be fucked by God.'

Boring

They saw the face of innocence then
As they'd not seen it since the black rocks cried
For the young woman and the young man
Drowned one September evening with the high tide

Ebbing. They'd often longed to see it,
Mentioning this fact as the bills mounted
And he looked as though he'd just fainted
Like he did with boy-excitement at its height.

They were nearing the Christmas of the black smog
With old people perishing of poisoned air
When they saw innocence on its knees, adoring, adoring.

They stood back, staring, long and long.
Then with tired eyes he turned to her:
'O love' he said, 'How boring it is, how boring.'

Intellectual

'McNamara is such an intellectual!
You should see him smoking a cigarette!
The delicate fingers of him!
The posh way he puts it in and takes it out

Of his mouth! O he had me mad about him,
Clean out of my head!'
It took me months to get him to notice me,
Months more to ask me to bed.

For the first time in my life, I really
Opened up for a man, I was big and deep,
There, I was there, all of me, pure cunt, body and soul,
                    I was there.

McNamara touched me. "Jesus" he gasped
"You're as big as a fuckin' elephant."
I shut like a trap. Men? What do I care?'

An Unsolicited Outburst in My Ear

'Can't stand her. Too demandin'. Bitch an' liar.
Wouldn't piss on her if she was on fire!'

Under the Blanket

'I never saw me husband naked.
Aengus Hayes and me were married forty years
We did what we had to do under the blanket
We had ten children and never once

Did we mention sex which as you know
Is tip-tops for a woman
But never never talk about it, just go
And do it, enjoy it, be silent, have the child

If it comes, keep quiet in the morning, do the work,
If he wants it again be quick
To give it to him under the blanket.
Listen, girl, not once in all my life
Did I set eyes on Aengus Hayes's prick!'

For All That

'For all that, she'll win through in the end.
Here she is in this fucking bughouse
And won't even admit I'm her friend
Though I've loved her for thirty years.

It's her weakness, she'll make it her strength.
She sits and cries.
Something's wrong, she says. What's wrong? I ask.
Something's wrong, she replies.

                    Something in me dies
When I think of the girl I walked with
Through Wicklow woods, near a river, over a bridge,

She was open then, talked at every bend
And twist of the road, music laughed from her mouth,
She began to get lost, fell over some edge
In herself. For that, she'll win through in the end.'

What the Woman Chooses

'His language is foul as mortal sin,
His ways like a mad animal's
Getting worse and worse the more he boozes:

How can any woman put up with him?
But she does, she does, God help us all.
It's a choice, I suppose. And that's what the woman chooses.'

The Names

'The names he gives me

   good thing
      fast bit
         born whore
            tight cunt
               snazzy bitch
                  would-be nun
                    dirty slut
                       sizzling witch
                       great ride
                           heart o' the home
                         snowy bride
                        randy spark.

Throw a bag over our heads

We're all the same in the dark.'

Get This

Open the door, see what's going on.
Get this: her brother is seventeen
Her father forty-one.
Brother and father fuck her

When they will, it's called abuse, but
No one can prove it.
One or two neighbours will tell you
The girl will grow to love it.

She loves the music of U2
And when only her heart is listening
She sings
Of red yellow purple green white blue
Of trees and the sea of love in the streets
And rivers wandering.

Who will open the door of her singing and crying?
Neighbours say she's all right; they're lying.

The Green Dark

I know, in the green dark, I have not solved myself.
Must I be someone you can praise or damn?
A nowhere traitor or the devil's dancer?
A randy trucker killing the road from Cork
Begging the lifted teenager for sex?
An ex-priest discovering man's work
Among our stinking spiritual wrecks?
      I am all, and none of these; and they are me.
The green dark is what you dream it to be.

H

Fish and Chips

Sex is fucking things up
And yet we need it need it
For the propagation of the faithless.
I have a cure for AIDS

But am keeping it to myself.
This fuckfuck world is all war and famine.
I often think of the night, I'm sure it was night,
Hitler was conceived:

His daddy has just grabbed fish and chips
Wrapped in the sports pages
Of the *Squirish Mimes.*

His mammy opens her legs and her lips
When daddy, vinegar-greasy, chirps,
'Come on, luv, let's fuckfuck for a laugh.'

The fun begins with a heart and a half.

'Down we goes'

The Minister for Unemployment in Hell
Is scared shitless some Christian Jew or Turk
Will come up with the notion that people
Would like to work
And begin to believe in dignity.
The prospect is too ghoulish to contemplate
So he keeps the youngsters drugged and boozy
Crammed with frustration and hate.

'So down we goes to the Quay in Dunleary.
Fiona is locked outa her mind when Mick
An' myself decides to rape her. Jesus bleedin' Christ!

Me head bangs when I wakes in the mornin'.
I think I remember Fiona got sick
When Mick belted her face with his fist.
Ah sure the three of us were curse o' God pissed.'

An Unlimited Company

I saw the knife shape itself in the vast cold
It took an arsenal of cries to make the handle
The blade was made of unchronicled pain
Not of humans but of beasts and creatures
Without a name.
As it formed itself it swung slowly round in the air
Like a moon aware of its reputation for lunacy.
I stood there
And watched the knife select an iceberg in the freezing sea.
It pointed itself towards the iceberg and began to enter it,
Piercing, piercing like certain memories of living and dead.
Now the knife and the iceberg are an unlimited company,
The knife in the iceberg, the iceberg in the knife
In the freezing sea, kisses and bombs and fucks and
Sniggers and judgments in my head.

The Fish of Darkness

'I coaxed your penis into me
While you slept. You explored me
Under my dark-waking touch.
Who are you? Where do you come from?
I don't worry overmuch
But as I lie and feel you in me
Like a rocket or a thrilling fish
I hear you breathe and sigh
And utter little cries at finding
Worlds beyond my reach.
You die in me, away from me
Not knowing what you give.
When you wake you vanish.
When you sleep you live.
There will be morning light all shy and fresh.
You are the fish of darkness now
Feeding in my flesh.'

A Snotty Moralist

Out there along the potholed muddy road
I walked with a man
Talking of a woman
As though he were God

If God knows what invigours the mind
Of a man planning something
With a woman's life while she's eating
Or sleeping or treading untreacherous ground.

I looked into a field, I saw grass and stones
And I thought, he'll do what he says
And I'll do what I can.

We went silent and sure as automatons
Though I sensed, gross, on the April breeze,
The crass blast of the spirit of a man
And I knew, sniffing the piffling schemes,
What a snotty moralist I am at times.

Lipstick-Letters

Nasty deeds and midnight secrets yanked into the light
Are no concern of mine.
My interest in melodrama is slight
Though spiced with elements of the divine.

Recently, however, I raised my head
On hearing why a randy
Friend of mine was dead.
He took a pretty thing to bed

Because she got him going in a pub.
They screwed till he felt sleepy-sick.
This proved to be an error.

She was gone when he awoke. In lipstick-
letters, large and red, WELCOME TO THE AIDS CLUB
Was scrawled upon his bathroom mirror.

A Bleedin' Scream

I've been reading *The Official AIDS Jokebook*
(O the tumour-humour of the age!)
Edited by Herod, with a pithy introduction
In which he deals with the victim's tough luck
And the perils of haphazard seduction.
Herod's jokes crackle with moral purpose:

What does AIDS stand for?
– Arse-Injected Death Sentence.

What was Rock Hudson's Dying Wish?
– To be buried in the arsehole of Kerry.

The book, published by Merciless Press at five
Ninety-five, is crammed with such gems, concise and merry.

Sex, argues Herod, is pantingly funny
Though intimately linked with Original Sin
Making brothers of Adam Saddam Marx Ho Chi Minh.

His *Joke-Book* has laughed into fifty editions.

Royalties come pumping in
Justifying his editorial claim
That every joke is a bleedin' scream.

Professional

My decent tipsy versatile GP,
Perceiving in my eyes the seeds of murder
Or some such crime he didn't like to see
Suggested I might have a perilous disorder
Of the body or the mind or both.
I was a boy, he knew me well, 'twas long ago.
That old GP, itching for the truth,
Took, one prosperous Christmas when the snow
Flourishedflowed like money or strong booze,
A sample of my urine.

For reasons of his own
He stored it in his deepfreeze. Next Christmas,
Over a jar together, that heart-seeing man,
Professional to the end, said 'I believe that this,
Beyond all reasonable doubt, is traitor's piss.'

Luck

A woman will tell her truth
(Even then it's a matter of luck)
In the small, horny hours of the morning
After the third fuck.

    In my loved culture, the poet sees
    All good things come in threes.

'O Judas Judas I love you I love you
How beautifully you betray
Every bitch of a son and son of a bitch
Who gets in your way.'

    In my loved culture, poets bless
    What they think is loneliness.

I swallow her horny happy gasps
With more salt than is good for me,
Satisfy my lady as best I can

Before rising to unadulterated apple juice
Such as Eve might have sipped in fruity Eden.
Then I set about the work of the Son of Man.

If This Was Fake

There are as many heavens and hells
As there are men
But I discovered heaven in a moment
When I slept with Mary Magdalene.
To be honest, I didn't think I had a chance

But when I put my case
                    she smiled, said yes:
When she made love the world was love
And all her body did was bless
My body as I died inside her
And she lived as I'd never seen a woman
Live before. She gasped, cried, moaned,
                    shuddered, stilled.

Something in her stillness made me ask
'Mary, did you fake that orgasm?'
I'll never know. She kissed my cheek and smiled.
I smiled too, my whole body longing to sing.
If this was fake, Christ, what is the real thing?

Sweetest

When you betray me, love, I know
I should surrender to the smell of rot
But sweetest memories come and go
Of my knife dipped in your honeypot.

On My Back

Hitler tells me skin covers a lot,
Shown only by careful peeling.
In you go, beyond flesh, blood, bones. To what?

Nothing, the study of which I find revealing
As a warm afternoon, on my back, grassed, staring at the sky,
Flawless, deep, unending, like a perfect lie.

Back of the Laundrette

I felt his tongue, the first time, like a wet
Snake on my neck in the tiny yellow-
papered room at the back of the laundrette.
A laugh-a-minute, tinkling, vodka-swigging fellow
He made his money out of dope
And had four thugs slugging for him,
They sported chains, sticks, knotted bits of rope,
They hovered, sinister and dirty-dumb,
I knew it was only a matter of time
Before they turned on one or both of us.
One Christmas day when it was pissing
Out of the heavens the four thugs came
And found us in the tiny room, kissing.
I escaped. They broke his back. Treacherous.

The More Human

I meet a woman with one breast.
My eyes question her body, I get no answer.
I acknowledge the mastery of cancer
And know she knows that she and I are dispossessed
Midgets wondering can it please
Heaven to witness this disease.

The best way to fight cancer is to eat it.
I don't tell the woman this.
The clichés tell her how to beat it.
Cancer lusts for metamorphosis
As does your dispossessed adventurer
Through languages and clubs and scarce positions
And stale tales waiting to be freshly spoken
Amid paid gestures of articulate liars,
Priests and poets, experts, critics and professors.

Do I deserve inherited derision?

Does a chopped-off breast bleed its way to heaven?

What do they do with these breasts?
Burn them? Bury them?
Leave them for sniffing beasts?
Have the women forgotten
How they were kissed and bitten?
Will their history ever be written?

I say goodbye to this pleasant one-breasted woman
I am a one-purposed man.
Of the two, she's the more human.
We both live as best we can.

Dangerous Pieces

I smelt my own evil rising
Like the most expensive perfume in the business.
I bought it duty-free at Jerusalem Airport
For Mary Anne Fatima McGuinness.
    She wore it like the gift it was.
    It became her inimitable smell
Throttling every other scent of her body and soul.
That's a long time ago, I remember it well
Because this morning my own evil
Poured out of me through doors and windows
Streets fields highways into the sea
Where it poisoned whales sharks nameless creatures
Made prisoners of waves and broke
Over shores everywhere in dangerous pieces of me.

Kisses

What a noble sign of love is the simple act
Of kissing, especially the version lip to lip,
Implying passion no lover can retract
Without envisioning himself a hypocrite.
And are there not, in this love-ravenous world,
A hundred thousand variations
Of that blessed essential sign
Among individuals and nations?

I have kissed but little: here and there, a mouth,
An eye, a cunt and, now and then, an arse
To ensure that I became the thing I am –
Not the victim of some spiritual drought,
A human lump dumped in a ditch, scarce
Glanced at by good folk who don't give a damn.
But I, damn me, I give a damn, I always did,
My heart experienced metamorphosis
Of passion rampant in the blood
So that I knew what should be is not what is.
Whispering to deaf ears is profitless
As touching words like, has it come to this?
It has. Authentic prophecy is a lucky guess
And we are still confounded by a kiss
In the dark or half-dark or drunken light
With the evening dying at its own pace
Like an old man too knackered-shagged to dream,
Who has forgotten the lifesigns in his face
That years ago seemed angelbright
Before his eyes drank deep an evil gleam.
      Alfonsus John O'Grady, friend of mine,
Will not frenchkiss
A member of the slopposite sex
For fear he might asphyxiate the lady.
He has, as well, a passionate objection
To the notion of sticking his tongue
Into a fellow creature's mouth.
He does not think it wrong
But quite ridiculous and unhygienic
Believing that behind sweet flawless lips
Germs bide their slime, expecting fun.
The thought's enough to make Alfonsus sick.
Therefore, no frenchkissing. 'Why should I swallow
Other people's germs?' he asks, 'I've plenty of my own.
Do you know how filthy people's mouths are?
Have you ever opened her jaws and peeked in?
You'll wish you were a far hygienic star,
Between her teeth fester black lumps of sin.
If that's the sort of thing you wish to kiss
I wish you centuries of stinking bliss.'
      For all I know, not much, this may explain
Why Alfonsus John
Experiences a small, recurring pain
At the prospect of not being turned on
By wet tongues flickering between white teeth
Brushed silverbright with tasty fluoride,

234

Bodies randymad with juicy youth
Clamouring for the muff-dive and the ride.
Instead, O'Grady broods on the first time
His mother's lips kissed silk into his cheek,
The gentle affirmation of true bliss,
The sign that leads away from sin and crime,
The love that understands why man is weak.
Home is where the fart is, and mommy's kiss.
   Kisses suggest emotion, a vastly
Complicated topic which I shan't go into now
Except to say it can have ghastly
Repercussions for the feeler and the felt.
I think of stab rip hack rend whip stick belt.
Sticky kisses of first love may help the whelps to grow
In confidence but their ferocity
Suggests a cannibalistic fury
Causing the approving heart to wilt,
Appalled such tenderness should lead
To such sweaty paddling in another's flesh.
Yet it is necessary, necessary
The young kissmunch each other,
The male one day may be a happy dad
And the object of his munching, productive mother.
Then stretch, young love, stretch limb and sinew,
In order to find out what's in you
The spittle-orgy must continue.
     How many kisses
Have you received in life to date?
How many have you given?
Do you love your wife
Or are your kisses to her spiced with hate?
(Remember the first night?)
Do you kiss her out of duty or relief
Or just the sense you'd better get it over?
Compare this dutiful peck with that volcanic kiss
When you saw yourself a lover.
The insured years are enemies of fire,
Duty chokes desire,
She's standing at the door, she turns away
Knowing you've all to do, nothing to say.
You no longer wonder how it came to this:
A corpse is no more dead than a dead kiss.
  A novelist, Hans-Christian Wurster,
Knocked at my bedsit door, came in
With a grin you wouldn't find in fiction,
Sat on a chair made by Joseph of Nazareth,

Sipped a cup of decaffeinated coffee
Said he wanted to write a blockbuster
About my strife and crimes.
                              Could he have a true
Heart-to-heart no-holds-barred let-it-all-hang-out
                    Interview?
He had his questions ready. They covered
Sex, violence, treachery, money, political intrigue,
The precise nature of the messianic impulse,
The passion to commit an ultimate sin.
'Well, Judas?' queried the decaffeinated grin.
'Fuck off, Hans-Christian' I said.
But he persisted. 'Wild horses
Won't force me out of here, Iscariot;
I'll not be shifted by car or bus,
By train, plane, donkey's cart or chariot
Till you reveal what my novel needs to know.
If you tell, you'll find it'll please us
Both. Why in God's name were you so
Brash as to plant a kiss on the face of Jesus?
Why choose the sign of love to be
The ultimate sign of treachery?
At that stupendous moment for mankind
Were you playing a game?'
I smiled and said 'One man in all this world
Understands that kiss, but modesty
Forbids me mentioning his name.'
        I once saw a modest kiss.
Herman's daddy took him to the zoo,
Showed him all the happy, trapped animals.
I was there too.
Herman called for an ice cream,
Sat on the edge of a pit
Containing several insatiable apes.
        Herman fell into it,
Broke a hand, a leg, was badly concussed,
Lay on his face, the apes slowly came.
One, a most ugly joe with great sad eyes,
Stood guard over Herman, kissed his head.
This world is not remarkable for modesty.
Herman was saved. I'm trying
To imagine the pain
Of a small, wild creature
Among trapped, happy men.

        When the podgy sub-editor turned

236

And planted a long, boggy kiss
On the gob of the tipsy Foreign Correspondent
Pale from his recent act of Cosmic Analysis
But responding with some guts to Podge
I thought the Christmas office party
Would crapple in disarray
Since I believe in local manifestations of universal decay.
Instead, that minor orgy became a hearty
Free-for-all. I had nothing to say
As I watched the lads guzzling each other.
What would any decent mother
Think if she saw this sozzled riff-raff,
Normally a most efficient staff,
Discovering an old delight in a new way?
The birth of Christ sets Dionysos making hay.
I reflected, as I began to laugh,
I might have been ten million miles away
Nightmaring on a charcoal planet
Watching the sober Russians dressed in white
Breaking all records in the sunless light
Of image and politics and starwars hate,
Goading themselves to absorb the thought
It's possible to run where sun cannot obtrude
But works in other worlds far away
To warm the last drop of human blood.
The Russians have run faster
Than any man has ever run.
Each runner's penis swells in pain.
Unstoppable women charcoal from the dust,
Each woman takes a penis in her mouth,
Sucks, kisses, kisses, sucks, again, again.
How assiduous the women are,
How glad-insatiate. No almosts, no near-misses,
I marvel at their skilled procedure
As they confirm themselves sweet thieves of kisses,
Suckers of the Russians' come and go.
In that virgin charcoal land
I see again, as I saw long ago
On earth, women in command
Kneeling in blithe postures of submission
To the gods of love,
Tired, ecstatic runners towering above,
Becoming now a helpless shiver;
I saw this first in the time that is to come
When we're more equal than we dare to dream,
When betrayal accelerates martyrdom:

Forgive me if I call it love,
　　Something I misunderstand forever.
Beyond words, certain kisses promise much.
There was a lover
Who could never cease, never find peace
Till she had kissed his body all over
And over, breathing Holy! Holy! all the while:
Feet knees thighs lips cock balls belly buttocks
Shoulders chest lips lips teeth cheeks eyes
Head. Holy! Holy! Old women kiss a crucifix
Thus, as if purifying their shook lined mouths
Of the weighty self-important stink of men.
I've seen these women in dark places
Thrown out like empty wine bottles.
Once, they were held, kiss-tasted. Now they kiss an
Image of the dead god buried in their faces.
Empty bottles clatter, break, love's sacrifices.
　　　Yet I must speak of tenderness,
Soulbreath emanating in a kiss.
Am I imagining it, has this feeling
Vanished from the world? I think once
I felt it, long ago, an evening
Smell of apples in the air,
A sense of youngsters, believing in love,
Strolling among exciting promises there.
Perhaps it didn't happen, just one of
My illusions designed to sustain
A heart incapable of warmth.
For one moment, though, I might have fathered
A child coming home to pain,
Making his way, like dad, through storms
The battered dead have met and weathered.
　　　In the wars that are to come
Children of love, indifference and rape
Will perish with the earth on fire.
Not even a mythical idiot will escape
To kiss and kill a king because
The pain of learning is the learning of pain.
Is there anyone, anything, we cannot kill?
It is a source of satisfaction
To know not even the shrewdest creature
Can outstrip the terminal aspect of our skill.
We've spent our hearts for this, we spend them still.
Victims may kiss our feet, adore our blood,
Breathe homage into every lineament and feature,
Knowledge belongs to one, it always will,

Who dares to recognise, to kiss and kill his god.
                    I go out,
A calm evening, the kind that brings
The sick to beg release from pain,
Believers in miracles with a sense of what
Ought to be, persisting in hope.
My steps are slow, deliberate, I cover ground,
I cast a shadow, a not unfriendly shape,
My thoughts are skimming over all I've found
                    I come to him
I kiss the tired legends in his eyes
I kiss the pleading lepers in his face
I kiss the mercy flowing through his skin
I kiss his calm forgiveness of sin
I kiss the women hovering at his side
I kiss the men who make him their cause
I kiss the money made and lost in his name
I kiss the murders committed by his children
I kiss the mob adoring him
I kiss the mob killing him
I kiss the treachery of men
I kiss the ways they will remember him
I kiss the ways they will forget him
I kiss his words his silences
I kiss his heart
I kiss his caring daring love
                    He seems relieved
He murmurs something about a kiss
Betrayal
The Son of Man

I have never seen him so peaceful and still
Hardly breathing
As living creatures do

Has he ever lived at all?

Living not living
He is led away

I stand
Doomed with triumph
Nothing to say

In the name of Judas
And of Judas
And of Judas

As it was in the beginning
Is now
And forever shall be
Judas without end

Amen.

Heigh-Ho

Judas Iscariot is buried and dead
Heigh-Ho buried and dead
And the heartbreaking worms work to nibble his head
Heigh-Ho nibble his head

Judas Iscariot has run out of cash
Heigh-Ho run out of cash
O give him a choice of the nail or the lash
Heigh-Ho the nail or the lash

Judas Iscariot has run out of hope
Heigh-Ho run out of hope
And he's casting his eye on this rogue of a rope
Heigh-Ho this rogue of a rope

Judas Iscariot would make a great cry
Heigh-Ho make a great cry
But he knows in his heart he'd get no reply
Heigh-Ho get no reply

Judas Iscariot with silence is one
Heigh-Ho silence is one
Questions and answers can't tell what is done
Heigh-Ho tell what is done

Judas Iscariot swings from a tree
Heigh-Ho swings from a tree
O he was the bad one the good ones agree
Heigh-Ho the good ones agree

Judas Iscariot grins at his doom
Heigh-Ho grins at his doom
Where did he come from? Out of what womb?
Heigh-Ho out of what womb?

Judas Iscariot is hanging alone
Heigh-Ho hanging alone
And no one can say where Judas is gone
Heigh-Ho Judas is gone

But I met an old goat who said Judas is well
Heigh-Ho Judas is well
And as long as that's true there's hope left in hell
Heigh-Ho there's hope left in hell

A Reported Sighting

Following my kiss
I visited a few pubs and clubs
And then went missing.
No word for a while then someone said
'Where's Judas?'
I stayed away, they speculated, I was invisible
As God, they wondered, I strayed through their eating and drinking
And grunted efforts at usual half-thinking,
They must see me soon, I hid, there was
A reported sighting in the Bekaa Valley, all
This was in the realm of rumour and pissful blinking,
I stayed silent as God, I began to tax their belief,
They quarrelled among themselves as to whether I existed or not,
Some said I breathed, others swore I was a bad thought,
One child prayed to me, I lightened her distress,
A boy invoked me, I whispered why he was blind,
I exploited my absence, discovered the most
Important thing in this world is to be nothing,
My own father, my own son, my own self-puzzling ghost.

Three Words

...and yet, and yet, someone loved me,
Incredible, incredible.
Further, to deepen incredulity,
She was beautiful, beautiful
And she told me not by letter, not by phone
But face to face
In a restaurant in Peter's Lane.
Three words, I love you.
                              I quit the place
And walked for miles and miles
Till I was lost, then hopped a bus,
Returned to bedsit, unrefreshed, dumb.
I love you. I have my own madness,
Don't need another's. Whatever love is
It's what I fly from.
My heart will never house an unexploded bomb.

NINE

I know I've arrived, can you tell me why I'm here?

A Dream of Keys

Down in the water among the black flowers
Among the Doolin dead the drowned boys' eyes
Like shining new pennies to entertain eternity

     The keys
Dangled ten centuries above my head
Like promises memories letters received and unwritten

     I said
These keys are mine   I will unlock

Myself healthy and sick

My father and mother my curses and prayers
My sex my sleep my relentless dreams
     My cute little arse

So I reached for the keys through the winter air
But they melted at my touch and threatened
     To burn my fingers, or worse.

As You Might Expect

My mother came to the tree
As I was hanging there
She began to cry
And tear her hair

          Greasy serpents of doom
          Slithered through her womb

I tried to open my mouth
No words came
The wind refused to help me
Say her name

          I was born with a caul
          My mother sold it to a fool

She broke out in grief
Accused the sky
Who killed my son? Who killed my son?

This, I take it, was love.

I continued to die
Hanging all alone, hanging all alone

As you might expect from the way
I'd been thinking, earlier that day.

I Shall Not Forget

I looked down on myself
After I hanged myself.
I took off my clothes,
The clothes of the hanged me
And carried them to a stream
Some fifty yards from the tree.
There, I washed
All the dirt out of my clothes,
I washed all the blood out of them
And all the sweat. I shall never forget
The smell of my own sweat.

Even if my mind is twisted for eternity
I shall not forget that smell,
My own smell, stronger than the thought of hell.

A Special Meeting

I attended a special meeting in Damascus
For all those contemplating suicide.
I sat next to Marilyn Monroe, she said she was
Going along for the ride.
She shone like a freshly polished Granny Smith apple
Before avid human fangs bite into it.
Hitler sat on my other side. Six million times
I heard him mutter 'This is Jewish shit.'

At my back, several aristocratic shoplifters
Listened. So did child molesters, bank managers, priests,
Disciples of Einstein, a novelist with a tubercular cough.

Why commit suicide? Fascinating answers
Poured from all corners of the packed meeting-hall.
I said nothing, being for some reason utterly pissed off.

Style Matters

Styles of suicide intrigue me since, in a fit of pique,
I committed it myself
And was considered by biographers
To be both treacherous and weak.

Style matters: in my case, a rope
Induced a feeling of being launched into inner space.
I cannot claim to have disported a look of hope.
In fact, a bloody pessimism flushed my face.

Hitler tells me that when he did it
He went on the pill.
Herod chose wine. That figures.

Attila the Hun slashed his conquering wrists.
The Ancient Mariner went for a long swim.
Hemingway stuck his favourite gun into his mouth
                      and pulled both triggers.

Neck

Prior to my hanging I made sure
My contribution to humanity wouldn't end
With my measured yet untimely demise.
I donated my body to medical science.
Wendy Ling, a budding surgeon of Vietnamese
Extraction, chopped me up,
Kept choice parts of me in a Woolworths cup
And made several useful discoveries

Which she explored at length.
Wendy is a tenacious girl with a methodical style.
Operating on the most abject human wreck
She adds to medical knowledge with a smile.
Just now she's putting the finishing touches
To a public lecture on the muscles of my neck.

Black Cat, I Dream of Ease

I'm modern, I understand nothing, you like me for that,
I'm ninety or nine thousand, sitting inside a window,
A rug over my knees, at my feet a black cat,
I'm a plundered mound, a ravaged chapel, do you know
My secrets, I don't, something has exhausted me,
I am trying to grasp something piteous beyond me,
A search for some kind of writing, I misunderstand
It all despite the evidence, someone else will see
Something else, true for him, it'll fit, he'll thank God
And be grateful for finding behind the snack-bar
Jars containing grain beans lentil smoked-meats bread wine
Given to hell-shocked heroes staggering home after
A hard day's fighting in the open plain. They eat
With the hunger of men who have played their part.
Between mouthfuls they speak of rape, a city betrayed.
Black cat, I dream of ease, this dream stings my heart.

Simply Divine

I went on a pilgrimage to Lough Derg,
Took the boat out to the island
On a day dead as Dante
Ignoring the glances of my fellow-travellers
Getting ready to fast and pray.
I prayed and fasted for three days and
Three nights, but sneaked an odd slug
From a vodka bottle full of poteen
Hidden in my massive black overcoat
Like a bomb in a supermarket,
Picked up at a Franciscan Sale-of-Work in
Abbeyfeale for a fiver.

On leaving
Lough Derg in the boat rowed over mud
Dead as Homer I pondered
The waves, breeze-ruffled, daubed with foam.
I couldn't see the point in believing
Anything, not even the foam, pilgrims have always wandered
For God, wandered lost as waves, I'd be better off
At home in Listowel making my simple
Beads and laces of treachery.
I drove back to my factory
Stopping in Limerick for an Irish stew
Washed down with a bottle of house wine
That tasted divine.

Even Now

Even now, out of the sexual dark,
       I could rise
And cut through the blindness
       Of my eyes,

Cut through the pathetic inevitable meshing
       Of men and women
In their God-ordained round-the-clock fucking.
       I could go on

And on through the sperm-riddled days
       And nights of those
Who love to increase their sorrows.

I could grope through fog to find what I never had,
       A glimpse cleaner than painlight
          Of the face of God.

Instead, my love my loss, I'll crawl home to bed.

Dreams of Perfection

I know in my heart I never perfected
Anything. Yet, like your hand under my head
Supporting my brief sleep too long denied,
Conceivable, inconceivable universes focused in this bed,

Dreams of perfection visit me
Like thoughts of happiness.
I want to say, Come in, come in, you're welcome,
Stay as long as you like, your presence is a bless-

ing, I have lived to see you enter in-
to me; but no sooner are these dreams
here than they're gone like youngsters emigrating

from places they'll always carry in their bones.
O I've seen perfection all right, roses in slums,
jewels rubbing noses with old County Council stones,
but it slipped away from my grasp the moment I started half-thinking.
I'm all flaws dreaming of some flawless thing.

Dear Doll

I'm creating a *lingua franca* of betrayal.
Words used by malicious, murderous, queer,
AIDS-afflicted Flanagans are of no avail
Since in their way these buggers are sincere,
Flinging cups of blood over prison officers.
Considering the obscene caution of politicians
And polite academic pornography,
Reading some of our less claustrophobic theologians
On the complex nature of the holy

My unholy gorge rises like a tinker's penis
At the sight of a bourgeois doll
Waddling her shrewdly-caloried bum.

Dear doll, whatever else may come between us
My *lingua franca* will ensure your full
Enjoyment when you decide to kingdomcome.

On a Stand

Caught, having got into a spot of bother,
I was upright on a stand.
They asked me to swear
To tell the truth, the whole truth, and nothing but the truth.
If these poor bastards are innocent enough
To believe that such a thing exists,
I thought, why then I'll tell it.
And I did, I did.

I told it as a blackbird sings its song
To the unlistening dawn. I told it
As any daddy tells his life's truth to his son.

I told it to the judge, such a strong
Wise man who seemed to wonder if I meant it.
It was a difficult case. I won.

Things I Might Do

I thought of things I might do with my heart.
Should I make it into a month like October,
A chalice for the sad madness of leaves
That I might raise in homage to the year's end?

Should I make it into a small white church in
A country-place where bells are childhood prayers?
Or a backroom of a brothel in Dublin
Where the trade of somethinglikelove endures?

Should I make it a judge to judge itself?
Or a caring face in a memory-storm?
Or a bed

For Judas dreaming of the tree :
          'There now, there now, rest as best you can,
          Darling, rest your treacherous head
          And when you've rested, come home to me.'

Gizzard

The judging world finds judging easy.
If I happen to be seen in a house of ill-repute,
Low dive, dirty pub, grotty café or sleazy
Joint, I'm judged and sentenced in a minute.

Can it be that the world is right?
I do not know myself, after all.
I have this feeling in my gizzard, however,
That I didn't fulfil my potential.

Even as a lad I blushed at that sense of power
Sweeping over me like sun and ice in a never-before
Felt surge creating this herodhitler sense of scope.

Now, peering into my private clean keep-out abyss, moody-broody as ever,
I ask myself if it was I closed the door
On myself. So. There's hope. There's rope. Hope rope rope rope

Sounds

Again and again, that hanging night,
I heard the sounds of my life
Galvanising the grass.
                    My mother's cry
Came razoring my head.
The first time a teacher beat me
With a stick that sang through the air
Like a lark packed with venom
Choked celebrating bells in my blood.
                    The first bird I killed
Toppled into silence that was its own cry.
The sun melted and I begged
For the mercy in its light.
                    Words I didn't know the meaning of
Towered black and important as priests
In tall rooms of majestic loneliness
And unquestionable authority.
                    The words of a healing woman
Were so true I knew the sound of a lie.

                    When love threatened to drown me
With words so soft I knew they must be the opposite
Of God knows what
I sought the saving rumbles of beasts;
They taught me to listen to men
Whose hearts were rotten
Yet fine
Compared with mine.
These were pleasing sounds, silverbright.
I forget them now.
Only the sounds of a kiss in the evening light
Will not be forgotten.

Bastards

he pales
eyes vanish into the skull
lips whiten
hands tighten
he trembles through all his body
head sags back
chest rattles
I hear the fright in the heart

two fishermen grab his elbows
tremble with him, branches of one tree,
cries break from the woman.
She
embraces his knees, kisses, moans, goes dumb.
The crowd vanish into him. I do not succumb.
The crowd are back. This had to happen.
Nothing satisfies these bastards but blood.
Bad bastards like me make them feel good.

A Dog Died

To be stripped to the bone
Beyond the bone
To have even the memory of things
Whipped into the never-happened no-part of the mind

To know the final darkness is light
Compared with the darkness beyond darkness
To realise the working generations
Live to kiss the lips of nothingness

All this and more I saw or thought I saw
When the woman pinioned to the priest
Ran her right hand through her hair

A dog died at a gate
People said its teeth were perfect
Everyone in the city was rotten
So rotten they had estranged despair.

I'm a stripped bone in the sun, nothing to fear.

Need

My beads and laces factory in Listowel
Was so thriving I decided
I'd exploit some other product as well.
I walked up and down the Square,
                scratching my head
Like a lice-ridden philosopher
Wondering, for I have preserved and nourished
                my sense of wonder
Refusing to let myself explain myself away
Like a poem or a picture, please
Understand why I've tried to resist the disease
Of explanation, I looked at the people, I
Pondered the two churches, Catholic and
Protestant, I stared from the bridge into the
Feale, waterstoneweedmudpollutionsand,
I knew then.
                'A Poison Factory' I thought
'Is right. I saw Peter deny Christ, I took
Silver, I saw Christ lost writhe and cry and bleed.'

Being Someone

I said to myself, Supposing my life
Were a comfortable overcoat
Capable of resisting the worst winter cold,
Would I have the heart to give it
To an old man shivering at
The edge of a village or in the dead
Centre of a Christmassy city street,
Shoppers lusting for goodies like Romans for blood?
    Suppose I were the old man himself
And a stranger charitied up to me,
Offered me his overcoat to keep me warm,
Would I accept this gift of seasonal love
Or would I look the stranger straight in the eye
With 'Fuck off, chum! Keep yourself free from harm'?
    Grant me the licence to be
A clown in a travelling circus
Fulfilling its destiny
Among the scamps and urchins of credulous
Provinces. There I bulge, waiting my turn,
My forehead so red the Big Top may burn.
Long ago I gave up daring to think.
Now, awaiting the ringmaster's wink,
I tumble through every laughable bone
Of my being into the swallowing eyes,
I'm Jackass, greased lightning, rainbow joke,
Bonfire Baggypants chuckling up in smoke,
Let me never again be conscious-awake
Cowed by what is and is not a mockable mistake,
But I am, and I look, and I lie
To the children escaping the massacre
For the moment, lost in the funny thunder.
    There's nothing as funny as a man
Who's not quite human.
That's why I cuddle the notion
Of changing from clown to Fat Woman.
    As a girl I was passably slim
But today these incredulous eyes
Feed on my boobs, my belly and quim,
My hot mythological thighs.
    Tonight, for some reason, I'm feeling volcanic,
Vesuvius, Etna, my buttocks are fire,
My mind a pit of lava-thick rage.
Pardon me, please, if I heave and get sick

In this ring of my waddling desire.
How some women nosedive into old age!

In this me of deaf girls, autistic children,
Blind telephonists planning an evening of beer,
Rainy angels grey on the pavement
I am my own blind man whitesticking through hell
Wondering what my morning shave meant.

An elbow-touching apostle approaches:
'May I help you, sir, to cross the road?'
Impulsive charities arrive like despatches
From part-time soldiers in the army of God.

That morning shave has worked, I feel the wind
Fingering my face like a cosmic masseur.
Brother wind, are we not blind together
Or am I the blindest thing in this land of the blind?
'Thank you kindly for your help, dear sir,
I find it hard to manage this treacherous weather.'

A girl cursed me once, I whitesticked into her.
Soft flesh, yielding, granitecurse her voice.
Days come I choose to be made of stone
Drawn from a quarry where children play
Games that will be politics one day
When money is the marrow of their bones.
I am majestic outside a famous Bank
A top Insurance Company thrives close at hand
I am the most pigeoned monument in the land
I have survived the appalling human stink
Even of my creator who was paid to think
I am happy to survey the haste
Of the same old conscientious mob at work.
Perched on my right hand, a blackbird sings,
It is a thousand years from now, the blackbird wastes
Itself, a boy prepares to blow me up
Because old monuments are threatening things.
                              Being someone
Is strange. That untraumatic morning
Long ago, I knew I was no one.
I might have grown depressed, gone into mourning,
Taken to muttering in the tolerant streets,
Paraded my sensitive soul as an artist
Or poet up to his rhythm in debt,
Invaded Impressive Gatherings to get pissed

In the slump any of Distinguished People,
Swallowed politics as Hitler's visionary sidekick,
Learned to deliver the most lethal
Insults to those who really hackle my wick,
Allocated Nobel Prizes to all who seem
To believe in some magnanimous dream
But I end up being this drably dressed
Non-being who can speak, gesture, smile
At others others others doing their best
To smile their way through the barely tolerable
Days, to hell with despair, so
I will not nag, complain or carp
At this idiot impulse to rise and go
Anywhere. I'm learning to play the Jew's Harp,
Neat touch, seems appropriate, besides
I've been informed that one of music's
Properties is deep, deliberate healing.
I may enchant non-beings on every side,
Provide a healthy interlude for the sick
If I play my little Harp with feeling.

O hear my music rise above the heads of men,
I play for... play for... Who am I, then?
A blind child stirs in me, begins to cry,
Her tears are mine, they burn, I don't know why
Her hurt is my heart, I must find her name
And let my music tell her who I am.
I must be someone, someone you'd say
Hello to, if I happened to pass your way.
My blind child cries, I believe she's near,
A moment, for a moment, let me know her.

Ringing the Baptist

I was working as an undertaker's assistant when I died
And was given the job of preparing my body for its coffin.
I sympathised with myself at my own wake, I cried
For myself, I reminisced about my life's performance:
Flawed, I concluded, could have been better.
I was, as you know, bald; a bald corpse.
I looked grey, hairless and dead, I thought it might be fitter
If I wore a new wig, so I rang John the Baptist,

He sent me one, made of the hair of his head.
I encountered some difficulty in affixing it.
I rang the Baptist again. He said 'Use glue.'
I did. The wig refused to stick. I felt mad.
I found a nail and drove it straight through my pate.
Wig fixed fast. I looked good, beautiful, true.
But for the nail I'd have been in a nice how-do-you-do?

That Lyric Evening

No more than I doubt my birth
Though not a squeak do I remember
Of that bloodyblind adventure
Despite what the records say

Did he doubt, that lyric evening,
Words are but a sign
Beyond the obstacle of flesh
Singing 'You're divine!'

All I know is that he heard it
In the garden of an evening
And though he never mentioned it

I knew that it was beautiful
And all-revealing
And far beyond my powers of telling.

Mr Dicky Everyman, Half-Assed Rapist, Contemplates A Nude Mannequin In Brown Thomas's Window, Closely Observed By A Female Guardian Of Morality

'So this is where Dicky gets his notions.
Staring at her stare, her small off-yellow tits,
Her perfect belly, satisfying thighs,
No wonder he looks half out of his wits
Thinking what he thinks he'd like to do with her
Cunt that isn't even a proper cunt like mine

But has the mythic symmetry that men desire.
Why don't they clothe her? Then she'd be fine
But he stares and stares at this naked effigy
Of woman surrounded by expensive things
Like bras and panties there for all to see.
The bastard is transfixed. What is he thinking now?
Look! He's turning from the window and his eyes
O heavenly Jesus are staring straight at me!'

Shy

Even my trusting darlings say I'm a cynic
Powered by self-loathing. Not so, my love, not so,
It is the age that's sick,
What sort of age will practise slavery
And call it freedom? What sort of age
Will sell itself for a bad dream
Then whirlwind into a rage
When one defines the nature of the crime?
I have a modest talent for definition.
Our natural element is the element we create
That is, pollution, though even in that climate
Someone doubtless finds himself saying 'I love you'
And he means it by God he means it.
Looking down on the city last night
In the shadow of an enduring tree
I saw what looked like rain but it
Wasn't rain, let me not say what it was, I'm very
Shy to admit some stinking truth I'm forced to see.
A disciple of the apostles has AIDS,
He was in Mountjoy Jail for six years
And now he's out, trying to get laid
By any scouting knockabout
He meets in the streets of the Capital.
'Mickser' I said, examining his eyes,
Aware that the most private part of a man is public
Though he be nicknamed after an archangel
Who has never fallen from grace,
'This will not do, this will not do,
You're sliding down the Capital drain.'
'Judas' said Mickser 'Give me some silver
And I'll refrain, yes, I'll refrain.'

If it be that I am guilty of self-loathing
Of the kind
That threatens the modestly defining mind
At such moments as we all recognise
It has to do with silver and what looks like rain.
If I hanged Mickser would that be a kind of loving?
Mickser is a prison full of cries
And hanging is an end to pain.
To-day in the Capital, no words but these:
'Help the handicapped, please! Help the handicapped, please!'

An Adjusting Experience

The morning after the Last Supper at which
Bacchic fracas some extraordinary things happened
I had a vision: a leper told me
One moment only of my life had mattered,
I was nearing the end of my allotted span,
My treachery, as it would come to be known
By those whose minds cut to the bone,
Played its own part in the divine plan
Involving birth, death, resurrection
And the redemption of man.

This vision was followed by voices:
First, a murderous peasant's: 'Cut out his heart';
Then a woman's, posh: 'Good idea, please hand me that knife';
And finally a chorus: 'He must be punished for his art,
Let's hack the creature into pieces,
Jolly slices of life.'

    That is exactly what happened
Except that I, all alone in Croke Park,
Enjoyed a seat in the clergy-politicians' box in the Hogan Stand
Where I watched myself die, die,
Tiddly-i-die-die-die
                    at the hands
Of that beautiful butchering woman
Who knifed me with care,
Cutting off my parts and throwing them to dogs
Milling about, sniffing her, sniffing her.

It was hard to see a divine plan there.

To watch oneself being eaten is an adjusting experience,
It jolts the sense of perspective
So that one feels brutally sane
Despite being distributed among fangs,
Seeing titbits of self chewed and swallowed
With a gusto reminiscent of the judgments of men.

That's my last Last Supper by Jesus. Never again.

All I Got

One of the greatest pleasures in death
Is cycling down a street in hell,
The damned air invigorating every breath.
One evening I cycled at full

Tilt to a meeting of kindred spirits
To discuss the implications of universal poison
In food and drink. Are there hidden merits
In this distressful state? Or is all wholesome fare gone

Forever? As I parked my bike at
The entrance to a laneway, a young demon
Strode up to me, took my photograph

And beat, before I could move, a quick retreat.
'Come back! Come back!' I shouted as he ran
But all I got was a resonant, mocking laugh.

Creatively Buried

Like a slow poem my funeral moved to the Potter's Field
(I'd never looked that Potter in the face
Though people said the man was quite a case)
Where a few oddbods waited to sink me.

260

It was a pleasant day (I hate rain at funerals)
And just before the diggers committed me

To the Mother, several men in para-apostolic uniform
Balaclavaed out of nowhere.
Then, in a manner disciplined and stern,
They fired several volleys over my coffin.

If I weren't a corpse I'd have died laughin'.

These volleys made many people angry
Including bossy official apostles who called

For a full investigation
Into this gunning over the abominable dead.

But a Senior Apostle replied 'One must be practical.
Official intervention at para-apostolic funerals
Can cause a great deal of trouble,' he said.

The wrangling continues. I lie, creatively buried.

Spectator of Myself

As my dangling carcass swayed in the breeze
Beyond indignation and rage
I wouldn't toss you tuppence for your thoughts
On the implications of my body language.
But since I am a spectator of myself
Even at such post-ultimate moments
I could see poems novels saucy dramas
Flow from my undulating bones.

And, bless the mark, I could see soap operas
Of a murderously bubbly kind
Spread from the Potter's Field

                    to all the lands of the globe

Taking possession of millions of eyes
With garish lies capsizing the minds
Of young and old

till my story
is a weary
joke.

The Stony End

Nothing cracked my heart
until that evening
at the stony end
of the healing garden
when you turned and said,
as if remembering a secret
known long ago and long forgotten,
'I love you.'

Disinfectant

Such, at times, is my sense of my whopping
Soulstink, my spiritfilth, the cant
And raggy lies of my attempts at uttering
Myself, I buy a bottle of disinfectant

From a musical suburban supermarket
With a parking-lot as universal as the Catholic
Church, also, in its way, One, True and Holy.
I manic flatwards on my nagging bicycle

And drink the disinfectant
Like a priest gulping the blood of God.
A few minutes later, I'm a different man.

I vomit and defecate with prehistoric gusto.
I shudder and moan as a hell-purged soul would.
In three days I resurrect, an ordinary treacherous sonofagun.

I'll Pick Stones

I am not a man of vision or of visions.
Torment me for fun, offer me a choice
Of dreams or stones, I'll pick stones.
I rub them together and hear my own voice
Telling an ardent young man
Who wishes to serve a master
That once, outside a small provincial town
In the company of a leper,

I saw a flock of griefs
Explode from a field behind his eyes,
Electrify the sky,
Melt, concentrate like leaves
Into earth, fierce seeking energies
Packed into a star without a name.

Do you blame me, then, that I pick stones?
Stones are guilty skeletons.

I Crossed the Street

Was it an imitation Roman chariot or a second-hand
Mercedes Benz nearly wiped me out as I began
To cross a street in the chief city of that island
Where I learned a little of the nature of man?
My death shot past like a Corkman looking for a job,
I froze on what I believe is the right side of eternity,
I thought I was dead, I was not, I felt robbed,
I was not, I looked after my death and melted quietly
Like I used to, a child unable to answer questions
From men smelling of Woodbines and hatred of work.
A few breaths later, my death was already miles away,
Bringing, I surmised, sustaining scraps of life
To a house called *Warm Horizon* among trees, off the main road.
Yolanda was there, whom a bullylover would betray,
Ben who'd make money from Portuguese property
Until the revolution came to stay;
Ted who'd seek, seek, never find a wife,
Daniel, strong Daniel who'd get interested in God.

I too was alive, left alive. I crossed the street, I breathed,
I know I breathed because I found in a bookshop on the far side
A battered copy of Sam Prunty's *Observations On Suicide*.

Peeling the World

I washed my body with grace and water
It remained caked with sin
I spent seven days and seven nights
Peeling the world off my skin.

The world had penetrated my flesh
Taken possession of my blood
I let the dogs of my mind loose in there
They whimpered back, afraid.

In deepening terror I sought any part of me
That hadn't been world-stupefied.
No part could I find.

I was banklink cashsave monetary policy
Success failure eitherway too proud
To sweep the rubbish out of my mind.

By grace, by water I would be defined
But grace and water cannot make me kind.

Closet Mystic

I am not the man to weep when the dreams
Of the two-legged ones are gouged by the cloud.
    Look up! Earth cries and screams
When the cloud poisons what's left of the love of God.
Yet there have been those who loved their own poison
And so shocked the hygienic souls of men
They created the cloud and said it would never rain
Death on the ignored slum and the open plain.

But it did and now it is pouring its successful self
On the mountains and seas
Flashy paperbacks and male models
Rhetoric and lies
And the deftly edited poems on the shelf
Of the closet mystic who once borrowed a pair of socks
From Thomas Aquinas.

Bad Company

I know a little about pain.
Bodypain, the tearaway thing,
Causes me to concentrate on the small
Of my back, hidden gut, such brain

As I possess. Not nice, must be endured.
I witness the mummified women
Sweating it out in the smelly corridors
Where nobody comes, neither the children they reared

Nor the men they tried to love. I find
A worse thing rending me, let me not bore you
With details, let me assure you
The demons screaming and shitting in my mind
Are everywhere like money
And bad company when they
Brag of making me their instrument of treachery.
If the demons make me, let the demons beware of me.

Rescue

Demons pester me like bills I cannot pay.
Days I know I'm made of dust
Accentuate my interest in men
Who live as if they're not.
     Memory helps me swerve away
Or I stop a man in the street,
Ask him what he knows of silver.

I am amazed at how much
Ill-dressed wretches with rotten teeth
And lips cracked as the Middle East
Have garnered over the years.

Myley Soames tells me that damages
For the life of a slave gored by an ox
Are set at thirty silver shekels.

Myley knows a Church of England Bishop with the pox.

Such titbits rescue me from myself, fox the demons.

A Reassuring Shock

It interests me to see my spirit so widespread.
When the red moon rages over the city in the morning
Like the blast we're waiting for, the promised poison,
I know I am hanged but never dead,

Especially that enterprising part of me.
I witnessed it last night: John Brett, Mel Dee, Mona Bold
Crouched in a hedge near the Eagle Golf Club
Waiting for Inspector Francis Ashe to go home.

Mona Bold shot him six times in the face.
Brett and Dee concentrated on his back.
I stood near the familiar pool of blood.

I am stronger now than ever I was.
This tingles me like a reassuring shock.
Homage swaddles me, multitudes my solitude.

Injection

Treating myself as my own guinea-pig
I'm making new advances in parasite control,
A quick injection that will clear the earth
From pole to pole.

Excising vital parts of one's system
May be done by others but I prefer
To operate on myself that I may know the man to blame
If I should err.

Blaming, however, is not a pastime of mine.
Watching parasites at work is much more fun.
They're a clever lot.

When the time comes to administer my injection
You'll marvel at the way parasites quit the scene.
And nowhere will you get the smell of rot.

Never Be Short

Even the shrewdest biblical scholars are not aware,
As I kicked and jigged in my hanging position,
I decided to make a quick, mid-air
Act of Contrition.
Mother of Jesus, it worked like a charm.
My soul felt scrubbed and clean
And though assorted blood-vessels were exploding in my head
I was free of sin

For the first time since I was a nipper
On my mommy's lap of a Saturday night
Snug and purged after my weekly wash
And the old girl advised me to land a job with a pension,
Ignore groupies spouting mystical shite
And never be short of cash.

Living

In another life (I'm nothing but other lives)
I'll be born a tinker in Killarney.
My father and mother will teach me to be streetwise
Because I live surrounded by beauty

And beauty is above all things an industry.
Therefore, out the window with truth and lies

Like all the poems about nature and her ways
I learned at school. Living is what I must do.

Living. But what kind of living is this?
I go to the door of a pub, a cinema, a disco-place
And there's a bull of a man with a kicking face

Spitting 'Tinker! Tinker's get! Out of here! Piss
Off!' I have to live this, die this too, before
I can be born as Hitler's most colourful biographer.

Taking the Air

I take the air for granted.
I breathe and never think of gratitude.
Last night I spoke to a shadow
On the wall of the house of Allo Kincaid.
                    The shadow said,
'This village may soon find itself without air,
People will find life difficult, I fear.'

The shadow sneered, vanished through the wall.
Allo Kincaid frayed at the door of his house,
Said 'I fear the gossip of men and women.
                    Words are poison in this place.'

Though each breath rhymes with death, I'm breathing still,
Relishing, as it kills me, what has the power to kill.

Whenever That Happened

Hell is the familiar all stripped of wonder.
Was there a moment
When wonder at the world died in my eyes?
Had I a friend I could recognise?
When did I take friendship for granted?
When did I get used to the thought of murder?
When did my flesh cease to astonish me?
When did my mind become grey-familiar?

Whenever that happened is when I knew
I could do anything.
When wonder died in me power was born.
I can change the world because I no longer dream of blue,
I can betray a god because I never heard a girl sing
Of steps in the street or sunlight blessing a field of corn.

If You Will, Sir

Unlike many men who have mullocked through hell
And managed to gutter out again
I am not what bright people call cynical,
I am, instead, distressingly sane

And would learn German for the fun of it,
Gulp evening lectures on how to think
In a way that sheds a kind metaphysical light
On a mind accustomed to soulstink,

Bodystink, bloodstink, talkstink of demons
Whose sole purpose in death is to lead me astray
On a proven diet of cool, mocking laughter.

No, for me, hell is an education
Convinced it has something stylish to say
To poor souls. Interpret, if you will, sir.

Another Life

I've no time for that reincarnation stuff
And yet I know a truth I cannot prove.
I was a bomb in another life,
Sammy John McGinley fell in love
With me, kept me, believed in me as
An instrument of justice. When he fingered me
I was touched by his boyish tenderness.
In time, I grew to magic in his eyes,
Rush-hour exploded when we had to part,
My heart splintered in a million pieces
When Sammy John decided our affair was over.

In my bedsit, at evening, memories spurt
And die. I have my act together now. Where is
Sammy John? Am I looking for another lover
Who knows love's genius is hurt, and being hurt
And living every hurt until
The heart is able to endure
What it was born for?
Or am I peeved love's puzzle is undecoded
Because I upped some former time and just exploded?

Why Did I Cut Myself Down?

I spent last night in the company of the corpse
Of myself. I was strolling along my favourite
Pathway when I glimpsed my corpse in the twilight
Swinging from a tree. Oak, I venture to suggest.
Hopping over the hedge I cut myself down.
I was a sorry sight, my heaven-kissing eyes
Bulging with bloody dreams and prophecies
Or just popping in a way that suited the occasion.

I knelt by my self, looked me closely all over.
The grass was damp, I put my coat under my head,
I saw an ambitious youngster, a cold man. I could have wept
But didn't. I sighed. I saw a tentative lover
Of...who was she? He? I bent and kissed my dead
Lips. Then I lay at my side and slept.
When I awoke my corpse looked better, younger.
'That was a long sleep' I said, 'Maybe you'll tell
Me now if there's anyone alive or dead you ever
Loved as much as you wanted heaven and feared hell.'

That old sly look came back into my corpse's eyes.
I continued, 'Tell me, now that you're gone
Beyond this world of treachery and lies,
Are you part of the earth the sun the moon
Or some reticent star I've never dreamed of?
Or are you what the evidence suggests, mere dust?
If you'd rather not answer, I understand.'

'Do you?' grinned my corpse. Then, 'Whom did I love?
Retrospection is treacherous, there's the problem of lust,

I'm your past, your future, your only friend,
The last, vigilant spectator
Of what you have yet to suffer.'

I should have been consoled; still my anxiety grows.
Why did I cut myself down? Curiosity, I suppose.

Last Moments

Wars before and after
Howl through the last moments of my silver laughter.

Glint

Equipped with my Penguin *Iliad*, some German beer
And a goodly supply of potatoes
I went digging for myself. Down through four
Cities I dug though plagued by mosquitoes

And recurrent bouts of malaria. Beneath
The cities was an arena. I listened
And heard the heroes confronting death
In each other. Down through the arena I pen-

etrated for two festering summers till I found
A silver mask. I lifted it, saw my face,
Teeth perfect, jaw firm, eyes speculatively bold.

I kissed my lips in that most holy ground.
I was perfectly preserved, the mask was flawless,
My silver has a glint not known in Homer's gold.

Alive

Towards the end of the fortieth century
In various countries, they were countries once,
A strange legend grew up about me.
Three persons, each of equal significance,

Were said to live in me.
                I was one.
I did something someone considered wrong,
I was handed over to the public executioner,
Right man for the job, didn't take him long.

Were three persons hanged? No. Just one.
                And one head
Bit the dust. Versatile to the end
I picked it up, it made an innocent moan,

I took it with me to the field of the dead,
Buried it in my own grave. I find
I'm alive when I make legends of my own.

Gods and Servants

It's what I must enjoy, this tripping among legends
Gathered by scholars from lands near and far.
The legends celebrate tenacious lights
And capable stars

Or so I think, hearing the legends told
At concerts weddings assorted fêtes.
I see the giants and the dwarfs converging
For their têtes-à-têtes.

The scruffy wizards preen themselves like sparrows
Waging World War Three in a suitable pool.
Sparrow-obscenities tend to shock me.

A summit meeting of yesterdays and tomorrows
Shows one last king and his obstreperous fool
Trying, failing to unlock me

For I was present when the legends said
They'd be my gods and servants if I trapped them in my head.

Comment

How could she know, that girl from the hot
Village at the edge of the legend-lake
Deep and rippling through her childhood
The ebb and flow of every give and take

Among parents sisters brothers and the one
For whom she knew that she'd give all
And all would never be enough, she thought;
Caring him when his day's work was done,

How could she know, opening under him
One sharp March night of witnessing stars
And the occasional slouching cloud

That in her body was the tame
Beginning of the man whose name still stirs
Comment for the way he treated God?

It Is Done

Betrayed?

I betrayed
Nothing or what has become
Nothing worth
Betraying.

Or I betrayed
What lay beyond my comprehension
Puzzled me
Made me feel foolish
Made my understanding of things and people ridiculous.

I betrayed another kind of mind
A tolerant emptiness
An obsession with death
A style
A hatred of money
An addiction to folly
A rage against what is necessary and inevitable.

I betrayed an impossible attitude to the world,
An absurd approach to the ways of men,
A refusal to understand
The complexities of genetic engineering
Or the Master Race that must happen
When the loony-bins in the head are evacuated and burnt to the ground.

I betrayed a monster whose words would have crucified
The efforts and hopes of decent men;
Who would have me walk naked in a murderous climate,
Whose alternative to plague and the grey face of cancer
Lay in a fabricated lambasting of the self
And too much mocking spittle for comfort.

Comfort!
I betrayed a restless isolationist
Too guilty or hung-up to be comfortable,
Who never understood the primitive,
Cosy weekends of desire and fulfilment,
Who had a talent for fucking things up at the wrong moment,
Who could never accept the happy humming of the fridge in the kitchen
Or the plans, the plans for the bright brats of the future.

I betrayed
Spirit-killing organisation
And all its crawthumping fathers and mothers and daughters and sons.

I betrayed
The maker of the money-climate,
The father of the white bankers of international skill and concern
The sustainers of famine
The grotesque moralities of happy men
The Concorde sky of sophisticated mayhem
The angels of heavenly hospitality
And the whores and pimps of too-much-to-eat.

I betrayed
The origin of my own defeat,
The inspiration that caused me
To be.

And I did not betray
Myself.

What I did
Is done.

I am not one in three
Or three in one
But myself alone.

So cut to the bone, launch the ship, join the club,
apply the knife, tighten the knot, get the divorce,
measure the drop, kill the poet, honour the censor,
clinch the deal, organise the camp, advance on the birds,
find 'em fool 'em fuck 'em and forget 'em,
refuse to think, live in the land of the should-have done,
help me to see myself,
o for a bursary a house in the country
a well heeled centrally-heated sabbatical,
fix the count, arrange the promotions,
turn might-have-been into bitchery,
get into line, polish the cat,
stand back and let the dog see the rabbit,
o the style of that chancer and my Johnny on the dole,
watch the fiddlers at their music,
pay the bills, kiss the mortgage,
screw the system, praise the daubers, decorate the interiors,
say fame though you're lame is the name of the game
and never never fuck the begrudgers.

Be he damned or blessed
Whoever has done it will say
It is finished, It is done.

Ite, missa est.

I Meet Myself

After twenty centuries of vigilant sleeplessness
I am alive and well
As your average unfortunate traveller who has
Sidled through hell.
I thought I'd put an end to me
When I dangled like a doll
In my agony-ecstasy.
Ach! Not at all!

I meet myself in Houses of Parliament,
Brothels, churches, pubs, igloos, bungalows,
Funeral parlours where old friends lie in state.

I am solving a teenager's bewilderment
I am the first suggestion of an overdose
I am a whisper in bed to an opening mate.

Am I There?

When you speak of me, remember this:
I was chosen.
Don't try to understand too much,
The act is frozen
In time, repeated in eternity.
There may be tenderness in rape,
Courage in murder, respect in blasphemy

But there's no escape
From those who make me human, satanic,
Divine, confused, lucid, alien from the good
While God's terrible secret is locked in me.

Drunk with insomnia and dizzy dialectic
You streel the streets of Malmö in your blood
Raving to join the Redeemer in hell.

Am I there? At the bottom of the sea?
At table with you, convivial as you'll find?
In your heart, prisoner in his cell,
A cold, elusive, blind
Image of freedom in your mind?

Long Trek

I made the long trek to my grave
And stood there looking at the luminous grass
Cheergirling from my corpse with a gusto
I'd rarely managed in my life
And I found myself saying to myself

     'Judas, old son, I hope you're OK
I hope you're at peace, I hope you're out of hell,
I hope you're not suffering there

What I'm suffering here, and if you can,
Give a teeny-weeny sign to say you're all right.'

A teeny-weeny sign. Well, as the knacker said, there's the rub.

No reassuring mutter or gurgle rose from my buried man.
I left my grave, walked away in the useful light
And consumed much bread and wine in my favourite pub.

There I met, pint of Guinness on his knee,
    Large whiskey in his fist,
    Jeremiah Michael O'Dee
    Stalwart follower of Christ
And champion gravedigger for parishes around.
    Had he not dug my own?
Jeremiah had a twisty subterranean mind,
    He was an earthy man
And when he told me of the bones he'd shovelled over his head
To make space for me, he laughed and said
'Your grave is comfortable as a featherbed,
    You won't feel the time passing,
While the likes of me is sweating and digging
Bone-idle you'll be lying peacefully disintegrating'

Why, with these consoling words, with bread and wine,
        Was I uneasy then?
I cannot say. My little grave is mine,
No different from the graves of other men.

The Back of My Hand

I know myself like the back of my hand.
I rarely glance at the back of my hand.
Question me not about the back of my hand.

Mix-Up

An old woman of the roads once told me
The inadvertent switching of name
Bracelets in the Morning Star Hospital
Led to a baby mix-up in which some

Stupid nurse gave me away to strangers.
That moment of confusion deepens my life's irony
And causes my gorge to palpitate with anger.

I am not the man I am said to be,

I am someone else, someone else is me,
I wonder what he thinks of his position,
Does he know who he is in his swapped heart?

If I were in my rightful place would I
Have earned my dubious reputation?
Did earth and heaven con me from the start?

The allocation of name bracelets is a difficult art.

Becoming

I am becoming myself, a nothing, a myth,
Everything you'll ever want me to be.
There was that story of being born in Mexico,
Reared by serfs, bought by a touring lady,
Exported to England, polished at Oxford,
Stand-up comic in the BBC,
Got shingles, hit the drink, recovered,
Dabbled for years in a fashionable ology,
Converted to the Church of England for a while,
Was priested, opposed the ordination of women,
Fell in love, dear Mary, lost, managed to survive,
Took to fasting, perfected a hermit style,
Died in my chair one winter afternoon,
A fellow mythmaker swears I'm still alive
Somewhere in North Africa, waiting for the opportune
Moment to resurrect and call the tune.
Time, o ye demons, for a trueblue screw under the moon.

Let Me Be the Thing I Am

Above all, I pray you, do not fabricate me,
Don't make me a butt, a scapegoat, a paradigm,
Ne plus ultra, sine qua non, epitome
Of this or that.
        Let me be the thing I am.
I'm not a dartboard to be darted at,
An old Nazi to be hounded, caught, tried,
Sentenced, hanged. I'm not Herod lying in state
Or Pilate turning aside.

I'm someone I don't know, yet I know this:
If you see my face blush till the blood
Is fit to break the skin while I try not to cry;

Should I shift from foot to foot, make choking noises,
Sweat like rain, disintegrate like faith in God,
Don't make my lie your truth, my truth your lie.

Future Guilt

The mountain is judging me tonight.
I've been hauled here into the Black Valley
And made to stand before that tribunal.
A few stars have scurried away in terror
And hidden their faces in darkness beyond darkness.
The moon spits, gives a sneering grin
That in a tick disfigures time and space.
What is my sin?

The mountain is listening.
Some new stars are giving evidence,
Their faces made of hate, their tongues filthy.

The jury of planets doesn't miss a thing
And the verdict makes sense.
Guilty. The mountain repeats it. Guilty.
I will be sentenced in the Black Valley.
When I hear it pronounced in appropriate tones
I don't know what to make of the sentence:

I'm to bear the weight of the mountain's shadow
Till my blood vanishes and my bones
Melt. Wherever I travel on earth
The mountain's shadow will be mine.
Day and night in sun and wind and ice and rain
Nothing I do will shake it off.
The more I struggle to be free
The more it will burden and entangle me.
I must never protest or question
Because when the mountain passes sentence
On a man, it's the end, or the beginning, as you will.
The shadow I cast now is mountain-huge, and growing still.
If follows me like future guilt,
Stretches before me like my past
A malignant judge who'll never rest
Till he's convicted me of waste
And sentenced me to a black hole
In the middle of my heart:
I'll be a lump of writhing dust
Hating the thought of what I am.

Therefore, one evening, late September,
Sauntering down an empty street
I strangle my own shadow.
        I do, I know I do.

Forever and forever I'll remember
My strangled shadow in the mild light.
If shadows die this death is true.
If not, shadows lie too.

Justifiable Homicide

Do you have much interest in people
Who kill each other because they
Twist something that happened on a hill
A long time ago?

Are you a reader of the longest history
Of perversity known to man?
Have you boils of prejudice? Lumps of hatred?
Are you wrinkled with condescension?

280

Are you taken by those honest joes who make
A living out of the blood
That flowed like the sheer
Outsidedness of God

Wanting not wanting to get through. There's no getting through,
There's happening happening happening
Leaves in a flood, kids in famine, beggars
In London and Dublin, begging.

And there's the loneliness that sees all this
And lets it happen without what we know of concern
Nor do I complain or comment because I know
The fields will change, the sun burn,

My foolish mind pick at fragments
Like sparrows darting among gravel,
Children will frolic with Satan, priests try to explain
And thinkers chance their arm at good and evil.

This unrepeatable morning a magpie swerves, plunges,
Rises, picks a spot, settles in a tree.
I'm thinking about people who kill each other.
Somehow, they're killing me.

Arrived

Judas, my age my love my self my art
My mortgage my job my pension my memoirs
My dreams my critic my radio my pen
My eyes my words my words

Refusing to say me, saying there's nothing to say,
Slipping down laneways like poets who know
Poems are no longer needed and little apples
Won't grow some later day.

Judas my school my holiday my official reading list
My summer job my fourth world my plan for killing pigeons
My books my footnotes my arthritis my inner city
My pub my career my bit on the side my plans for retirement
My lump of concrete flung from the terraces

My broken bottle in this drinker's grip
My nuclear reactor my shrink my greed my fear
My hands my lips my tongue my stink my mortality.
I know I've arrived, can you tell me why I'm here?

TEN

Some lads

Out there in there

Bomb is tired squatting there, doing nothing,
Just waiting for that ultimate ecstasy.
This morning, Bomb said it was planning
To play with modern poetry.

'Out there in there where the last word won't go
Where no word has ever been
I would like to hear a poem ticking
Like my heart. Let the Tick
Be tender blunt uncouth obscene

I will study it more mercilessly than anyone
Has studied me. Tick, tick, I will make
That tick my own,
Plant it in a word I will menace into being,
A word to do with known, unknown,
In me of me beyond me
Breeding a new ancient poem
Tick, tick,
I will study
Until it merges with my bone,
Bonepoem, bombpoem,
One-word-poem-tick-tick-way-of-seeing
Into the flash that is beyond all believing.'

Deep

Much of it seemed inspired conjecture
Yet I was animated that logical afternoon
When Dr Rufus Moon
Gave the special Easter Monday Lecture
On *The Nature of Self*. It was splendid
And perspiringly attended.
Dr Moon was deep, so deep
Three lady academics were seen to weep:
Sibyl Killitt, Sowena Glume, Devina Heepe.

Intellectually spent,
I betook me to my couch of legend

In my bedsit
Where I dreamed
I drank my piss from a golden cup
And ate my shite from a silver plate.
Dr Moon has popped into the world of light
And I am left with this funny appetite.

Guess

I met Gee-Gaw Chatterton in Holland.
He's a traveller through the world. He told me
The best way to raise cash nowadays
Is through forgery. Gee-Gaw had forged three

Copies of the Kabala, two of the Koran
And was at work on *Much Ado About Nothing*.
This he described as throwing the shit in the fan.
I decided to try my hand at forging

One of the Four Evangelists, masters of bonny prose
Who translate badly but get a grip on people's minds
With their fetching versions of that remarkable story.

I set to work, I toiled for heady days,
I sold my finished text. Flawless. Scholars find
It magnetic. Which of the Four is it? Guess. Go on. Try.

Terms of Revelation

Professor O'Paytreat is getting eighty thousand
Sterling
For a preface and postscript to The Sparrow Edition
Of *Ulysses*.

Professor Tegrotty has signed a contract
For three million dollars flat
And a monthly expense account of twenty thousand
For a life of Sam Beckett.

And what in God's name is the life of Sam Beckett?
Don't we all know he taught French, played cricket,
Joined the Resistance, got stabbed, wrote books,
Was economical with the truth?

And what about me? It ain't fair, feck it,
Who'll pay me for my poem about
My investment in God and other ticklish matters?

Who'll reveal me to the lewd-studious mob
In a preface an intro a shamelessly honest biog?
When terms of Revelation are legally agreed
How much will the bugger get paid?

The Dinner

James Joyce had dinner with the Holy Family
One Saturday evening in Nazareth.
Mary was a good cook, her Virginsoup was delicious,
Joyce lapped it till he was nearly out of breath.
The Holy Family looked at Joyce who said
Nothing, he was a morose broody class
Of a man, his glasses made him look very sad,
It was next to impossible to get him to talk and
The dinner was uncomfortable as a result.
'How're things in Ireland?' asked Joseph. 'Ugh' said Joyce.
'What're you writing now?' persisted Joseph, 'I couldn't find fault
With your last book. Perfect.'
                                        Joyce seemed to sulk.
'A large work' he muttered, 'Like the Bible. The sea. My voices.'
'Am I in it?' queried Jesus. 'Yep' said Joyce 'Pass the salt.'
'Is it too much to enquire about the rôle I play?'
Continued Jesus. 'It is' said Joyce.
Mary changed the subject. 'Are there many grottoes to me
In Ireland?' 'Countless' replied our hero.
Joyce's short answers were buggering the dinner up.
'The Society of Jesus' queried Jesus 'How's it going?'
'Who knows Clongowes?' said Joyce 'Could I have a cup
Of Bewley's coffee to round off this occasion?'

'Why did you leave Ireland, James?' queried Joseph,
'The Swiss, French, Italians are just as lousy
In their ways.' Joyce pondered. 'Crime'
He replied, 'Of non-being.' Jesus butted in:
'In that case you must have sinners in plenty.
I think I should visit Ireland, sometime.'
'I wouldn't, if I were you' said Joyce.
'But you're not me' said Jesus 'Though there
Are times when you behave as if you were
The Son of Man Himself. You get in my hair,
James, from time to time, with your pretentious
Posturing, sitting on a cloud, paring your toenails
In an orgy of indifference, pissed on white wine.
Though I readily admit your prose is divine
With touches of Matthew Mark Luke and John,
Why can't you be an honest-to-God
Dubliner, go for a swim in Sandymount, spend
Sunday afternoon in Croke Park or Dalyer,
Boast of things you've never done,
Places you've never been,
Have a pint in O'Neill's,
Misjudge the political scene,
Complain about the weather,
Miss mass, go to Knock,
Take a week in Killarney,
Listen to McCormack's records,
Re-learn to mock, jibe, scandalise, sneer, scoff
And talk your head off.
James, you have a block about Ireland,
You're too long on the continent.
In some strange way, James, you are,
If you ask me, bent.'

'But I didn't ask you, Jesus' replied Joyce,
'It so happens I think things out for myself,
I had to leave Ireland to do this
Because no one in Ireland has a mind of his own,
I know that place to the marrow of its bone
And I insist that people are dominated by your henchmen,
Those chaps in black who tell folk what to think.'

'I beg your pardon' said Jesus 'These men
Are not me.'
       'Would you put that in ink?'
Asked Joyce.
       'In blood' Jesus replied.

'This is getting too serious' Joseph interrupted.

'Shut up, Dad!' said Jesus 'The matter *is* serious.
It's precisely for this kind of crap I came and died.'

'But you're alive and well, son' Joseph said 'You're not dead
And we're the Holy Family. That's what they call us.'

'What family is wholly holy?' asked Jesus.
Joseph looked about him, then at the ground, perplexed.
That honest carpenter didn't seem comfortable.
There was nothing he couldn't do with timber
But this was a different matter.
                              He said nothing,
Just poured himself another cup of Bewley's coffee.
Mary said, 'Let's finish with a song,
Mr Joyce, I understand that you
Took second place
To Mr McCormack at a Feis.
But that's a long time ago, a long
Time ago.
Though second place is not the place for you
Perhaps you'd give the Holy Family a song.'

Joyce brooded a bit, took a deep breath,
Straightened his glasses gone slightly askew,
Coughed once, then sang *The Rose of Nazareth*.

The Holy Family loved his voice.
It was pure and clear and strong,
The perfect voice of the perfect sinner

And the perfect end to the dinner.

Every Decent Family

Every decent family should have a brothel attached
Instead of a half-hearted garage.
How else can they be expected to survive
In this age of hate and rage?
Keep a whore instead of a car
Your man is happy
Driving her to work
Nearly every morning of the year.

The whore keeps the wife alive
The wife hates the whore
The whore screws the man, the man loves the wife,
It is always possible to entertain a guest,
The garage boasts old tyres and plastic bags
Though there are times when the desire to burn
Everything to the ground can scarcely be suppressed.

A Game Lad

Pontius Pilate did his Ph.D. on the theme of
Crucifixion in the Post-Post-Modern Novel.
He ensconced himself in the British Museum
And waded through oceans of relevant material
Much of it, sad to relate, drivel.
But Pontius persisted for he was a game lad
Pouring, year after year, body and soul
Into the task; and he came up with the goods.

The External Examiner, Oxbridge man,
(No equal in the field,
It was agreed)
Gave the Governor a rough passage in the oral exam
Yet, in the end, he covered Pilate in glory
Noting, in his report, that here was a fine
Scholar incapable of even a teeny-weeny sham,
An academic colossus who'd doctored the authentic story.

K

Table for Two in a Hurry

'We'd just escaped from Portlaoise
And were on our way to Dublin
When Dicky suggested we try the New Paladin.
We had chicken liver paté and melon for starters

Followed by turkey and ham.
Dicky kept glancing at the door.
All dishes were accompanied by lettuce
Tomato and coleslaw.

A Garda streeled by the window.
Dicky had meringue glacé.
I had hot apple tart with cream.

We finished with a pot of tea.
Dicky said he was ready for Dublin.
The Naas dual carriageway was a dream.'

No Time for Answers

Of the dubious creatures slouching on this earth
Flanagan intrigues me most:
He'd edit Nature, adjust the nameless planets,
Sell bibles to suburban housewives
Then give them the fuck of their lives,
Make a cock's hat out of the Holy Ghost,
Demonstrate the exact ways in which anarchy is order,
Explain why Judas is not a popular Christian name
Explain the fallacy of fame
Breakfast on the morality of murder
And discourse on the origin of the sense of shame.

Turning on me those eyes which on this winterday
Are marine green daggered by freezing blue
He asks 'Judas, what is fear?'

This is no time for answers, I snake out of his way,
Here's an airport ticket, I'm gone, where am I now?
Wherever it is, thanks be to Jesus Flanagan isn't here.

Faces in the Crowd

The hideous visibility of the faces!
>Flanagan laughing
>Flanagan weeping
>Hitler sniffing
>Hitler speaking
>Herod musing
>Pilate washing
>Pilate judging
>Pilate bleating
>Barabbas eating
>But worst of all
>On an icy morning
>Knifing the bone
>Nightmare over
>Daring the mirror
>– My own.

Interest in Systems

Pontius Pilate's interest in systems of Penal Law
Began soon after he'd washed his hands
Of the man who kept his mind to himself
As though bored with questions
Or suddenly knew he had nothing to say
Of the slightest interest to a Roman (or any) Governor.
Pilate lusted for dusty tomes on various Penal Codes
Till he achieved the mask of an erudite cadaver.
How his eyes would squint with knowledge, his voice waver!
He studied intricate systems of humiliation and degradation,
Dispossession so intrigued him he wondered at his own nakedness,
The imposition of utter dark on tenants caused him to sit alone
Unconsoled by anything but a few Mongolian love-songs
Which to other ears would be chastely lyrical
But cut informed Pilate to the scholarly bone.

The Wrong Finger

On one of these divine mornings
That never fail to augur well
For blind mankind, I attended the wedding
Of Heaven and Hell.
Hitler and Eva turned up, I sat with Marilyn
Who was pregnant with delight.
Heaven sublimed in a skyblue suit.
Hell was all in white.

The world was a church that morning
The congregation, drawn from history and myth,
Emitted gasps of adulation.

Hell blushed when Heaven slipped the ring
On the wrong finger but we all drowned in joy
Knowing without contraries is no copulation.

Stag Party

Limbo was Heaven's best man.
He organised the Stag Party the night before the wedding.
This Men Only affair got off to a good start
With Limbo cracking jokes and Heaven drinking

As if he wanted to forget something.
In that male, celebrating room
Limbo made a speech full of happy stories
Slanted to poke fun at the bridegroom.

Heaven responded by drinking more.
No wonder next morning
Heaven was in no fit condition to follow what was going on.

Limbo, also in the throes of a hangover,
Was muzzy throughout the entire wedding

But Hell, radiant, smiled on that tipsy scene
Of sacred binding

And the road ahead,
                winding,
                        winding.

A Rough Honeymoon

Heaven and Hell had a rough honeymoon.
Hell had a sense of humour
That Heaven frowned on:

> *There was a conductor called Hass*
> *Whose balls were two small spheres of glass*
> *Which tinkled toccatas*
> *And fugues and sonatas*
> *And on Sundays the B Minor Mass.*

Heaven didn't like Hell's banter
And exhorted her to be more serious.
Otherwise, said Heaven, the world will think you're a cod.
Fuck the world, said Hell, I believe in God.
Heaven pushed on: Your breakfast jokes are vulgar.
'How do you like your eggs?' 'Unfertilised.'
That sort of crack is in bad taste.

Perhaps it is, conceded Hell, but we must get to know each other
And jokes point the way to the heart of the matter.
Let's reconcile me laughing with you being scandalised.
Otherwise our marriage is a bit of a waste.

First Year Tiffs

During the first year of their marriage
Heaven and Hell bickered night and day.
You'd see Heaven biting his lip in rage
When Hell was giving out the pay.
On the other hand, you'd see Hell squirming
When Heaven was in a bitchy mood.
At such moments Hell's heart kept yearning
For bitchless solitude.

Teeny-weeny matters sparked instant quarrels.
'You pick your nose' snorted Hell.
'You curse in your sleep' Heaven sighed.

Glances they exchanged were predictably baleful.

'You snore' hissed Heaven.
'You fart' Hell replied.

Despite these tiffs, Heaven and Hell persisted.
They did not take lightly the fact that they were married.

The Main Thing

Heaven and Hell were at a dinner-party one night
And met Micky Moggerley and Sheila Nagig.
'How's the crack in Leeson Street?' said Sheila to Heaven.
'Fine' replied Heaven, 'though Hell is a bit of a prig

And objects to whores shunting up and down
That sparkling thoroughfare'. 'Well then,
I wouldn't worry too much about that' said Sheila
'Whores have a funny effect on women and men.'

'Don't they, though?' mused Heaven. 'It's almost as if
Whores were men's mothers in dreams,
Laying the whole deal on the line once more.'

'Hadn't thought of it that way' said Sheila,
'I wonder if that's why Micky, at times,
Makes me pretend I'm his mummy first, then his favourite whore.'

'Keep it up, Sheila' said Heaven, 'the main thing is don't be a bore.'

What It Means

'By Jesus' gritted Heaven, 'I'll make you suffer
As much as you made me suffer all these years.
I'll make you know what it means to cry to die,
To scream for any form of oblivion.'

'You're nothing if not inventive' chuckled Hell
'I love the way you make things out of nothing,
I haven't a clue what you're talking about but all
The same you intrigue me with your imaginings,
Your ability to concoct images from the abyss
And make them serve whatever purpose
You're promoting at the time.'

'Liar!' exploded Heaven, 'Has our marriage come to this?
Am I living with someone who won't take me serious-
ly? O you fat slug, you rat, you bellyful of slime!'
'Feel better now, my perfect darling?' queried Hell.
'No!' fumed Heaven, 'You grow more and more execrable.'
'I know' said Hell, 'I am fulfilling my rôle.'

Tut-Tuts

'How long are we married?' queried Heaven.
'Feels like eternity' smiled Hell.
'Do you remember?' honeyed Heaven 'You were an
Angel all in white, the belle
Of all the balls that were ever held,
You were radiant, fab, something else,
Out of this world, a picture
To electrify the deadest pulse

In Christendom, you were divine, Hell, divine.
Just thinking about you makes me excited.
Jesus, Hell, you drove me nuts,
Up the wall, round the bend, out of my perfect mind.'

'If that is so' mused Hell, 'Why have you reduced eternity
To a spirithood of polite tut-tuts?'

Preparation

'Communication' insisted Heaven, 'There's such a thing
As communication, you know. No Hell
Is an island, no Heaven either. It's simply
A question of how we illuminate each other.'

'Zat so?' Hell dulled.
'Yes' breezed Heaven, 'And if this
Marriage of ours is to begin to discover
Even a shred of conjugal bliss

You must learn to communicate, you must
Rouse yourself from your infernal torpor
And plant excitement in my brain, my blood.'

Hell's belly swayed, bloated with lust.
'Communication' mumbled Hell, 'is a gar-
rulous preparation for silent solitude.'

'I hear you' said Heaven, 'And I fear what I hear is not good
For our future nights and days.'

'Forget it' slurred Hell, 'There are ways, there are ways.'

A Dream of Hell

I dreamed last night you murdered me said Hell
I was sitting here watching TV
Worried about how in God's name
I'd manage to pay the electricity

Bill for the bad winter months when
There came an educated knock on the door.
I opened it, there you stood, a mad glare
In your eyes, a Hopalong Cassidy Colt 45 in

Your fist, without a word you pumped me
Full of lead, a heavy feeling, I've known
Worse, I remember thinking that as I died.

Then I awoke and here you lie, divinely drowsy.
Thank God I'm alive, I'll have a glass of pure
Unsweetened orange juice, steaminghot coffee and
        brown bread lightly toasted on one side.

So get up, you lazy bastard, and swallow your pride.

That dream, said Heaven, rising, shows you have something to hide.

Smiling Hell

Don't you like my savage smile? smiled Hell,
Isn't it more renewing than yeast-free Vitamin B?
Doesn't it make you feel hellishly well
After you've been split in pieces by

The ravages of good living? Have I
Not seen you glum and lonely on virtue's path
Stepping painfully on the callous gravel
Crushed by goodness and your heart's pure worth?

Ah you are a perceptive devil, conceded Heaven,
You notice many things untainted souls ignore
Though you stink of double-think and vile guile.

One must be what one is, grinned Hell, that's one
Sure five or six, I am what I am, more
Or less, I'm glad you've grown to like my smile.

Put the Kettle On?

'...till death do us part' mused Hell, 'Fascinating phrase!
Till life do us part might be more fit or
It might not. Death gets all the blame these days
For the bad sunderings. But you will never

Part from me, Heaven, will you? If I should
Set up drunken residence in the gutter
Where I feel most at home, whiskey in my blood,
Victim of the filthy truth, mistress of the bitter

Word, stinking ten times worse than usual,
Nailed with the worst name ever spittled in this town,
Whoring in quayside dives that make you frown
Because they separate God from man

And woman, will you, dear Heaven, when all
The known universe has cast me down
And out into universes unknown,
Please whisper, 'Darling Hell, rise up, come home, I'll put the kettle on?'

And Heaven replied: 'I may, and then again, I may not,
But I probably will, my little infinitely stinking pet.'

The Old Days

Having been married for five thousand years
Heaven and Hell parted for a while.
Separation is necessary, they both agreed,
If one is to retain an individual style

And not have it swallowed by the other
Coming too near
To exterminate, lovingly, one's character
And so be a cause of hatred and fear.

Hell went to an island off the coast of Donegal
To make Aran sweaters and home-made marmalade.
Her mental state remained brutishly unwell.

Heaven started a Ph.D. on *Man Before the Fall*
But gave it up, nonplussed. The couple re-united.
'Thank God' sighed Heaven. 'Just like the old days' smiled Hell.

Best Interests

The marriage of Heaven and Hell was bound to crack.
Incompatible, that's what they were, querulous and wild.
When they split, therefore, it came as no shock
To those in the know. Heaven and Hell had one child,

A boy called Navv, that's the Irish for Heaven.
The pair went to court to contest custody.
The judge, who knew both parties well, said
It was in the boy's best interests to go to Hell.

Heaven looked haggard as he brushed past reporters
And later announced from one of his many mansions
The judge had taken him for a ride.

Hell, by contrast, smiled divinely on all comers.
Dressed in white, angelbright hair swept back in a ponytail,
She strode from the Court, laughing, little Navv at her side.

Best of All

Flanagan thought he was Jesus Christ
And Sylvester White was the devil.
Flanagan took a scythe and sliced
Sylvester down the middle.

'It's all over' said Flanagan, 'the world is at an end.'

He wiped the scythe with a fistful of hay.
'There now! The devil is dead, I am man's only friend,
The light, the life, the scythe, the truth and the way.'

Psychotic, the doctors agreed, that's what Flanagan is.
Guilty, concluded the jury, but insane.
Lock him up, growled Sylvester's ghost, throw away the key.

Why must people always want to be Christ
Or the devil? Why can't a man be a man?
Or, best of all, why can't a man be me?
Murderous romantics must be contained, you see.

A Bottle o' Brandy

'an' there was the poor fucker in the hospital bed
dyin', an' the doctor had told him five years
before that if he didn't give up the jar
he'd be dead
in no time. Well, he lasted exactly
five years gettin' pissed out of his mind
in cities all through Europe an' America
but of course he came back to dear old Dublin

to die 'cos it's a marvellous bloody city
to get corpsed in. This was accomplished
for your man when a lifelong friend

smuggled in a bottle o' brandy
to the hospital, your man drank it like a shot
an' that was the end, my friend, the glorious fuckin' end.'

poemprayer

he escaped then from the prison of his body
out into the decent air
leaving behind the pathetic rubbish
that was all right in its own way
and he made a poem to his Lady
that was a true and beautiful prayer

this poem was made out of all his longings
scattered like shells and stones on the shore
it was made of moments after lies were told
and he feared love might be no more
it was made of words lost at night and the tired eyes of women
and shadows gadding on the kitchen floor

it was made of moments of betrayal and wonder
and mockery and slander and pain
it was made of dead friends and enemies
and stories of this man and that woman
it was made of every defeat he had faced or ignored
and hurts known and unknown

today i heard an old man say the poemprayer
in a clear strong voice
that turned this battered world for a moment
into a warm-hearted house
and the clouds of heaven and the stones of the road
were glad to rejoice

The Right Colours

Flanagan asked me if I'd paint the room
The right colours for him.
He might settle in that room, he said, he'd been
Wandering a long time.
Red, I said to the men. They painted red.
It looked good. Yellow, I said.
They painted yellow. Green, I said.
They painted green. I stood

Back. It was a different room, it was wrong,
It stank of betrayal, someone was crying
Behind walls, the air began to bleed.
Black, I said, black it all, the whole damned thing.
They painted black. The room stopped lying,
Told its truth. Black is your man, I said. Flanagan agreed.

Two Picnics

'Bad Bomb! Bad Bomb!' I scolded, seeing
That missionary look in his eye.
'What are you planning? Where have you been?
How many are going to die?'

'Two picnics' retorted the Bomb, 'One in Dallas,
Th'other in Siberia.
At the first picnic I scoffed money and grew callous,
At the second, I chewed a heart-warming chunk of ice.

Siberia has potential, is rather virtuous in fact,
A certain chastity pervades the place.
Dallas is so rotten Dallasians cannot see
Their dreams need to be wrecked.'

'And how will that happen?' I asked, looking the bomb in the face.
'Me' chortled the Bomb, 'Little old picnickin' finger-lickin' me.'

Correspondence

I began my correspondence with The Bomb
Because I sensed we were two of a kind.
'Dear Bomb' I wrote in my opening letter
'Did you ever feel you were going out of your mind?

By that I mean did you ever find yourself
In a place or state where your mind was not?
I hope, dear Bomb, my simple question
Will give you bread and wine for thought.'

'Dear Judas' responded The Bomb, 'How sweet
Of you to write such a candid letter.
My mind, though my thoughts prowl every road,

Is fine. At times, however, I feel a bit of a wet,
Sitting on my arse, waiting. I'd feel better
If I could do what I'm best at. Explode.'

'Be patient' I replied, 'There are bright sparks in our hell
Who'll give you the opportunity to show your style.'

Consequences

'When a man explodes, be it in poetry or love
Or at the Annual General Meeting of shareholders
Feeling screwed because they've not profited enough
In Foreign Exchange, there are consequences'

The Bomb wrote in a thoughtful letter to me.
'Such consequences,' went on The Bomb, 'Can be dire,
Spreading ulcers, causing heart-attacks, oodles of hypertension,
Driving sensitive souls to suicide.

I ponder consequences, overmuch, I think,
But it's all I have to do as I squat here
Like a hunk of Sunday mutton

Wondering what well-trained finger will
Finally, acting on the orders of President Fear,
Push the button.'

A Teeny Bit

'If even a teeny bit of me exploded over London'
Wrote The Bomb one frantic Christmas Eve
On the back of an expensive card,
'Those who'd still be capable of grief

Might see, had they their eyes and
Sufficient thickness of skin and underlying
Tissue, steel surfaces melt, concrete explode,
Fire having a heyday, bridges
And multi-storey buildings destroyed.

And someone somewhere would be overjoyed

To see the tourist industry badly hit,
The class-structure dismantled. Worst of all
Would be the total loss of hope

Not unlike yourself, you miserable shit
When you tried to cope with your treacherous soul
And solved nothing with your coarse rope.'

Final Letter

'If you ever' purred
The Bomb in his final letter
'Realise that in the end will be The Word
And The Word is me

You will Judasout into the desert
And suck the cactusweed to shoot higher
Than any bod has ever been before.
There you will see it all, the entire dream

In the mind of God, you'll see the beginning
None has dared remember, you'll see
The sun dancing with a girl who never heard of sinning
And you'll be the ecstatic naked boy you fear to be

Because you created me. Beware,
Judas, of what you create, although you must create.
Live in the desert where there are no words
Or stay at home and sing "Too late! Too late!" '

I read that letter to my famished heart,
My heart said 'Don't bother to reply.'
I went to the edge of the desert but didn't go in
Because the magpie sun was jabbering in the sky.

More Liver

The mobby afternoon Barabbas was released from prison
He headed straight home to the wife who stared at him
As if he were a heavenly or infernal vision
Or a disturbing blend of both in the heart of her home.

'Darling' said the vision, 'Hop into bed.' She did.
Afterwards, Barabbas said he'd like his favourite dish,
A slippery mountain of lamb's liver and chips.
She watched her munching man. Between gulps he spoke of his release.

'Chap called Jesus' he said, 'Gloomy sort, didn't open his lips,
Didn't complain, either, though the poor sod was pushed about,
Not a protest at every spit, curse, hiss, kick, sneer, jeer, trip, shove.

In prison I'd heard stories about a miraculous prince of peace
But all I saw was a bloke with his mouth shut tight.
Didn't seem to care. He's for it now. More liver, love.'

Heaven

Lazarus and Barabbas slipped out for a *Table for Two*.
The heart of Lazarus began to droop
As he surveyed the chomping undead in the room.
He opted for Resurrection Soup.

Barabbas had *fruits de mer* in a béchamel sauce
Dusted with freshly ground nutmeg. Scrumptious.

Main course: Lazarus had a young Moscow cock
So butterly succulent it gave him a shiver.
Barabbas whose taste made some people sick
Chose creamed calvary of lamb's liver.

Next, a melon of well-nigh decaying ripeness for Lazarus
And a light lemon livercake for Barabbas.

They managed five bottles of the house red:
Heaven for the ex-jailbird and the ex-dead.

Shit-Kicker

An epileptic fish-and-chip shit-kicker from Tralee
Dreams of being an actor, wishes
To play the part of me.
I meet him, stringy, all pimples and rashes,

Flushes, quick glances, false teeth, stinks of B.O.
Powered by vanity.
We talk, I let him escape from himself
To look down on his uncertainty

As yet unscrutinised. He does this,
Doesn't like what he sees, turns away,
His truth white spittle on his lips.

'You shit', he hisses, 'I could stab your eyes.'
'Do not', I said, 'Be wise. People are hungry,
They don't need acting, they need fish-and-chips.'

The shit-kicker's brush with acting is done.
He is himself, no playing, no masks, real natural,
Up front,
Sound man.

Second Place

I never cease to be appalled at how people are forgotten.
I've known outlandishly gifted lads who could
Confront a sceptical mob and wow the sods
With words burning straight from the mouth of a critical god.

And I've known girls, Miranda, Amanda, Jasmin, Bop, Lucy
Who could speak in a way to put godhot prophets to shame.
Where are they now? Drowned, I fear, in the drowsy, cosy, juicy
Pit of marriage. Have a nice day. Enjoy your trip to Rome.

Deirdre has the flu, Deirdre takes to her bed,
Wee Jim and Alanna frolic on either side of her skin,
Neesha is going to Brussels to live at a hectic pace.

Brussels is where people practise how to be dead.
Their skill in this matter so shatters all expectation
The dead themselves are beaten into second place.

Relic

Myths flutter thinking wings about a man,
Theorems from Euclid, plans from Pythagoras.
Of the stories concerning Flanagan
My favourite, epic in its way, has

To do with his Aer Lingus pilgrimage
To the Holy Land where he went on the piss.
Out of his mind, Flanagan had the urge
To bring a relic home that would impress
A hosting of fellow-mythologists.
So off with our hero to the Potter's Field
Where he dug me up. I was less than beautiful.

Flanagan didn't mind. He bagged me. Back home, pissed
At parties in his flat, he drank poteen
Amid a giggle of myth-makers out of my skull

Swearing
As he sucked the good stuff
Through the holes of my eyes
That only a drink from the skull of Judas
Will make an Irishman wise.

Upset

Pilate, darling, I'm upset all day
I didn't want to wake you in bed last night
I had a dream of the man's innocence
I want to speak out
I saw a flower in the middle of a field
I saw weeds organised like armies
Black battalions closing in for the kill
                   I saw a cheese-and-wine party
You'd gathered ambassadors and their wives
             At a jolly function to celebrate
Styles of conquest in different lands

I told you about the flower, the weeds in murderous waves
Converging.
            You turned peevish
'Fetch a basin of water, woman' you snapped
'My hands are filthy, I want to wash my hands.'

An Exemplary Guest

Whenever Hitler visits my bedsit
I share with him my views
On the family customs, sexual habits
And business skills of the Jews.

I find him an exemplary guest,
Quiet little man, likes to shave closely,
Circumvent his moustache, choose
His few words precisely:

'Please, no trouble on my behalf, I'm just
Happy here, thank you.' He goes to pains
To compliment me on my conversation,
My self-portrait, my home cooking and baking.

I feel at ease here with this gentlest of men
Though sometimes outside my door I get the notion
Someone is quaking.

Step

Hitler said 'Judas, I hate the way I walk
When I take a few steps I feel tortured.'
'Walk' I said. Hitler obliged.
'You move like a ruptured duck' I ventured,
'You must walk like the man you are
As the wind performs in its own style
As a star is itself and not another
As a bolt of lightning defines the sky.'

'That is a shrewd outburst' Hitler said,
'I want you to teach me the Hitlerstep,
When I take that step it is me, no one else.'

For a year I trained him. Times he cried
And swore he'd give up but he stepped
His own step in the end, all false
Steps disappeared. When he took
One step of his own
Onlookers froze to the bone.

308

Pigeons

Hitler is pigeons.
Every Sunday morning he's off with Sinbad Kelly,
Cocoa Brogan, Boyo Coll, Ructions Kane
And other members of the proletariat
With hundreds of pigeons in small boxes.
This is how your honest worker whom
Hitler loves to befriend, relaxes.
Heavenwards the pigeons roar, the game
Is on, the Sunday workers and Mein Führer
Gape at the spectacle, the pigeons vanish
In the blue or grey or black, will they return,
Will instinct betray them, have they art craft guile,
Can the birds of the air be trusted or
Will they betray these honest men?
                    In time, a pigeon
Appears, settles on Hitler's shoulder. A smile
Radiates Mein Führer's face.
In pigeons, as in all things, he loves first place.
The place for others is in the shade.
Luminous the pigeon-hero stands, trusting, unbetrayed.

The Other Side

Three-quarters pissed,
I long for the hard-hitting
Visionary cartoonist
At his most cutting.

I've seen apostles in situations
Of which evangelists knew not the half;
I inform Hitler, he says
'I'll cartoon them for a laugh.'

Off he moustaches to his rented
Cottage the other side of Hackballscross,
In two days, fat with cartoons, he returns.

I devour the cartoons. Talented
Is not the word. What a comic genius
Is that fussy wee man. My heart burns.

Height

Others, interpreting gnomic utterances,
Employ devices of ideological weight;
I, following my foxy senses,
Marvel at men of a certain height.

Listening to Hitler speak of his plan
To wipe all Jews off the face of the earth
I was prompted to ask 'What height are you, man?'
Mein Führer turned haughty, all trace of mirth

Scarpered from each angle of his moustache.
'Five foot three' he sniffed, 'And you, Judas,
What height are you?' 'Five foot four' I replied.

'What height is Jesus?' Hitler asked. 'Six foot dead.'
'Is he too tall for his boots?' the Führer probed.
I looked down on Hitler, waited, nodded, sighed.

Winston Added Brandy

Whenever Hitler discourses on the skill
Necessary for war and the extermination of the Jews
He reflects at length on Winston Churchill
And that great man's epic love of the booze.

Winston, says Adolf, hated the taste of water.
It had an emaciating effect on his mind
And might have tampered with his plans to slaughter
The infernal enemies of humankind.

Therefore, adds Adolf, Winston added brandy,
Never in a craven way, to every glass
Containing water. This made him brainy, brave,
Inventive, witty and occasionally randy.
Churchill, moans Hitler, shoved bombs up my ass.
Drunk as a skunk, he learned how to behave
In ways that brought him his immortal glory.
Now, if I'd behaved like that – a different story!

Through a Pleasing Mist

One dreaming morning through a pleasing mist
In the Garden of Eden I saw Adam
Pissed.
At first I was tempted to kid him

But noticing a knifey look in his eye,
Refrained.
'Christ, Judas' he moaned 'I'm fit to die!
That cider! It's bombing my brain!'

'What cider?' I asked.
'All the little apples of Eden' Adam replied
'I made cider of them, drank the lot.'

He puked. 'That's knowledge' I remarked.
'That's cider' he wailed, 'Bad cider.' 'Knowledge' I insisted.
Adam sobbed. 'Knowledge or cider' he wept, 'It's all bloody rot.'

Tonal Departure

Sometimes when I speak to Herod of trivial matters
In a slight tonal departure from my customary style
A look of horror and disbelief improves his face,
He treats me like a favourite child.
'I know' says he 'a psychiatrist in Foxrock,
Quite inexpensive, despite the address;
A specialist in typical Irish problems
And a whizz-kid on aberrant Jews.'

Three days later I confront Dr Shamme,
Hands purged like his desk, three teeth boasting gold,
Looks concerned but does he give a damn
About anything? 'Are you cruel, Judas?' he asks.
Silence. 'Cold, do you feel cold, Judas?' he asks.
'No' I reply, 'I don't feel cold. I am.'

Hours later, Shamme stands, a thin professional cough,
Mentions a fee. I stand, smile and say 'Fuck off.'

So Many Names

'Hello, Judas, you whore's melt!'
Is how this jumped-up knacker
Flacks my eye this trumped-up morning
In this snakey place, this bad corner
Where knackers nurture insults like grudges
And fling them at me...why?
Whore's melt? How solid was the lady
To begin with? With what spark did she lie
To spawn me, scapegoat, sinbag, spat-on-myth?
What was the deciding factor when he fucked her?
What did she look like in her sweating pelt?

This prick is right
But I hate him like the sin I'll commit
To give him and his breed the chance
To christen me whore's melt. I have
So many names, names by the bitter score.
Before you were born, I had foul names,
Each name vile as a leper's sore.
There'll be more.

Like a Child

I met Hitler in Grafton Street, he looked grisly.
'Hello' I said 'Old cock, old sport, old stock,
Old trick-o'-the-loop, old throw-me-in-the-thistles,
Old bamboozle-my-brains-with-gas, old rattle-my-bones-with-shock,
Old slash-me-to-death, and how are the balls of your feet?'

'Mein Gott' he replied 'I'm like something the cat
Would bring in and forget to carry out.
But Judas my friend, how come you're so merry?'

'Because' I said 'I have found a job for you,
Your first job since you had to quit Berlin:
You must exterminate all the enemies
Of Jesuits throughout the world.'

The Führer's aspect changed. He was like a child
Who had found his long-lost whore of a mum.

312

'Do you accept?' I asked.
'Six million enemies' he mused, 'Ja, ja, I accept.
And thanks. Six million... May the Jesuits' will be done.'

Scared Shitless

I ran into Hitler escaping from Berlin
Scared shitless, that's understandable, not knowing
Which way the winds of revenge were blowing.
'I've decided' he said 'To come to Dublin,

Good Catholic city, people are just and fair, a
Real advantage to me in my present position.
I'd be honoured to meet Mr de Valera
If you could arrange it, Judas. He's one man

Who appears sympathetic to my cause,
A frequent caller at the Embassy
Enquiring if my Mission is going well or not.'

'I'll do my best, Hitler' I said 'But for Jesus'
Sake please lie low for a while. I'm trying
To nab all Nazis. We Jews are a sticky lot.'

Restraint

Though Flanagan's acting style is not in fashion
– Such volcanic words! Such knottings of the brow! –
He was asked to play Jesus in the Passion
Play at Oberammergau.

Flanagan accepted, rehearsed the part for months.
                On opening day
As Flanagan-Jesus staggered under his cross
                On the way to Calvary

An amateur assassin stepped out of the crowd,
            Spat on him, punched his face
        Screaming 'You perfidious fucking Jew!'

Jesus-Flanagan restrained himself. His voice, when he spoke, was not loud.
    'Wait' he hissed 'Till after the Resurrection
And by Jesus you'll see what I do to you!'

Trial by Television

Pilate objected to the television show
Close-upping his washed hands as though
He had no real interest in being just.
'When people see that show' he said, 'They must

Conclude the Roman Governor doesn't know
How to govern. Look at it! The accused stands there
Looking noble, the mob lusting, the climate grow-
ing murderous, myself seeming only to care

For my own comfort, wanting to be rid
Of this chap, please the politicians and priests,
Wash my hands clean of the entire messy affair.

I'm shown in the worst possible light, a spineless sod,
A well-dressed nincompoop who simpers and bleats,
Jesting 'What is truth?' and won't even wait for an answer.

I'm tried already, sentenced to blame for Calvary,
Schoolkids will jeer me through all eternity
But show me the man who knows the whole story.'

'Too bad, Pilate' I said, 'You are what you're shown to be.'
'O Christ, Judas' anguished Pilate,
'Is the whole damned show TV?'

The Calvary Crisis

Crucifixion is depressing but it makes
Fab television especially if it's a rainy
Day at the seaside or near the Black Lakes
Where you repose in hope of becoming less weary
And bored with tedious accounts of endless
Catastrophe.

314

Sky News' minute-by-minute
Coverage of the Calvary Crisis
Together with the Beeb's incisive and comprehensive
Bulletins should keep you up-to-date
With every detail
Of this horrific but fascinating event.

There'll be an open discussion on the Late-Late
Show, dealing with some if not all
Of the consequences. Don't miss it. I won't.

Isn't it like getting a promise from the Son of Man
That we'll never be bored again?

Steely Midnight Peace

'Flanagan!' breathed Barabbas, 'Ah! Flanagan!
For how many years did I die in the next cell
To that renegade spacer? Next cell to Flanagan
Was melting in a suburb of hell.
He had AIDS or believed he had AIDS
And liked to broadcast this fiction-fact
To screws and prisoners of all classes and grades.
Everyone said he was crackt

And when he slit his wrists one night
(Ah the steely midnight peace of prison!)
He poured blood into a cup, flavoured it with piss
And started to roar with all his might:
"Wake up, you sleepy bastards, get into line,
Queue for my cup, step up, and drink of this."'

Worst of All

'What was it like in jail, pet?' Long Moll said
To Barabbas one winter night when the wind
Howled like souls who know they have sinned
Against heaven and are suffering. Long Moll's sleep was bad

And she longed for a post-midnight chat.
Barabbas stretched, opened his eyes. 'Jail!' he spat, 'It
Was like being buried up to your nose in shit.
My best friend was a fat thief of a rat

Who shone a starved eye on me in the dark.
I was locked up for eighteen hours a day.
There's only one word for the toilet facilities: hell.

There was no sex, darling, so I had to jerk
Off all the time. The grub was rubbish but worst
Of all was Flanagan, raving in the next cell.

I could write a book about Flanagan. But hang me if I will.'

That Divine Performance

Barabbas, a more involved man than your average historian supposes,
Got stuck into the Prisoners' Rights Movement
And wrote an opera for the men in Portlaoise
Entitled *Barbed Wire and Roses*.

He produced and directed the show himself.
On opening night
The best people, including the Taoiseach and President,
Said the thing was a delight

Making the heart leap, eyes weep, spine tingle,
Mind think twice about goose-pimples
Sprouting like tiny bombs in the audience's flesh.

Barbed Wire and Roses travelled to prisons in Cork,
Limerick, Dublin: 'But crucified Christ!' beamed Barabbas
'Will you ever forget that divine performance in Long Kesh?'

The Ticket

Barabbas who'd been in jail for fifteen years
Found it hard to adjust to the outside world.
He thought people were staring at him in the streets,
Their fingers pointing, eyes jeering, lips curled

In contempt. He said to Long Moll, his wife,
'I need a break from this accusing town,
There are tongues everywhere judging my life.'
'We'll pack our bags' said Moll, 'And hit for Ballybunion.

We'll go for long strolls on that happy strand
I'll show you the castle, the great cliffs and
I'll tell you the story of the Nine Daughters' Hole.'

Barabbas and Long Moll spent a month by the sea.
Barabbas' persecution complex faded slowly but surely.
The day he left Ballybunion he had a healthy soul.

With his eyes seabright and his skin sunbrown
And the Nine Daughters' story the rage in his head
He laughed scorn on the judges of the accusing town.
'Ah, the sea is the ticket' Long Moll said.

Understandable

On a package tour through eternity
I met Christopher Columbus trying to discover
Something. Isabella, Queen of Spain, shrewd lover,
Gave Christopher the cash to find the Indies
In the Santa Maria, the Niña, the Pinta

But he stumbled on the Bahamas instead.
Christopher and his crew had almost died
Of these diseases you meet when you're at sea.

It is understandable, therefore, that his men
Should set about raping the Indian women
And by the grace of weapons shedding some Indian blood.

'Out here in eternity you've had time to brood on
Such matters' I said, 'What did you bring these people?'
Christopher smiled: 'Pox, poverty and the word of God.'

The Old Solution

Hitler is worried about the brats
'They have no manners on them' he spits
'No please, no thank you, just grab what they can get.
Some nice Corporation man plants trees in the streets,
The brats pull the young things up by the roots.
This is a generation of louts.
I locked one up for a month for breaking a window
Thinking he might experience a certain sorrow,
A brief transfiguring moment of remorse.
Not on your nanny! The bastard got worse!
The old solution returns like a dream I can't forget,
My brats need a chastening whiff of gas,
If the dream won't happen you must make it come to pass,
I'll put manners on my darlings yet
And though I'm not as young as I was
When I wrote my stirring little book
I am patient and passionate still
If I know the cause is good.

　　Not for ages have I been so convinced
Of the need to get something done:
If the brats refuse to learn manners
Barbarism is come again.

It is time for the airing of strong wills,
The clean execution of a purpose
Thought-out and expressed.
It is time to resurrect the old skills
Which, properly applied, leave the loutish millions
Impressed.'

Picking Blackberries

Hitler is blind and vital as a man
With a thesis about poetry or the gospels.
He knows he knows what happened
And why. He could turn women into gulls,

Gulls into submarines, submarines into men.
He burns with wisdom and skill.
Language is a slave in his presence.
He respects the Commandments, except *Thou Shalt Not Kill*

Which is, he says, a wishy-washy bit of thinking.
He adores perfection.
His favourite colour is white.

When we yoga together or go picking
Blackberries in Connemara, he murmurs
He's glad he's seen the light.
When he bids the mountains move
The mountains move.
He has a thesis to prove.

Holiday

Exhausted after the Fall of Man
I packed my bags of sin
And took a fortnight's holiday in hell
Hoping to find my origin –

al soulgusto. In the lower depths I ran
Into Charles Stewart Parnell.
He looked tired and sad. 'The Bishops spun
A yarn about you' I remarked, 'Your whole

Dream of a humane island was wrecked.
Isn't love wicked? Eunuchs' envy is fierce.
They nailed you to their Celtic cross despite your gritty

Fight. You poor thing! You still look shocked.'
No words. And then 'I am' he said, 'What's worse,
Though I scour every hole in hell, I can't find Kitty.'

A Foggy Night

Once, strolling through myself, I met The World.
Though it was a foggy night, I could see clearly.
The World said 'On those rare days when I'm not muddled
I perceive that you have cost me dearly.
My best occupants do not trust me as they should
While others, grosser, gorge themselves on me
Forcing their digestive tracts to think I'm God.
You, however, are clear-eyed, you know what treachery

Is, you see through me, note how I'm exploited,
Misunderstood, an abused bellyful of myth, enduring
My difficult weathers, yet you gave me a bad name.'

I said 'World, you've gone a bit soft in the head,
Too passive, tolerant, put up with anything.
Be sinister, rumble, spit fire, growl, go naked and fierce again,
Scare them shitless, steep the bastards in the ancient shame.'

A Costly Enterprise

When Hitler hellforleathered out of bombed Berlin
We decided to rebuild the city,
A costly enterprise, as you can imagine.
My brothers sniffed the possibility
Of making silver and gold out of this.
Upset by the spectacle of greed
I wrote a morality play called *The Need*
For Gas, starring a Jew, Slyluck Preiss
Who concentrates body and soul in grabbing cash
And land and more cash.
                Some say Slyluck is sick.
An enviromentalist wants to send him to Auschwicz.
Opening night, some of my Jewish friends rush
The stage, shouting 'Judas is anti-semitic!'
They scab my carcass with anti-theatrical spits.
Did I ever dream my brothers would treat
Me and my small morality play like this?
It wasn't theatre in the round or theatre in the square
Or anything a man might be crucified for.

It didn't even get the chance to fall flat.
The Need for Gas never began to exist.
It was exterminated at birth
As Adolf had considered it a must
To wipe my tribe off the face of the earth.
(He told me once he knew what we were worth.)

Enough survived to exterminate my play
And so my heart begins to entertain
Thoughts of revenge against my brothers prejudiced and blind.
I may not act, but then again I may
And if I do it's likely I'll cause pain
To spitting kin who do not know my mind.
What should one do, betrayed by one's own kind?

Patron Saint

There should be a patron saint of rubbish dumps
Especially when rubbish dumps are people
Who receive a stunning overall majority
In the election of Baduns to take all
The blame for crimes accomplished and imagined.
In a world aglow with perks and privileges
You'll understand how nakedly deprived I feel
In the matter of certain small advantages.
        I've been a rubbish dump a long time now,
Hungry gulls alight on me to pick
Choice morsels of guilt, blame, recrimination, remorse.
        I think of my patron saint's illumined brow
Listening to my prayer mumbled from centuries of shit
But all he hears, clean Jesus, is an old reeking curse.
If my patron saint won't hear me right, who will?
If prayers are curses in my mouth why should I talk at all?
If blood is spilled, blood must be chosen to spill.
If men believe they're fallen someone must exemplify the fall.
Suppose I change places with my patron saint
And he has reason to mouth a prayer to me
Shall I listen and reply? Shall I ignore him?
Choke the words in his throat? Pretend his words are true?
Suppose he has a problem as some saints do
Shall I give the man a compassionate hearing,
Assure him he's not a rubbish dump, a condemned house,

A homesick unemployed AIDS-blasted male prostitute
Subject to cruel tirades of public jeering
('You'll be buried in the arsehole of Tubberneering')?
Shall I open to his pleading, soon or late?
No, I'll be myself, must be, locked self, locked Judas.
O saint of God, what man dare know thy state?

If the Tide Is Right

As any half-assed philosopher will tell you
Without being stimulated by kiss drug knife or gun,
To betray is indistinguishable from being true
If the tide is right. I wanted a son,

No, not a son of God, but a son of man
Nappied at the start, learning to chat with me,
Play football, think, drink, do everything I can
Including betray when necessary.

At birth, however, he proved a monster,
No legs, hands, a hideous grinning stump.
I stuffed it in a bag and drowned it.
Had he been able, he might have said 'Thank you, dad,
For not letting me see the world in which you live.
It must be tough.' With that thought, I wince a bit.

The Light of Men

I saw the light of men in the corner
Of a pub. I was doing the crossword
In the less backward of our evening papers
When a tipsy out-of-work actor

Began to mumble about his lives.
Out of his eyes shone the life that is the light of men
Exhumed from dark theatrical archives
Where old gods snore in the Equity den.

Aspiring gods are gone on strike
Looking for better conditions in heaven.
Hell is satisfied with itself. Well, hell, why not?

The light of men is a laser beam through my mistake,
I read the signs, billions unborn wish to get even
With me. My mind is clear. I'll be here after all the actors rot,
Doing the crossword in the adjudicating light.

Special Decree

'I, Judas Iscariot, am assuming special powers
to take over the authorship of this Book
from my collaborator, Brendan Kennelly, who is a sick man.
I will be working with an Emergency Committee
to run the Book while he is unwell.
                                        The Lads and I
sincerely hope he will soon be better, and that
he'll be able to finish the Book without much
further help from us, once his health improves.
His work on the Book has taken its toll: he's suffering
from exhaustion and judasfatigue, and is presently
convalescing at his summer retreat in Ballybunion. We will
of course let you have further news of his progress.

Until he returns, we will need to make certain changes
to maintain the smooth running of the Book.
Captain Flanagan will be responsible for law and order
in the Poem, assisted by his deputy Major Dicky
(late of Portlaoise) and his team of volunteers.
All religious matters must be now cleared with
Cardinal Caiaphas, representing the Bishops of Ireland.
Literary allusions will be controlled by the Ministry
of the Interior, headed by Mr Harry Novak, who'll have
special responsibility for compound words, neologisms,
references to sheep, puns and other acts of linguistic treachery.
The Ministry of Plagiarism under Mr Barabbas
will look after thefts and borrowings from other books.
Mr Hitler here will deal with your questions, and has
already decreed that question-marks are now banned,
so there can be no questions. I am taking over
personal control of the first person singular.

I am sorry to have to tell you that Dr Pilate
has decided to step down, for personal reasons.
He wishes to spend more time with his family.
We will have to proceed with the Poem without
the benefit of his sound judgment of a line.'

Judas and his Apostles faced the Press
and several Renaissance artists in the Upper Room
from a long table lined with loaves, chalices
bottles of Bulgarian Red, and clusters
of microphones (which the painters chose to ignore).
As he was wishing his fellow author a speedy
recovery, an armoured car and a Crossley tender
burst into the courtyard below, followed by twelve
motorcycle outriders and a Rolls Royce tourer.
The dapper, uniformed figure of Michael Collins
leapt from the car to the rostrum, saying:
'Judas Iscariot, I am arresting you for high treason
and for hijacking this Book. I wouldn't be
in your boots now, for you're sure to hang,
unless I'm mistaken.'
                              A haughty Judas scowled
defiance: 'Micky Collins, you won't pull this
one off. What makes you think Captain Flanagan
and the boys here won't just blow your brains out?'

Collins was either brave or barmy:
'Sure, they won't shoot me in my own country,' he said.

Time

Despite madness and heartache
Despite white supremacy and black magic
Despite heaven's rage and earthquake

Let's take a commercial break.

324

ELEVEN

He will be mist

In They Swept

What I did for the politicians will never
Be properly evaluated.
Once the troubles were over, the miracles
Accomplished and acknowledged, the man dead,

Buried and resurrected as he said he'd be
To spectators at home in sin,
Terrified of grace in exile,
It was time for memory to be exploited
And politicians to move in.

And in they swept like a tide of leprosy
Like a plague of smile smile smile
Like an army of scabs to their own drill
Like a nightmare of handshakes
Like an unkillable smooth lie
Like me standing there, cold, looking up the hill.

Herod's Hiring

Herod nearly came a cropper on the matter.
Senior Members of the Party were furious and gave their reasons.
Worst of all was Herod's hiring of boy
Prostitutes for spanking sessions.

This, Senior Members felt, was really ripping it up.
This was Herod striking a base and stupid note.
It was arranged, therefore, that Herod's membership
Of the Party be put to a vote.

As a mere backbencher, I'd no doubt of Herod's loyalty
And though I've little time for spanking sessions
I couldn't see much point in the fuss.

What do we want of a man? His genius but not his kinky
Needs? Take him kinks an' all, say I, or leave him alone.
I voted for Herod. Isn't he one of us?

The Old Style

I gave up treachery for Lent
And forced myself to meditate
On what sincerity meant.
I gazed long and long at the Irish Free State

Seeking a sincere man or woman.
Sincere. Sin seer. Won't do. I couldn't find
A single soul in the whole island
Whom I could, with all my heart and mind,

Dub sincere. But I tried, I tried, I really tried
Because I am a sticky lad
Once I get something into my head

But I failed, I failed, I really failed, and I sighed
Briefly before releasing the Judassmile
With 'I think I'll return to my old style.'

The Situation

In America when they want to know anything
About the situation, they ask him.
In England when they want to know anything
About the situation, they ask him.
He's the Great Authority, the Big Voice,
The High Mind in the know,
The Source that bright, bewildered men seek out
To find what's true

About the situation. And meanwhile I
Who brought the situation into being
Am left unquestioned in my chair, alone.

Why won't they ask me about the situation?
He's a slick articulate pig, I'm a king
Of fact and language, I'm the man, I cut to the bone,
I took part, I looked, I saw, I heard every word.
Why won't they ask me then? Why am I being ignored?
He's the Judas in the house, I'm the knowledgeable Lord.

The Budding Pharmacist Broods On
The Second Biggest Problem In Ireland

'We had a two-day seminar on shit.
Professor Shaw
Speaking with his delicious Oxford wit
Said there was no discernable principle or law

Governing the ideal shit; yet he would say
That the conical-shaped, soft-textured plum
Replete with roughage and common in the
Fields and ditches of nineteenth-century Ireland

Was it.
Today, however, laxatives and purgatives
Are all the Irish can find.

It is the second biggest problem in the land.
Why, asked Profesor Shaw, do the Irish not realise
That shit is all in the mind?'

Flanagan's Crony

He drank his grief from a glass darkly.
It's a mercy he was taken quickly.

Christy Hannitty

Christy Hannitty was the most accomplished
Castrator of God's creatures in our pious island.
Ever since childhood, Christy wished
To perfect this most demanding craft.
            Bulls, pigs, rams, boys
And countless men victim-witnessed Christy's skill.
            If he could castrate women
Christy would've done that as well.
            Bloody hell!
He was known from Kerry to Donegal

For the gentle way he did the job,
Working his heart out, this most sensitive of souls.
He had one unwavering simple conviction
Which he enunciated with papalbull precision:
'I have all God's creatures by the balls.'

A Mystical Idea

Christy Hannitty thought it would be a blessing
If he cut the balls off all the Bishops of
Ireland because debollicked Bishops are less
Prone to the terrible temptations of love

Than those who are well-hung. Christy
Wrote a letter to Their Lordships, outlining
His plan for The New Purity Among Bishops.
Their Lordships read Hannitty's letter, noting

The crystal prose, the exact expression of a mystical
Idea, the juicy logic of the notion. They
Concluded, as a group, that they'd rather

Keep their balls intact, little as they used them.
They thanked Hannitty for his suggestion. Christy
Decided he'd take the matter up with the Holy Father.

Special Cases

The problem of what to do with the balls
Of all the Bishops of Ireland obsessed Christy Hannitty
To the point of endangering his sanity
Which was always a shaky commodity, anyway.

For Christy it was a deeply human problem
With philosophical and moral overtones.
If God gives a man balls what's he to do with them?
Thank you, God, for balls. Christy spent years

Pondering the problem. He interviewed many people,
Read revolutionary South American theologians,
Probed Flanagan, Joe Soap, scrutinised the faces

Of lechers, boozers, rapists, whores, wankers, all
The usual victims you spy in cities and towns
But he found no answers. Bishops are special cases.

A Short Paper

Christy Hannitty attended a Conference on Castration
In Hackballscross. He read a short
Paper entitled *How to Cut the Balls off Young Fellas.*
The paper was a model of its kind

And showed Hannitty's mind at its most acute,
Logical-lyrical, clinical-intense.
The paper was substantially footnoted and
Was instantly translated into twenty languages.

(Why wouldn't it, for God's sake?) Christy
Had put years of thought and practice into the thing,
His prose was spot-on, grave yet light.

He was confident his paper would be
Significant to all those devoted to castrating
Youngsters. He was right.

A Stirring Account

Jesus took Christy Hannitty out for a meal
And wrote a stirring account of the event
In *Table for Two* in the *Squirish Mimes*:

    'The décor was Last Supperish, the waiters vaguely
Apostolic. I started with peasoup. Excellent.
Christy Hannitty had Dublin Bay prawns
Which looked radioactive to me but
Christy enjoyed them so I said nothing.
For the main course Christy had coddle.
I've rarely seen him look so contented.

I had colcannon. Succulent.
I changed some of the local water into wine
Pretty good though I got some dubious
Looks from the other customers. We finished off
With infinite cheeses, coffee, Napoleon Brandy, for a laugh.
The bill, which I paid hastily (Christy was inclined to pilfer
The spoons) came to thirty-one pieces of silver.
Strolling home, Christy sang *Roll Me Over in the Clover*.'

Hot

Don't tell me the world isn't ruled by liars
Like me. Schultz put all the rebels to rout,
Organised a dinner for the sellers and buyers
Of truth because truth, says Schultz, will out.

Pilate, recently, in a petit bourgeois setting,
Phantomed among sheets and shirts flapping about his head;
Schultz, passing, asked Pilate what he was getting
Up to. 'Hanging out my dirty washing' Pilate said.

By all means let us have a Last Judgment.
Let bank clerks and shopkeepers comprise the jury,
Let the sharpest minds analyse this cosmic rot

While for the umpteenth time the veil of the temple is rent
And I, neat as a flea, fresh as a berry,
Coax the whore truth to bed and fuck her while she's hot.

With Such Passion

The Church bugged the room where the Last
Supper was held because it wanted to know
Down to the final detail, exactly what the most
Wanted men in that part of the world were up to

On that particular evening. As the night wore on
The apostles grew more and more tipsy,
Tongues loosened, old rivalries flared in
The usual way and it fell to Christ

To keep the men in a tolerably harmonious
State. He talked about bread and wine, body
And blood. He asked to be remembered in like fashion.

The Church was listening to all this
But couldn't quite grasp it. 'Has the wine gone to
Jesus's head' muttered The Church, 'that he should speak with such passion?'

A Pitiless Scrubbing

My knowledge of politicians is limited
To the private but passionate conviction
They're more attractive dead than alive.
One politician informs me he thinks
Pontius Pilate a fascinating figure
Capable of governing many lands.
My own experience of the Roman suggests
He's rather too fond of washing his hands.

Winter and summer, by day and night,
Before, during, after drinking and eating,
Following peaceful strolls through green

Unpolluted countryside, Pilate can't wait
To give his hands a pitiless scrubbing.
You'd swear he believes they'll never be clean.

A Motion

I decided The Church's name should be changed
To the Losers' Club. I put the motion to The Church.
'Why?' queried The Church.

       'You've become unhinged
With caution' I replied, 'You've lost the sense of search –
You're out of touch with your origin, the man
Who died for me, you wear pompous clothes,
You eat too much, you're too fond of money,
When did you last smell the Mystical Rose?
Everything you do smacks of vanity and defeat,

You take heaven for granted,
You need to get back in the gutter, you need
To bleed profusely for a while,
You need to dynamise your style, you need to admit
You're the Losers' Club before you're new again.'

'Motion rejected' smiled The Church, 'Let us now pass on.'

Purified

Pretend to be what they believe you are
You are what they believe they think
They want a guiding star you are that star
Want hope, be hope, exist to rise and sink

And listen to the wind that knocks the house.
They want a victim, grab the victim-role
They need a traitor then be treacherous
And feel damnation amplify your soul

They're nothing
But won't allow you to be nothing too.
You must be someone, that's your fate.

Walk where the cliffs are crumbling
Towards the sea so murderously blue
It looks like eyes eyes eyes purified by hate.

One Thing

'I'm sure I'm speaking for all Judas fans
Who've turned out in philistine rain
With the loyalty of Peter and the patience of Job
To see this mortally misunderstood man
Retire at last from the political scene
He has graced through rough and tumble, thick and thin,
From the trusting age of nineteen.

He had his ups and downs
His triumphs and catastrophes
He hit, was hit, booted, was booted, kissed, was kissed.
But, ladies and gentlemen of near and distant regions,
There's one thing we'll all admit about Judas:
He will be missed.'

How Able Is Abel?

Saxon shillings, Yankee dollars, Irish mist:
Cutest hoor that ever pissed.
Turns muck to amethyst.

I Wondered

When they whipped the blindfold off me
The black girl started to sing.
I looked at the circle about me.
Each man was young.

Was that why they tortured me
With boyscoutish enthusiasm?
Were the young men impressed when I
Enacted my deathspasm?

I've always admired this quality in youth,
Scrupulous imitation becoming individual skill.
Under its touch the gangleader died.

The black girl's voice was lusty, almost uncouth,
Yet her passion balmed my lashed soul.
What would she look like, I wondered, crucified?

Thought for Today

Rational suicide, he said, is gravely sinful.
      What right has a lad or lass
In full possession of his/her faculties
To terminate what God has brought to pass?

On the other hand, I can understand
Why a man sticks a rifle in his mouth,
Gets his position right, pulls the trigger and
Blows what's left of his brains out

If he happens to have no work,
No hope of working ever again.
Why is work so important to men?
Without it, only the self, the self's raking pain.
We have hundreds of thousands of unemployed
Potential suicides in our land of busy rain.

Hundreds of thousands. Will they? Won't they?
Well, that's my little thought for today.

The World Shivered

Where were you at the death?
I was watching Aston Villa murdering Liverpool
Having earlier dipped into a Russian novel
About the mysticalmurderous potential of a fool.

Then I glued my brain to the radio
Enunciating the saga of Pablo Dias
Strapped to a billiard-table,
Electric wires leading from his toes

To his mouth. He cursed his captors to the end,
Refusing to betray himself and others.
All through the city, worse things were happening.

After six years, an insurrection of wives, sisters, mothers
Brought trials and judgment. The world shivered
But didn't trouble to notice the other dying.
I hear him crying
True notes of agony amid all the torturing, lying.

The Line

Here's the line, he said,
Cross it, you're a goner.

I looked at the line:
Straight, black, absolutely there.

Stay at your side of the line, he said,
Or it's curtains for you, chum.

Why, I asked, did you draw the line
Down the middle of the bed
Since the bed is big enough to contain
Without bother to either, two grown men?

I sleep this side, he said,
You sleep that side. Right?

Right, I replied, I swear
I'll never cross the line.

If, however, he said, my leg strays across
The line, you'll understand, won't you?

That'd be an accident, I said,
How could I blame you for that?

Thanks, he sighed, I feel better now,
Knowing I won't be punished if I go astray.

Sweet and deep be your sleep, I murmured,
The line is there between us to keep us together.

You have a way with words, he said,
And dozed off. So did I, the straight
Black absolute line down the middle of the bed,
Down the middle of my head.

A Modest Advertising Campaign

You would think, would you not, that it would be
A most difficult task
To get people to purchase my Pure Poisons
Manufactured in my personal factory
In Listowel. In fact, all I had to do
Was mount a modest advertising campaign
Stressing the value of Judaspoison to all who
Are interested in the true nature of man.

Within three days, my poisons found their way
Into the mouths of lawyers teachers priests
Doctors executives entertainers clowns bores
News announcers continuity girls actors poets
Shopkeepers publicans professors editors bishops
And the busy cunts of profiteering whores.

Impossible

Conspiracy is impossible to disprove.
Am I involved in one? Are you?
If you are, are not, how do you know?
I/you go about our work, eat
Sandwiches at breaks, face every task,
Draw the pay, pay the tax, enjoy
The weekends, endure Mondays and never ask
Is this a conspiracy?

Can I prove it's not?
Will you insist it is?
Victims? Perpetrators? Or someone not like
Either? Do we love the rut?
Break it, have we friends who'll write
To the papers if we go on hunger-strike?
Start a 'Free Judas' campaign
When prison-doctors find
I'm going blind?

Blind. I'll never see you again
And all I see in my starving dark

Is open to question.
Question me under a blinding light.
Ring me with lie-detectors, skilled perjurors.
I'm a hopelessly ignorant man.
I have no answers, none.

Coup

I know the men behind the coup.
You. You. You. And Judas Trueblue.
Government? Failures in crime:
I'll name them all, one by one, in time.

TWELVE

The true thing

I've Only So Much Blood

Dear me, to have reached such heights, such depths,
And then to find a mosquito
Has the upper hand in the hot, foreign night.
Cute little bloodsucker, specialist in vertigo,
Dive-bomber close to my ear,
Such a mighty whine from such a little thing
Creating one more tiny civilised fear.
I've only so much blood. Therefore I sing
Of languages I cannot learn
Dream-images I'll never understand
Neighbours I never dare to know
Delusions of logic among philosophers
This notion I have of living where a few
Decent moments flourish and grow.

Taste

To savour the full taste of betrayal
One must half-love one's victim
And be wholly loved by him
Or her or it or they or all together in a shining choir

Such as, old voices say, surrounds the heavenly throne
In eternal perfection. I take a lamb,
A sheep, a cat, a man, a dog, I call the thing my own,
I savour nature, I betray therefore I am.

Language is a farce.
The fascist flesh rules you and me.
No words can shape the curse.
I lock my lips on nothing and go free

To mope at street-corners
Give pet-names to stars
Ruminate on the factors
That influence the blood of traitors.

Words and Silences Betray

Madness is a monologue. Show me a man
Not mad in deep sleep or crude light
And I shall explain why this woman
Believes she is with child
By Jesus Christ
Or Che Guevara
Who left his shirt and trousers
Hanging on her bedroom door
Before he vanished forever;
Or why this boy,
Believing himself the worst of wasters,
Sits in his room all day listening to the chill river
Talking to his own silence.
There are others I have known,
Masters of monologue, kings of unrelatedness,
Brooding where sunlight touched
Every word, non-word,
Not caring if they were heard
Or lived and died unheard.
Both words and silences betray
The small heartwhispers they are trying to say.

Favourite

My favourite painting is *The Last Supper* by
I forget. Names of painters don't matter a salvation.
Aren't we blessed that paintings are immortal though painters die?
I decided to steal *The Last Supper* one
Leafy October morning from a museum in Rome.
It was Sunday, people were feeling like bed.
With my old IRA rifle, I entered the museum,
Whispered to the dozing guard that he'd be dead
If he didn't part with the masterpiece straightaway.

'In Sardinia' he replied, 'We don't accept such rubbish,
Take the thing and welcome. I'll report it later.'

'You're a fucking moron' I said 'With foul taste.
See! Judas looks inspired.' He looked, pondered, agreed.

The Last Supper hangs happily in my bedsit
Where I sprawl gazing on that handsome
Image of myself, holding myself to ransom.

Field Day

I once tried by hook and by crook
To collect the scattered thoughts
Of the Apostles and their apostles
And publish them in one helluva book.
It was a massive task involving
Research among thieves robbers hitmen whores,
Disentangling strands of public rhetoric
Barbed whispers behind closed doors.

Let me say this: I had a field day
Digging up these thoughts from everywhere
Writing them down, knocking them into shape.

My book says what I've heard people say
At guarded and unguarded moments here
And there. Get it. Read it. There's no escape.

Parodies

The more real the man is the more intent
The pigs are on reducing him
To a crucified parody of himself.
Terror of the real deepens their cry for killing.

I have an unparodied beat in my blood, whether
Good or bad, well I'll leave that up to yourself.
But don't forget, we're in the crucifying business together.

Where I come from is nailed with old stories
Like a field studded with thorns and stones.
We heap mockery on skeletons.
I heard a yarn today grinning through a circle of men:
'Down Baggot Street I saw a tinker's pony

Cartin' a load o' dung. "See!" I said, "Paddy Kavanagh
Is lookin' for digs. The fuckin' poet is homeless again!"'

The lads broke their arses laughin'.

A Ridiculous Song

Pray for the slaughterers of language,
For crimes against rhythm in acquiring minds
Shut and important as Civil Servants
On holidays with gloves and umbrellas
The few good days we get in this part of the world.

Pray for a loosening
Of the arthritic limbs of the spirits
You laughed close to when you were young.
God in heaven,
What is the source of the hardening
And the closing and the deadening of the hearts
That electrified the night with a ridiculous song,
                              So ridiculous
It took the pain from your blood
For a moment, a single, free, forgiving moment,
Enough for you to hear a music
You'd all but forgotten?

A Chanting Ring

The words, sick of folk like you and me,
Escaped, hid under seaweed,
Green weed bloodblackening in decay.
If birds gulped this, they'd die.
Should fish flounder here, they'd gape
Like snotty poets who can't take their drink.
If ailing women crutched here, they'd melt
And spread their sickness like the ways we think.

And who's this man of the horse and cart
Gathering weed now the sea is away
Balancing the world, giving the other side a chance?

He packs the weed into the cart, drives
Over the sand where the sea will be
And not be, and be again, like missionaries
Working on children in a chanting ring,
Acolytes glowing near gods who teach them how to sing
Of matters happy beyond all understanding.

Within Bounds

You know now what it means to be ditched.
You know the presence of the phantom limb.
'Listen to me' you say from your bed near the desk,
'I was Professor of Metaphysics

In an ancient university, I forget its name,
I loved and struggled with philosophy for forty years,
I achieved a certain fame
Among my peers

But now, forgive me, it is all a dream
I am struggling to remember. Why didn't my friends
Visit me? Where are the philosophers I knew?'

I take your hand, tonight you'll rave and scream
In your sleep but that's allowed, that's within bounds,
Whatever else is false, that much is true.
You'll scream your screams, I'll do what I will do.

Once, somewhere

Language hides its face in shame and is no longer willing
To speak of earth or hell or heaven
Or the bloodmarvel of ordinary feeling.
'Look at the lovely picture the child made out of nothing.'
It's a beautiful morning for a killing,

The patriots have struck again, it takes seven
To murder a man, and now they're cheering
Down the lane where he walked as a boy,
As a man with the extraordinary intention of
Working in hopes of settling with his girl
And fathering children to grow in love.
Love! Jeers flood river and lake
Cheers ripridicule the countryside
The sun pukes mockery on roads fields hills
His girl begins to break
The patriots have found a place where language cannot live
The hills are splitting into lunatic screams
The child's lovely pictures are obscene dreams
There is no word that is not a bad mistake.
    Someone prayed once, somewhere, o for God's sake
Don't make me laugh, I could die laughing
At words twisting in their pain,
Murder cheering down the lane.

From This Angle

I commandeered the philosopher, made him stand on his head
So that his penis dripped into his mouth
Like a fountain in the pleasant sun.
'What do you see from there?' I said.

'Your bedsit' he replied with that bullet-mind he had,
'The walls are easier to see from this angle,
There you are in your broody chair, tormented-contented,
And yes I see into your mind, it's full

Of non-thoughts, you're trying to think, you can't,
Why don't you give up, your mind is a rubbish-dump,
Stand outside yourself shouldering a placard, STRIKE ON HERE.

It's time you pulled some creative stunt,
Burn the rubbish, be a politician, a pimp,
Turn me rightside-up please, I am an established philosopher.'

A Winner

Outside the Bank of Ireland she stood
And gazed up at the statue of Grattan.
'Excuse me, sir' she said, 'Don't think me odd
If I read you a poem from the Latin.

Though it was written quite some time ago
These lines will touch your stony heart
For in your day you could be moved, I know,
By choice specimens of the poetic art.

The poem concerns a lady who must choose
Between putting her tongue in this chap's mouth
Or up his arse. She chose his arse. 'Twas cleaner.'

So saying, she read the Latin poem. My views
On poetry are amateur. It has to do with truth,
I hear. Grattan froze. I smiled. The lady picked a winner.
The Bank of Ireland glowed like a belly after dinner.

Bad Language

'One fine day, a scrupulous anti-pollutionist
Dumped all the poets in a river,'
The playwright said.
                    'The river was deep
Enough to swallow each self-scratching creep,
The poets began to gasp, splutter, flounder
Like flies in melted butter, they
Started to sink, it was sad, I was tempted to weep
Because here, drowning before my eyes
Were the spouters of all that's true beautiful wise,
All the creators of beauty in my time.
I stood on the bank, gazing, feeling my soul
Rapt-tragic. Suddenly I saw a log come

From nowhere like a poem, the poets saw it too, they began
To grab the log but there were too many drowning
Bards whacking and strangling each other like madmen
In a black parody of inspiration,

346

They sank in their own clatter, groaning curses
Such as you might find enshrined in satanic verses.

I have never seen so many poets sinking together
Amid such bad language, in such chaste weather.
That mass-drowning shrieks in me. May I never spectate another.'

Dirty Water

I'm slaving away here in the chilly fire of language
My little traitorous bum all frozen stiff
Perished is the cheeky rhythm of my buttocks
My heart is breathing ice through my infamous lips
My fingers have grown stone, I sculpt them with my eyes,
I sniff the tasty cunts of my youth, virginal and hot,
I am chipping out the eleventh commandment in my granite skin:
'Thou Shalt Not Get Caught
Or be the hokey if thou dost
Thou shalt toddle off to hell
Along with the tight-assed
The self-important
The puffed-up wise
And not a word of mercy shalt thou ever hear again.'

I'm in digs now, in this language beyond language
Where all I hear is the sun's rage
Swearing to melt my ice
Into dirty water
Infected-pathetic as language using men
In ways they don't suspect.
                              And this is well
For who could bear the torment
Of one fiery-icy syllable?

Original Manuscripts

'I ran into Paddy Kavanagh one mornin'
And asked him how he felt.
"Fuckin' awful," he replied, "I'm kilt shakin',
Half-blind, bloody bored, in terrible health
'Cos I was up all night writin'
The Great Fuckin' Hunger
For a Famous Institution
Interested in buyin' original manuscripts.
Sure I often claned me arse with poems
Not realisin' I was wipin' shite with cash.
I'll wangle money outa these bastards:
They think they're buyin' me fuckin' classic."

Course we all know his poems sing like a bird.
Isn't that the gassest yarn yez ever fuckin' heard?'

Baptism

Three businessmen, roused, threw the poet
Kavanagh into the Grand Canal
In Dublin. Enraged by hit after hit
Of his venomous persisting wit,
Animated by his ridicule,
They drowned him one misty November night.

      Down in the accommodating waters
Kavanagh called on his won't-take-no-for-an-answer God
      Who was pleased to display His might.
He plucked the poet from the murderous cold.

Kavanagh got the loan of a suit from a friend
In a merciful flat in Pembroke Road.
      Spick and span
      This poetman
Returned to the pub where the businessmen
Celebrated the drowning of the gadfly.
They gulped at the ghost who ordered a large whiskey
And said 'Thanks for the baptism, lads. I'm born again.'

Send a Letter

Out of the awful silence of the God of nothing
A voice, then voices: 'Of course, you pig,
You dare not know it,
Judas is the ultimate poet.'

I'd heard that vilest of bad rhymes
Before, in a sacrificial slum,
But now...ultimate? H'mm.
                              I'd never dreamed
There's nothing as treacherous as poetry
(Musical expression of the total man)
Not even the poet. Fly lads! Fly lassies!
Who suffered for this? Not the concern of these
Fly-by-night lines sparking a damned head
Convinced the sense of waste ends only when you're dead
And morning coughs in like a sub-editor
With a style like a leaking coffin,
Flush with an apt quotation
From *The Third Coming*,
Tubercular with the notion
That something important is being said.
Nothing I've ever read, said, heard said
Deserves to be remembered.
Another amateur Judas achieves a catharsis.
Say it. They'll gulp it. People are customers.
Old customers die hard. Say it. You'll feel better.
Who suffered for this? If you know, send a letter.

New Deal

Birds dropped it on Peru.
For a long time it grew
On hillsides, near villages, out-of-the-way places.
A boy plucked it one day,
Tasted it, paid for the experiment
With his life. A ferret-minded
Butcher with marital problems
Despatched his wife with it.
Its taste is sweet, its effects lethal.

Distinguished members of Church and State
Are conscious of its properties.
A trader out of my country
Which has a long problem with poverty
Did a deal recently.
It's on sale here now, getting popular,
Becoming part of our culture,
Deadly in certain respects, in others a boon.
Nearly every family will be growing it soon.

Frenchpolish

Suffer the little clichés to come unto me
And I'll frenchpolish them all
As they shamble like constipated chemists
Into the succulent dining-hall.
The pale dears cannot eat, they cannot eat
Because they conspired against fresh air
The day they started selling cures for piles
And how to keep your hair

Or when the ulcer acts up like a teenage son
Booting Dad's legacy in the groin.
This expensive tyke strikes out on his own
One prodigal morning, a randy paragon
In search of the Rose of Tralee or Mooncoin
To lend him an ear and soften his bone.

Again

Language Pathology, scrupulously pursued
By erudite women and men,
Is likely to come to a sticky end
Unless the word becomes flesh again

And not the flesh of sheep or cows
Or horses past their prime
To be scoffed in eating-places and watering-holes
By the plushest bellies of our time

But the flesh of the words of condemned men
Waiting on Death Row
For an end to the farce

Or the words of a whore in Merrion Square
Whose reputation as an AIDS-carrier has no
Visible effect on her eloquent arse.

Mercy Fund

I am opening the Judas Mercy Fund for Clichés.
I meet them everywhere, the poor sad battered
Old folk of language and time. I want to raise
Their overused hearts, give them an unfettered
Holiday away from dictionaries and tongues,
Away fom poems stories novels plays
Newspapers lectures letters sermons songs
Radio telly Official Statements Important Speeches
Critical articles scholarly tomes Orders of Merit
And Papal Encyclicals on the Holy Spirit.
I've applied for a grant from the Arts Council,
My application was clichéd, the signs are good,
Shortly we'll all have a breather by the sea.

After a few days, the clichés will start to feel
Immortal again, take on the tanned look
That seduces a poet's solitude
And mocks the pallor of pathetic suckers like me.

The Fundamental Question

A critic I respect grows hot
With the belief that most of the experts
At the Judas Iscariot Summer School
Are a vain, opportunistic lot
Dribbling a coy, pedantic, exhibitionistic snot.
They have quite forgotten
The original aim of the Summer School,
The fundamental question: is Judas a rotten

Traitor, lowest of the low, vilest of the vile,
Such as one would never find in any College anywhere
Even as one infects the young with a poxy lecture?
Or does Iscariot embody a certain style
Which most of us imitate with limited flair
As we publish our way between passion and prudence?

Who dare answer this question here or hereafter?
Let the experts assemble each summer.

Let them not, please God, be opportunistic and vain.

Disentangling Judas takes the brightest men
And women. They must be incorruptible as well.

Otherwise, let experts go to hell,
Gut the judaspoems, deduce what to buy and to sell.

A Startling Light

Taking the poet by the singing throat
The novelist hung him up on the washing-line
That long had dried the poet's shirts
Mostly black like Hamlet's, yon dithering wet
Who'd neither piss in the pot nor get off it
Like many a sensitive soul airing his agony
The better to achieve that gabby, narcissistic
Poetry of the crucified boring heart.

As the poet dangled from the washing-line,
Black shirt dishevelled, fair hair askew,
Metrics berserk, rhythms over the moon,
The novelist stood back and gazed.

A startling light emanated from the hanging man.
It said, 'I am dead, therefore I am

New.' The novelist, hardbacked at the sight, was dazed,
His style renewed, his future prizewinningly phrased.

The throttled poet (how can this be?) seemed finally pleased.

Next Time Round

Since I learned Yiddish at the age of three
And found that language is ridiculous
And not for me
I've been thinking of re-incarnation.
              Who was I? Am I? Will I be?
I know that I endured starvation
And made a fortune out of music-hall
But lost it to a trollop from Bangladesh.

              In a house of sin, Constantinople,
I read the hypnotic banality of women's flesh
Then died for centuries till I became
A Florentine, poor and most unhappy.
I was a thief, betrayed, forced underground.
His saviour, perhaps, next time round?
From my spirit-poisons what graces may abound.

The Present Writer

I saw the present writer stretched face
Down on the floor of a mucky place
In a posture of moan-and-groan disgrace.
       I studied him.

His face was unctioned in the muck
Like a speculator's mind in the Stock Exchange.
I couldn't see his eyes, they drowned beyond my range,
A feasting creature squatted on his neck.

His fingers flicked like rats among the filth
His odour caused the world to block its nose
There was some blood but no, the genius was not gory.

Others fled, I approached and said, 'Your health
Is vile, your vision slanted, your style uncommon. Rise
Up, you stinking get, and tell my story.'

As from the dead, he upped. The rest is commentary.

Blowjobbed

I saw the present writer blowjobbed with recognition.
Wankers ringed him, all shapes and sizes.
I neared and asked 'Why do you write, old son?'
He answered 'Prizes.'

Since this admission was profound
And honest beyond the statements of our time
Which often have a hollow sound,
He paused, I waited. 'Collecting prizes is no crime'

He said, 'I gather them from every side,
From honest Saxon and from gushing Yank,
From over there up above down under
From critics scholars patrons of the trade.'

I asked, 'What is your wish for the years ahead?'
He smiled, 'That no one steal my thunder.'

A Voice at Last

I had this fierce impulse to be a spokesman once.
I looked around for a cause: the poor, the sick,
The inexplicably shivering, the blacks, the Irish, the AIDS
Lot, starving millions, alcos, the blind, the dumb,
Tinkers, illiterates, the homeless, the Rock
Of Gibraltar victims, occupants of our choice jails,
Battered wives, battered husbands, battered pig-castrators.
All these sprang to mind, to nose, to eye.
Should I speak for them? No, I thought not,
They had their spokesmen and women, I pondered, I
Suddenly decided to be the first spokesman for

Nothing, I studied it in my breast, in yours,
In all the victims I have mentioned elsewhere,
I spoke out, nobody listened, everyone
Thought he was something, I persisted,
Slowly, the scene changed, my best endeavours
Tell me that nothing is coming into its own,
Nothing has a voice at last. Listen! Listen!

Ah, wrong again, Judas, old skin!
Jesus, why am I always getting it wrong?
Why can't I just up and say
It is not the voice of nothing
I wish to hear, to let speak
Over the valium towns and crammed
Cities, but the perfectly human
Voice of the fleshy damned?
And to what, my soul-mates, are we damned?
Nothing spectacular, I assure you, nothing
To excite emetic revulsion or epic shock;
Only, at certain moments, the sight and smell
Of accumulated shite
On a babbling Atlantic rock.

To Yourself to Imagine

A man is a story. Who will tell me?
Who will sit by what was once a fire
In God knows what about-to-be-bombed country
And gazing at the faces near,
Begin,
     'There was a child born of a serious woman
In a house in a village of gossiping tongues,
The boy grew, the woman told him stories
Of snakes and hills and kisses and human wrongs'?

     Or it may be quite a different beginning
Which I leave to yourself to imagine
For you also will tell it as you will.

Did you hear an inexplicable bird this morning?
Do you have it in your heart to finish a man,
A man you admire, perhaps, who leaves you feeling
You must prove to yourself you've the upper hand?
What story are you? Who dares know your style?
Who will listen when you are spoken? And
Of those who listen, who will understand?

Their Intended Stature

Why do passionate words grow weary?
I like his language, it speaks his bones.
When he says glory he means glory
Or he means what I think he means.
He's a great man to tell a story;
He'll stand on the steps of an old courthouse
Or row a boat out into the middle of a lake
And there begin to talk of revealing mountains and pits
And sunlight revealing water and rock.

And the people pay attention as though
Nobody had ever spoken to them before
Of where they came from, of what lies ahead.

I've seen his words melt people's hearts, I've watched the people grow
Into their intended stature.
That's a long time ago, the words live, the people are dead,
Their melted hearts earthed in a touchingly ignored solitude.

Revelations

It is true I fail at the level of language
When I try to translate the various parts
Of myself into words to be read by others
Interested in verbal revelations of the heart.

My gizzard, for example, my colon, my lights
Functioning in my body's darkness
Remind me of those nomad desert tribes
Moving through silence out of silence into silence.

Are they escaping a doom? Or embracing one?

Consider my brain ticking like a nailbomb
In a bag outside a supermarket
Winning the present phase of the prices war.
Who'll be passing when the nailbomb kicks?

There's the odorous slot in my bum,
My veins bearing the sign 'Rare blood to let'
And my lips, my God, what shall I say of my lips?

Teach Me

I understand the terror on the face of silence
Confronted with my clichés.
From the timber and steel of words I try to
Construct a few bridges.
I might as well be mangling the carcase
Of a myxomatosis rabbit brutally skinned
Or mooching backwards up a spiral staircase
Or pissing into the wind.

Is there a language on earth my use of it won't betray?
No wonder the silence is afraid of me.
And you, word-spotter, are you true to the bone?

Would you give me lessons in fidelity?
Teach me to be true for a year, a month, a day?
A minute? A second alone?
It's hard to be true, even all on your own.

Matthew's Answer

Words play tricks for/on any mindless blighter
Be he a slowcoach or a chancer in a hurry.
I wish never to write. Were I a writer
I'd say 'No need to worry, Judas, no need to worry.'
I've seen writers at work, I'd like to cover them in shite or
Spittle, with a measured ritualistic hate.
I'm not worried. Such aspirations are never too late
To fulfil. Writers see only with their eyes
Yet what they see they present as truth and beauty,
A pair of rotten duck-eggs in the corner of a yard
Hatched to dragons by a constipated bard.

    Matthew Mark Luke and John
    Went to bed with their nightshirts on.
    Matthew got up in the middle of the night
    Bent on dropping a writer's shite.
    Out the window he stuck his bum
    The moon shone down from Kingdom Come.
    Strolling below, I looked up high,
    Got Matthew's answer in the eye.

The Music That Others Make

One of the bad names in our place is informer.
Have I ever met one? Can't say for sure.
One thing I can tune you in on, however:
I talked to Gleeson who had the misfor-
tune to get the name whatever he did
Or said. What he said to me made good sense
But bad music, the kind he had to face when the word
Backfired on him and the men wouldn't give him a man's
Death or even an animal's if you want
Comparisons. It was, among bad ends, the worst
I've come across.
So much for that, there's nothing I'd care to add.
The music that others make is a weird business
Though it touches one's own in unexpected places.

The Years Are Words

Being your own hangman demands
A poetic sense of timing.
In that final stanza you discover
Sweet secrets of rhythm and rhyming.
While the blood speaks in your ears
A true blessing, a true curse,
The logic of your life is clear
As the argument of verse.
Dancing spots before your eyes
Are metaphors on a spree,
Your true music is heard at last,
The years are words grown bright and wise,
Lucid, right, ecstatically free.
So hang yourself and celebrate your past.

The Impulses

The impulses escaped through my eyes
And scoured the world for ways
To say themselves. They hid
In bones, skin, skulls, hearts,
Fists, wrinkles, feet.
They were tame at times, then ran amok,
Some blasted the green fields, some cared and loved,
Some said, screw mangle grab fuck fuck,
Some licked arses, got on, got on,
Some twisted themselves into those fascinating
Patterns only hypocrisy can achieve,
A few limped back from the desert to haunt me
In words no one has ever heard before.
That's why I believe what I think I believe.

A Hot Knife

A man is writing a poem about me
Raping paper with me in his head
Thinking he knows something about treachery
And anarchy blackening my blood.
Can he tell loneliness from solitude?
Does he know what I believe and cannot believe?
Does his notion of God touch my notion of God?
What has he lived of love?
                    I'm tickled to death
By people who think they know
Shallows and depths of somebody else.
                    I have such a pain today,
A hot knife in my wrist, my back, my head,
My heart, my eyes, my unpredictable pulse,
I think I'll hide somewhere and sweat away my pain.
If that man finds it, it'll chutzpah his poem.

Hometown Boy

'I saw the city die before my eyes.
Though I'm a hometown boy at heart
I love to go to foreign places
And, y'know, savour those famous works of art

Like O my God seein' a Giotto
In a really nice church in Assisi.
But as I watched the city die
The kinda colours explodin' before me

Were never seen nowhere by the eyes o' man,
Colours you wouldn't even see in a dream
Never mind Vienna Paris Venice Rome;
I watched the colours God the colours then
Knowin' for sure the job was done I said
Well, Enola ole gal, it's time for home.'

W.H. Goes Walking

Of course it's you, in optimistic mood,
A Hellenised Jew from Alexandria
Visiting an intellectual friend.
You're walking together, your way takes you

Past the base of Golgotha. Looking up
You see an all too familiar sight –
Three crosses surrounded by a jeering crowd.
Frowning in distaste, you say 'It's disgusting

How the mob enjoys this sort of thing.
Why can't the authorities execute criminals
Humanely, in private, put hemlock in their blood

Like Socrates?' You're upset. Then, averting
Your eyes from this vile spectacle,
You resume your discussion of the True, the Beautiful, the Good.

Spiritflowers

I decided at an early age that everything
I touched would be artistic.
I would teach my demons how to sing
I would transform all my sick
Moments into poems of my spirit
Seducing the petty mind and shrunken soul
Out of their natural inclination towards rot
Into spiritflowers flourishing in full

Glory. I planned to take my mean heart,
Make it a magnanimous work of art
Where every spat-on outcast might belong
And even old injustice feel at home.
This dream I had of myself. My dream said 'Come.'
But I could not. Why? God knows. Something went wrong.
Who knows what horrors go to make a song?

A World Record

A thousand and five years after I died
My self-portrait was hung up for sale.
That timeless object had been a source of pride
To me, I loved its power to console
My heart beating at a distressing lick
Harbouring yet another treacherous thought.
The auctioneer said it was a splendid image
Known and loved by the man in the street,
Hung in schoolrooms for the benefit of children
Reproduced on posters Christmas cards calendars
The most riveting image in modern art.

I'm not surprised it fetched thirty-three million
Pounds, a world auction record for any painting.
What would you pay for a painting of my heart?

A Modest Effort

When the effects of the wine had worn off
And I'd enjoyed a little snooze
In the cosy privacy of my bedsit
I wandered about contemplating those

Grave self-centred words, *Hoc*
Est enim corpus meum.
I'd plenty time now to take stock
Of their meaning. Soon, with the name

Of each apostle clinking in my mind,
I abandoned thinking and did a pencil-sketch
Of the Last Supper. It was fun.

Only yesterday that same sketch, a modest effort,
Was auctioned at Sothebys for thirty million pounds.
Strange how trifles attract such attention.

Milk

One morning in my bedsit, being visionary,
I began to paint a picture –
Baby Jesus at the bare breast of Mary,
God drinking milk from his mother.
I have never seen a more beautiful breast
Nor has there ever been a more sustaining milk,
Creation thrilled me, blood in my fingers,
Heaven warming my heart, I was blessed,
I know I was blessed but hell appeared, millions of devils
Opened their mouths, black teeth unwashed since God knows when,
Throats howling 'Mary, we thirst! Please! Please!'
Mary looks down, takes her breast from Jesus's mouth,
Squirts milk on the devils, they drink like hell,
I like the picture, it's called *A Moment of Ease.*

362

Reader's Report

At first I thought this a typical New Realism job
But I warmed to the writing as I read on.
A great deal hangs on the portrayal of the central character,
His pained involvement with the world about him,
His attitudes to women including his mother
His deft way with miracles, concise use
Of imagery in those punchy little parables
And his complex relationships with Romans and Jews.

Supporting characters are, on the whole, credibly drawn,
The style simple but effective, the plot
Swings through various worlds, heavens and hells.

That grisly scene on the hill verges on
Melodrama but the aftermath has a joyous
Magic. I recommend a large paperback edition.
I'll bet it sells.

What's That?

What is God but ourselves
Hearing in eternity
The voices of those we loved
In the poor opportunity of time?

             Not a bad start
But there I go again, never able to finish anything,
Betraying the promise, the beginning.

          This morning's quizzical clouds are works of art
Flung out as carelessly as the salutations
Of schoolkids to each other but here I sit
Turning the key in the lock
Of my heart. In there, maybe, I'll be able to listen,
I may even dare to finish what I set out
To say. What's that? Tell me or by Jesus I'll go on strike.

Light Verse

Mentions of me in the literatures of the world
Are not of a flattering kind,
Too much emphasis placed on my neck
Trite enquiry into my mind –
I may make some statement about myself
My handling of the human curse
Write a poem like one of the prophets –
                    Light verse! Light verse!

Light as the feel of a hundred-pound note in your fist
When the world is a belly dragheavy with greed
And only money will do;

Light as a kiss on the face of your Christ
Or other God's creature whose ways have an odd
Effect on you.

I Read a Poem Once

Those who believe they deal in revelation
Are sometimes traitors.
When I see their attempts to give body to vision
I recognise my brothers
Rehearsing in lyrical terms that death-rattle
Characteristic of emotional has-beens.
I am touched, or almost touched, by their prattle
Of integrity, whatever that means.

Therefore, my brothers, embrace a cause.
Champion the fascist or revolutionary dance,
Herod, Judas, Hitler, your bittersweet affair with God.
Suffer the chaos but observe the laws.
Be sullen and poetic, complain, I read a poem once,
Incoherent stuff, written in blood.
How can bad eyes recognise the good?

Not Everything

Not everything is mentioned in the Good Book.
How much should be said? How much remain untold?
I'm piqued that so few details are given about myself,
For example, that I'm bald
As a baby's bottom. I met a bold
Bitch-witch at a dinner-party,
She got furious at something I said,
She leaned forward and clawed hefty
Lumps of hair out of my head,
So hefty, in fact, I look like Yul Brynner now
(A forgotten hero of the twentieth century)
Deadly-bald leading the Magnificent Seven
On a mission of justice and peace.
        Only yesterday I purchased a wig
(Another fact not noted in the Good Book)
And covered this head that will not cease
To breed such thoughts I'm glad that they
Do not appear in print. God knows it's best
Not to give everything away.
The rest, God help us, is poetry.

There, If Anywhere

A rough man began to shout near the temple,
'Woe to the city! Woe to the nation!'
Day and night he bellowed warning to the streets.
Roused by his noising, prominent citizens
Grabbed and beat him. He would not apologise
Or accuse his attackers. Mere fear he did not show.
The district magistrate ordered he be flogged;
Later, judging him mad, let him go.

        The rough man continued like this, seven years.
One day, walking under the walls, he shouted
'Woe to the city! Woe to the nation!' Then, 'Woe is me!'
A stone, fired from somewhere like nowhere,
Hit him and killed him. He bellowed
No more woe. Where did I hear that story?
Why am I owned by this clumsy art?

If there's a way to fight the nothing in the heart
It must be a story. O I have mine but when
I try to tell it to a man or woman
It's all bits and pieces
Like walking by the shore alone
Some winter morning when the tide is out.
I have a plastic bag to put my story in:
Bits of driftwood first, polished by my favourite
Sculptor, the sea. Here's a dead widgeon
To hang around my neck;
Here's a stab of green glass smooth and wicked
As a persuading tongue;
Here's a terrier pup drowned near a rock,
Frozen hard as the sense of wrong.
My bits and pieces accumulate; the story makes itself;
There, if anywhere, I am trapped enough to belong.

Like Rhythm

Poets? Are they not the smug-with-suffering traitors to top
All traitors? Can you imagine someone
Imagining truth? Come, it's a dark morning
In the village of Black Waterfall, a man

Drives a car down a twisty byroad to the sea,
Takes a parcel, leaves the car, dumps the parcel in the outgoing tide.
The man is being watched, he drives away,
Another man retrieves the parcel, opens it to find

A foetus. He dumps the foetus in the outgoing tide
Or no, he takes it home (he lives alone)
And buries it. No one has ever seen him weep.

A poet hears this. He makes a poem. The poem is sad.
He speaks it as if he believed it's true.
It's not. If you must speak, say the sea is deep.
The foetus drifts like rhythm through untroubled sleep.
Yet there are some who hear the voice, and weep.

Hellhot Cakes

It takes a solitary scholar like me, not a tribal
Dabbler like Hitler to translate
The tricky Termonfecken Bible
From the Hebrew Irish Greek and Aramaic.

All through the work it was my wish
To eschew the gross familiarities of slang
For undefiled and dignified English.
My footnotes, thick with scholarship, rang

True. All indelicacies I brushed aside.
My Jesuit advisers suggested I
Review the book myself, taking whatever line

Seemed wisest. I prayed I cried I prayed.
And then 'Fuck it' I said 'I'll give the thing a try.'
My review was critical but benign.

The Professor of Bibles at Oxford
Objected on the grounds
I should not write about my own production.
He made pedantic sounds.
My version failed, he said, at the level of language.
'Fear not, it is I' Christ said
When he went for a walk on the water.
My translation ran 'I'm in deep, above my head.'

I wonder if people understand
Water-walking is advanced aquatic art
Perfectible only after millions of mistakes.

Even then a man might sink at any time.
I told the Professor of Bibles to go fart.
My paperback is selling like hellhot cakes.

Parnassus

You are a master of the freak erection
You murdered your wife the weapon was boredom
You traded skill for kicking up ructions
You knocked on every door but no door opened

You got what you sought you died of success
In vino veritas became brandy-and-port
You took experience and made it bitterness
And wished all the youngsters under the Dart

You played it safe and found true danger
Unwritten poems were pits where you drowned
Aiming your curses and eunuch's anger
At whoever stayed true to the foolish end

You lacked the guts to give your gift a chance
You took the chance to spill the guts of your gift
All over the days of your sense and nonsense
Stale and ailing as your tattered craft

You bitched ad nauseam of the true and beautiful
You downed living women to serve a dead muse
You died of drink you died of sobriety
You knew revelation was your bulldog views

You shared with the angels a true soulmusic
Or so you claimed for your psychic whine
You try to look tragic and you're bollox-comic
Go soothe your whingeing with more bad wine

You're an amateur monster I'm professional
I wouldn't touch you with Homer's pole
Though I smile at your show of red-eyed evil
And the small sad grace-notes astray in your soul

Normal Size

When he started talking his head was a normal size.
He had, be it admitted, the merest hint of a beerbelly.
He spoke clearly and calmly,
Visions of heaven emanating from his eyes.

That morning, his topic was Church and State.
He exhorted his audience to think
About corruption, widespread of late.
Suddenly, his head began to shrink.

'Betrayal of trust' he said 'is an art.
To achieve mean dreams, men poison and kill,
Strangle every last shred of innocence in their hearts.'
His voice deepened. His head grew smaller still.

Smaller and smaller it grew till it became
A perfect little head, big as a pin,
Booming out indisputable truth
That morning of breezy sin.

I was the only one who saw it so.
He finished speaking, the mob felt holy and wise.
He sat, bathed in his own indignant glow,
His head once more its normal size.

Satisfied

During a recent pilgrimage to hell
I was entertained by the spectacle
Of one poet eating another.
Some poets eat devilishly well.

Poet number one knifed poet number two,
Sliced and nibbled his left testicle
Then cut the tongue, a cool parnassian blue,
Chewed, savoured, pronounced it delectable.

Poet number two emitted epic cries
Knowing his paradise was lost.
Poet number one looked at him askance,
Tried some brain, sipped some blood, guzzled the eyes
And then, satisfied (I thought) at last,
Performed a dandy iambic dance.

Fizz

Though I'm not a community man
I wrote some touching hymns in my time
And was pleased to hear them chan-
ted in a large building in Rome

N

By lusty Italians at their most
Sublime, placating the Father,
Consoling the Son, praising the Holy Ghost.
My themes were simple, my style rather
Rhetorical in the manner of *Mein Kampf.*

Hymns need a certain spiritual fizz,
That Hitlerthing sweeping the crowd along
And upwards till they perch on heaven's rafters,
Transfigured by the knowledge that they've ris-
en from the dead on shining wings of Judassong.

The Sound

Show me a story that's not a crafty lie
Sucking the marrow from some bone of truth
And I'll show you a detached evangelist
Telling the story as he believes he heard it
From travellers dusty with parables
Homing at nightfall on a desert wind
Where gods and demons, born by candlelight,
Excite his mind.

All day long in the fevered valleys
This young man has been tending the sick.
Composing in his patient room
Words flickering at his thoughts' boundaries
He tries to catch the sound of *Judas, rock,*
Hosannah, father, John, salvation, doom.

The Point

Now let me see...

A man I distrust frequently begins his sentences
'The truth is, of course.'
His grin confirms possession of the truth
While you are a floundering barbarian, or worse,
Some garrulous nitwit infected with enthusiasm

Of the more unfortunate kind. So shut up, you.
He goes on to reveal the essence of everything
While you melt with respect in the presence of the true.

Living in the sweet grip of revelation
May be a challenge for some, but not him
Quietly content with total vision,
Tolerant, also, of the blind and dumb
Surrounding him, although among the dumb and blind
Lie truthful titbits he may never find.
The same gentleman is fit to wet his pants
If, in listening to your talk or reading what you write,
He cannot quickly see 'the point'.
Ah! The Point!

> *I read a poem last week*
> > *And I couldn't see the point!*
> *I heard a song last night*
> > *And I couldn't see the point!*
> *I looked at all these prisoners' paintings*
> > *And for the life of me – no point!*
> *I read that Northern woman on how we live down here –*
> > *What on earth is the woman's point?*

May one man kiss
Another and enjoy his own snake's hiss?
Blood on your white bread?
Steely creatures chewing the insides of your head?
My youngest brother with a petrol
Bomb in one hand and a stone in the other?
O days when times and crimes are out of joint
The point is your damned terror of the point
Whatever that may be.
Now let me see...

All the Terrified Strangers

Anything but this!

> I peel away the bandage
To reveal the wound, I peel away the skin
To show the flesh, I strip the flesh,
> > the bone

371

Blushes at my touch, I see a face then,
The eyes cry for all the terrified strangers
Living in me, in you, me, you, men, men.
I love you. No, screams the bone, never say these
Words again.

An Absorbing Theme

All kind of scribblers find me an absorbing theme.
Among the fascinating aspects of my character
My suicide most engages their attention
Causing them to speculate in a manner
That tickles my outcast ghost
Giggling constantly
In comic corners of eternity.
I've read poems and novels, attended
Films and plays investigating my case.
Pathetic efforts! I should, I suppose, have been offended
By such feeble scrutiny of my character in action
But I realise most men manage only
To talk about themselves and their simple
Obsessions. I am completely myself. That's why
I inspire such helpless imitation. Consider
The incidence of teenage suicide, for example.
What mind can grasp the ignominy of the pimple?

Humanpoem

I have tried to die but you won't let me.
I went to the hell of a lot of trouble
To end my experiment in misery.
This was no off-the-cuff arrangement,
No sudden twist at the top of the stairs,
Dart into the bathroom and Bob's your uncle
Behind the door; nor was it a slow
Mangy erosion of my personality
Culminating in farcical vertigo
And an irrefutable affirmation
Of that much talked-about ultimate erection.

This was, like all I did, a work of art,
A sculptured commitment to the notion of oblivion,
A humanpoem, flower of a human seed
There in the open air for any traveller to read
And interpret according to his need.
Physicians of my youth, darlings of my first thrust,
Victims and witnesses of my not innocuous lust,
Chief influences of my contemplative brow,
Where are you now?
For I have failed to put an end to what
Has constantly disgusted me, the thought
Of myself. Here I go
Lurching down Bride Street with a reeking
Drunk, listening to an over-taxed teacher
Railing against the hooligans he pretends to educate
('There's one cunt I'd crucify on any wooden gate');
And if I risk paper, television or radio,
These political voices I adore-abhor, I heard them
In better weather two thousand years ago
Or more. It is for these
Recurring delicacies you keep alive
This eternal judasflower, humanpoem. You are my
Nourisher.
Am I the answer to your prayer?

A Beautiful Mind

Recently I met
One of the unacknowledged legislators of mankind.
He struck me as being a bit of a wet
Though he had a beautiful mind.

He loved everything, especially himself.
His voice souped out of a dream.
He fidgeted. 'What's wrong?' I asked.
He said 'I can't find a theme.'

Now if there's one creature who moves me to the core
It's an unacknowledged, themeless legislator.
That's a hard double-burden for a singer to bear.
I was so moved I could endure no more.
'Take me as a theme' I offered, 'Dig! Explore!'
'No!' snarled the bard 'You're bad news for my Muse.
Vamoose! Piss off! Scram out of here!'

As I gazed on the trembling spirit standing there
Sensitive behind his beard like a poetic God The Father
I mused on the power of poetry
To capture bright sparks of eternity
And I mused also on how little
Love and hope there is in our world,
Certain parts of which persist in some distress,
And I thought how poets wage a spiritual battle
To shed some light on the unprofitable mess,
Blessing what others curse, cursing what others bless.
I wanted to utter my thoughts to the nervous
Representative of that sublime art, themeless before me,
But I held my tongue.

Instead I offered him a cup of Eden applejuice
With which to quench his Parnassian thirst
And refresh him into song.

He drank the juice. Now I must wait to find
What flowers startle from that beautiful mind.
And wait I will, for I'm a patient lad
Willing to sniff all flowers, good and bad.

Sole Encounter

I'm the last man on earth to blame those folk
Who swear to Christ that I'm again 'em.
Feeling my life's poison encircle my neck
I decided one morning to swallow my venom,
The most arduous exercise of my life.
My belly bulged with the immensity of the thing,
My guts groaned like famine pits, concentration camps,
I was the accumulated sewage of defecating

Humanity, sorry about that, the picture suggested
Itself like a nasty pressure on the brain,
Fine resting-place of recorded fears.

Suddenly, out of unspeakable me, arose such music
Angels kissed my spirit, danced and were gone.
This was my sole encounter with the music of the spheres.

We Know About Rembrandt

The pavement is trying to help him
Bent above Rembrandt in October mist
Trying to give an old name a new name.

In this mist, self-portraits are on the go.

John Clohessy of Ballinasloe
Fingers on the pavement those lineaments of love
That grab the last tourist's eye
And persuade her to swell his dwindling coffer.

We know about Rembrandt. Will John Clohessy die?

So it's not immorality but a kind of dole.
Rembrandt helps a man out of work
Michelangelo too will contribute his bit

To Angela Keane whose jeans hardly warm her
As she works the pavement to stake her mark,
Pay her rent, buy her food, save her soul, make her shit.

I Have My Doubts

Suppose there's nothing that is not a sad mistake.
Suppose my own version of the Good Book
In which I play a part of tragical bad luck
Though promising at the start, is but a fake.

Suppose all the talk of truth is a bag of lies
Like ripening tumours in an honest brain.
Suppose love with its sweet agonies and sighs
Is a gadding cancer through available veins.

Suppose dear god's a devil with a sense of fun
– who's reading this? –
And wrote the script for us, his natural actors,
To play the parts until the play is done.
It never is. My mind is melancholy because
I have my doubts. And there are other factors.

Play

I once tried my hand at an old-fashioned morality play.
Following long haggling with the management
The thing was performed at the Gabby Theatre.
The play was called *Whoever Said I Can't*.

The three principal parts were myself, Jesus and God.
I played the part of Jesus and he, me.
God played himself and was a howling success.
Some of the audience got riled because they couldn't see him.

I found it hard to get into the part of Jesus.
The heart of his matter was somehow beyond me
And my delivery of his parables lacked passion.
He, on the other hand, was a startling Judas
As though he knew my soul so completely
Every word gesture silence revealed me as touchingly human.
He brought me into the light
From the darkness of a thousand graves.
The play was vigorously reviewed, several raves:
'Jesus a revelation as Judas'
'Judas captivatingly ambiguous as Jesus'
'God impresses with his invisibility'.

         After long runs in Dublin and London
We decided to tour the Irish provinces
Encouraged by a fat grant from the Arts Council.
In towns of Ulster Leinster Munster Connaught
Whoever Says I Can't proved that it could
Touch the hearts and souls of the common people.
Their nightly applause was passionate and long.
'D'you think they know what's happening?' I asked God.

'They think they do, and that's what matters' he replied with a smile,
'Great actors will make people believe anything
They choose
From Peace In Our Time to the Conversion of the Jews.'

I was pleased, but didn't let it go to my head,
Happy that simple, old-fashioned morality was not entirely dead.

Certain Rhythms

I was devouring a Western by Zane Grey
Borrowed from the Donegal Travelling Library,
Sipping, while I read, pints of Smithwick's beer
Which added to my delight in gunplay.

There was a rustler named Zeb who knew the value of a steer
And a lean hero, six foot, greased lightning on the draw.
Turning a page I found a lost poem by Shakespeare.
You could have knocked me over with a straw.

Signed 'Will Shakspeer' the very sight of it made my skin tingle,
Scholars would gut each other for it, reputations would be made
And murdered. But I just started to read:

The fucking poem was a queer silly jingle
Dizzy with that wordgasm at which skilled Will excelled,
Guaranteed to make the hearts of all true poetry-lovers bleed.

There are certain rhythms impossible to forget
I thought, as I cycled off into the sunset.

The True Thing

I don't know anyone who knows what became of the true thing.
If poets think they sing, it is a parody they sing.
In the beginning men of common sense
Knew that for the damned dream to grow
Wholesale massacre of innocence
Was necessary, prophets' blood must flow,
Thieves of little apples be crucified, rebels be put down,
Conspiracies of messianic troglodytes be strangled
And saviours be given the bum's rush out of every pub in town.

Out of the smashed cities
Works of art adorn the Vatican walls
A comfortable living is right for the Archbishop and his wife
Lads and lassies study till their eyeballs burn and their souls know
One must never heed the bitter cries, forsaken calls
Of the man in the beginning burning fear

Like old papers, kissing his death, having given his life.
Yes, and we have double-glazed hearts and committees and promotions and
        pensions
And time off to enjoy and bless
The kids shining out to discos and parties
In the holy light of progress.
And we have learning, we could put Hell in a couplet, Eden in an epigram,
Dish out slices of epics like gifts of land in the Golden Vale
And sweat blood or what feels like blood
To get the right rhythm and thereby hangs a tale
Of an abortive experiment in love
That began in bestial company and ended in public shame
And started all over again in a sad parody
Of what cannot be understood

Only followed as a blind man follows his expensive dog
Through visionary streets of fluent slavish traffic
Calmly-crazily living the rhythms of my mechanical blood
Yearning occasionally, nevertheless, for dialogue with God.
I would ask, to begin with, what became of the true thing
And after that, well, anything might happen.
I can even imagine a poet starting to sing
In a way I haven't heard for a long time.
If the song comes right, the true thing may find a name
Singing to me of who, and why, I am.

Index of titles and first lines

(Titles are in italics. The numbers refer to pages.)

A Time for Voices
SELECTED POEMS 1960-1990

BRENDAN KENNELLY

'A voice and a vision...wild and unafraid – unique in contemporary poetry'
– MICHAEL LONGLEY, *Irish Times*

'With *A Time for Voices*, Kennelly can be included among the Irish greats'
– HAYDEN MURPHY, *Scotland on Sunday*

'With considerable honesty and bravery Kennelly enters and becomes others in order to perceive, understand and suffer...always moving, probing and doubting, never willing or able to settle on any one certainty. There is clash and conflict, cruelty and irony, sardonic wit and passion...a unique book from a poet whose range and vision is not pigeon-holed' – AIDAN MURPHY, *Sunday Press*

'Kennelly has always had the courage to write in bad taste...to move into areas that other poets seldom approach, and this selection maps a unique, and often a savage, terra incognita...a troubling book, exuberantly engaged, vital, and sometimes threatening; its poetry is authentic, not authoritative...Kennelly's energy remains unabated' – PETER McDONALD, *Irish Times*

'One would hate to be one of the warty lads, the fine liars, whom Yeats and the Muse prefer. All honour then to a poet who has ploughed decently and with sobriety through the Fifties and Sixties and so on, and who has attained the position of a genuine and major poet' – PETER LEVI, *Independent*

'Kennelly is a medium: he makes bread, sand, water, silence, history and people speak in their own accents...this selection from 30 years of poetry is overwhelmingly bleak...the most cheerful of our poets is also the most desolate'
– AUGUSTINE MARTIN, *Irish Independent*

Hardback: ISBN 1 85224 096 2   £14.95
Paperback: ISBN 1 85224 097 0   £7.95

Also available in a special limited signed slipcased edition
of 100 copies (ISBN 1 85224 081 4) at £50.

Cromwell

A POEM BY
BRENDAN KENNELLY

'This is an astonishing book...an intense poetic outcry. It is energy and honesty that make this book of horrors humanly tolerable' – SEÁN LUCY, *The Tablet*

'Brendan Kennelly has got guts. And a large portion of those are served up here. This book is not for the squeamish' – MARK PATRICK HEDERMAN, *Irish Literary Supplement*

'One of the most extraordinary books I have ever come across in my life' – GAY BYRNE, *The Late Late Show (RTE)*

'What marks Kennelly out as a writer of extreme psychological subtlety is the give in his treatment of Cromwell: an exacting judgement on the historical truth is tempered with mercy in the shape of comedy' – GILES FODEN, *Times Literary Supplement*

'These poems are shocking...he only deals, and can only deal, in strong poisons' – MARTIN DOGTURD, *The Guardian*

'*Cromwell* is explosive, expansive, prolific, explicit' – EDNA LONGLEY

'For Kennelly, a poetic voice, like a nation, is never itself alone, and *Cromwell* provides an important and unsettling example of this difficult dependence, an openness to history that does not rely on the self as an escape-route from nightmare, or upon the integrity of the individual voice as a guarantee of poetic value' – PETER McDONALD, *Irish Review*

'Kennelly has invented a Cromwell for the modern conscience, a figure to taunt the comfortable soul of a progressive Dubliner' – PETER PORTER, *Observer*

'*Cromwell*...where all the voices that are in Brendan Kennelly are let loose to cry out against one another. That is how he thinks of poetry' – PETER LEVI, *Independent*

Paperback: ISBN 1 85224 026 1   £7.95

EURIPIDES'

Medea

A NEW VERSION BY
BRENDAN KENNELLY

Brendan Kennelly has turned this classic tale of betrayal and vengeance into a text for our times. The sorceress Medea marries Jason after helping him and the Argonauts steal the Golden Fleece. When Jason deserts her, she punishes her faithless husband by murdering their two sons, after killing his young bride and her father with a robe of fire. Medea carries out her bloody revenge in the name of Justice, but in the spirit of rage. The rage of many modern women, including Irishwomen, electrifies this highly charged and deeply personal play. First staged at the Dublin Theatre Festival, Kennelly's chilling new version of Euripides' great tragedy has delighted and devastated audiences in Ireland, Britain and America:

'Medea's revenge upon Jason takes place on "one sweet, vicious, vengeful, devastating day", and the vigour of Brendan Kennelly's translation can be gauged from those mouthwatering words. He has a superb feel for the language' – THE TIMES

'Marvellously achieved...delicately honed, full-bloodedly direct and timeless in its relevance' – IRISH INDEPENDENT

'A poetic drama that leaps across the centuries with astonishing force and fury ...the exhilarating, spare language confronts crucial issues of our time'
– CITY LIMITS

'A homage to womanhood, orchestrated against a backdrop of love, power and jealousy, an engrossing tale to fuel the mind and senses' – IRISH PRESS

'Accessible, immediate, urgent...his language makes you feel the force of Medea's passions as closely and vividly as Euripides' audiences would have done'
– THE GUARDIAN

'He has created a modern Medea with classical touches who epitomises contemporary woman as much as a mythical heroine' – EVENING PRESS

'Great verbal virtuosity...rich, unpredictable, provocative...Susan Curnow's Medea is terrific and terrifying' – OLIVER TAPLIN, *Times Literary Supplement*

Paperback: ISBN 1 85224 189 6   £5.95
Hardback: ISBN 1 85224 188 8   £12.95

Brendan Kennelly was born in 1936 in Ballylongford, Co. Kerry, and was educated at St Ita's College, Tarbert, Co. Kerry; at Trinity College, Dublin, where he gained his BA, MA and PhD, and Leeds University. He has lectured in English Literature at Trinity College since 1963, and became its Professor of Modern Literature in 1973. He has also lectured at the University of Antwerp and in America, at Barnard College and Swarthmore College. He has won the AE Memorial Prize for Poetry and the Critics' Special Harveys Award.

He has published more than 20 books of poems, including *My Dark Fathers* (1964), *Collection One: Getting Up Early* (1966), *Good Souls to Survive* (1967), *Dream of a Black Fox* (1968), *Love Cry* (1972), *The Voices* (1973), *Shelley in Dublin* (1974), *A Kind of Trust* (1975), *Islandman* (1977), *A Small Light* (1979) and *The House That Jack Didn't Build* (1982). *The Boats Are Home* (1980) is still available from Gallery Press and *Moloney Up and At It* from the Mercier Press (Cork and Dublin).

His best-known work – until now – has been the popular and controversial book-length poem-sequence *Cromwell*, published in Ireland by Beaver Row Press in 1983 and in Britain by Bloodaxe Books in 1987.

His books of poems translated from the Irish include *A Drinking Cup* (Allen Figgis, 1970) and *Mary* (Aisling Press, Dublin 1987), and his translations are now collected in *Love of Ireland: Poems from the Irish* (Mercier Press, 1989). He edited *The Penguin Book of Irish Verse* (1970; 2nd edition 1981), and has published two novels, *The Crooked Cross* (1963) and *The Florentines* (1967).

He is also a celebrated dramatist whose plays include versions of *Antigone*, produced at the Peacock Theatre, Dublin, in 1986, and *Medea*, premièred in the Dublin Theatre Festival in 1988, toured in England in 1989 by the Medea Theatre Company, broadcast by BBC Radio 3 in 1991 and published by Bloodaxe Books in 1991. His stage version of *Cromwell* played to packed houses at Dublin's Damer Hall in 1986 and 1987, and in London in 1991. His selection *Landmarks of Irish Drama* was published by Methuen in 1988.

His other books include *The Real Ireland*, a book of photographs by Liam Blake with text by Brendan Kennelly (Appletree Press, Belfast, 1984), and *Ireland Past and Present*, edited by Brendan Kennelly (Chartwell Books, New Jersey, 1985).

He has published five volumes of selected poems: *Selected Poems* (Allen Figgis, 1969), *Selected Poems* (Dutton, New York, 1971), *New and Selected Poems* (Gallery Press, 1976), *Selected Poems* (Kerrymount, Dublin, 1985), and *A Time for Voices: Selected Poems 1960-1990* (Bloodaxe Books, 1990). His epic poem *The Book of Judas* is published by Bloodaxe Books in 1991.